RELEVANCE
RAISES
RESPONSE

*How to Engage and Acquire with
Mobile Marketing*

By

Bob Bentz

RELEVANCE RAISES RESPONSE

How to Engage and Acquire with Mobile Marketing

By

Bob Bentz

Relevance Raises Response:
How to Engage and Acquire with Mobile Marketing

By
Bob Bentz

Editing by Elizabeth Thorlton

ISBN-10: 1942489110

ISBN-13: 978-1-942489-11-5

DEDICATION

I wrote a book 23 years ago and dedicated it to my father, Kenneth F. Bentz, who passed away when I was still in my teens. For this book, I am dedicating it to my late mother, Bonnie (Edwards) Bentz, who always was, and will always be, my biggest fan.

I would like to also dedicate this book to my friends, colleagues, coworkers, and associates through the years. Throughout my career, I've had the tremendous privilege of working with so many fantastic people at the following companies around the world: Advanced Telecom Services, ATS Mobile, Purplegator, Advanced Federal, Advanced Mobile, Spark Network Services, Overture Interactive, and Olympic Internet.

I have always lived by the mantra:

Our people are our greatest resource.

And I've always believed that these people were working *with* me, never *for* me. Thank you for making going to work every day (almost) as much fun as going to a baseball game.

TABLE OF CONTENTS

FOREWORDS

*F*inally, someone has taken an extremely broad subject called "mobile" and made it understandable for marketers. Bob Bentz has successfully taken extremely beefy subject matter and delivered it in snack-size portions that are easy to digest. The worry in reading a quasi-business book is the dryness factor and whether or not you have the interest and desire to slog your way through the chapters. The good news is that *Relevance Raises Response: How to Engage and Acquire with Mobile Marketing* has a brisk flow as it takes the reader on a journey through the arcane world of mobile technology while delivering valuable insights on how businesses of any size can leverage the mobile phenomena in their quest to acquire more customers. In addition, Bob Bentz manages to weave in his unique sense of humor that makes turning the pages that much more fun.

Understanding all the various aspects of mobile is daunting. Anyone who has the word "marketing" associated with their title or has such responsibilities within their company should view this book as a must read. In it, you will learn about incredibly powerful marketing channels, such as text message marketing, social media on mobile devices, the importance of mobile-optimized websites, mobile SEO, mobile search, mobile ad buying, apps, the power of video, and how to leverage the 800-pound gorilla called Facebook, plus much, much more. Not only does the book do a great job of educating the reader on all the companies and their technology that play a part in the mobile ecosystem, but it also gives practical advice on how to use these technologies to build your brand and/or directly acquire customers using mobile marketing.

I have had the pleasure of working alongside Bob for the last 27 years. Bob is the classic early adopter, as he never met a new consumer technology—especially in the area of mobile—that didn't pique his curiosity and desire to sign up and become an actual user. I recall him telling me about a burgeoning Internet service called CompuServe and how he found himself unknowingly burning hours while playing around with it at nights. Our first e-commerce B2C sites were two ringtone websites that we created in the early 2000s, MonsterTones.com and RingingPhone.com. Here, Bob learned the art of SEO and SEM to capitalize on the incredible demand by consumers to personalize their mobile phones. Bob was insatiable in his quest to understand the pay-per-click model offered by Overture at the time (who was later acquired by Yahoo). I recall him traveling to attend three-day seminars on pay per click and SEO; he would return totally amazed at how the material had kept his undivided attention for the duration of the seminar. During this time, we saw firsthand the potential of using the Internet to drive traffic to various e-commerce websites that offered mobile services. Outside of baseball, Bob had found his new passion: mobile marketing.

In 2007 we experienced the dandy duo disruptors named Facebook and iPhone. Both companies created services that entertained, informed, and served as a utility in people's daily lives. Bob could barely sleep at night as he tried to wrap his head around the awesomeness of these revolutionary innovations.

The advent of the iPhone was a game changer in so many respects. The iPhone ushered in an age of 24/7 Internet. Before the iPhone, people stopped working when they left their computers. For better or worse, the iPhone blurred the lines between work and home. Non-voice communication using one's mobile phone became a round-the-clock habit. It also created new opportunities to market to people staring at their small screens while on the go.

With Google and their Android operating system phones quickly following Steve Jobs's blockbuster iPhone's footsteps, smartphones were on their way to ubiquity, and an exciting new marketing opportunity was created called *mobile*. The new ingredient that smartphones offered marketers was location. From Bob's and my perspective, the smartphone changed the opportunity from offering features on the mobile phone to offering advertisers the ability to target consumers based on online and offline behavior.

Facebook was another major market disruptor and game changer for marketers. With about 39 percent of the world's population currently considered active users, including 60 percent of North Americans,[1] Facebook deserves its share of any advertising budget. They have made ad buying on their social media network simple by providing easy-to-use tools for precise targeting and custom audiences. The precision of target marketing can actually be scary, as it basically culls text written and shared by members and algorithmically uses that text to enable advertisers to target their messages to just the right audience. Add the location of the mobile device that is in everyone's pocket to Facebook's marketing algorithm, and the marketer now has incredible precision in delivering their message at the right time, the right place, and to the right person.

Call it the mobile majority. Facebook generates roughly 80 percent of their revenue from mobile advertising.[2] Mark Zuckerberg, the visionary, saw that mobile was where the eyeballs were going, so he invested heavily in being able to offer Facebook users with an unequaled mobile experience while accommodating advertisers with tools in which to display pertinent and useful advertising, a true win-win. Facebook embodies the concept of *Relevance Raises Response*.

Without a doubt, an archaic approach to advertising still exists, meaning many advertisers continue with the "carpet bombing" or "spray and pray" approach to advertising—no analysis or research of whether the user is interested in the brand and therefore likely to click through, but rather putting out as many ads as possible in the hope someone will bite. It's an incredibly expensive way of getting your message out there, and, if anything, it can be detrimental. Consumers, who expect relevant marketing messages (especially if they are on a paid app), are likely to be irritated by intrusive, irrelevant ads, especially as they are increasingly seeing marketing messages tailored to their interests. Therefore, the risk of not using relevant advertising techniques is greater than ever.

The timing of the book *Relevance Raises Response* is ideal. As we enter the third decade of desktop Internet and work through the first decade of mobile Internet and downloadable apps, consumers are getting progressively savvier. Marketers are increasingly able to build profiles of people based on their interests and what they share across the open web, and are serving relevant ads accordingly. Consumers have reacted well. They understand that they are going to be served ads online these days—it's what makes the Internet tick—so why not make the ads useful to them? And, as mobile marketers, why not deliver the right ads in the right format to the right potential audience? The tools are there for the using; just do a little research (such as reading this book) and become skilled at the art of mobile marketing.

Bret Dunlap
Senior Vice President,
Mobile Division, Autobytel Inc.

I have known Bob Bentz over 10 years and have always been impressed with his hands-on expertise. It came as no surprise to me when he mentioned he was writing a book—I thought, ah, of course. I've always known him to constantly be searching for a way to satisfy his hunger and curiosity to learn more about the digital world. He has placed himself in an industry where the only way to learn and grow is to do it. And he has done it. Bob proves his excellence and knowledge inside these pages—it makes me think he's finally satisfied that curiosity.

This brilliant book on the optimization of mobile marketing is extremely timely, since in May of 2015 Google announced that mobile searches were more than 50 percent of all searches.[3] That will only continue to increase. Also, as Bob points out, Google "near me" searches have increased 34 times in the last four years, which highlights the benefits and explosive growth of location-targeted mobile advertising. With mobile phones transforming through the decades—from devices designed purely to accomplish a simple phone call to our most translatable identifiers—they have become personal devices attached to our hands. We never go anywhere without them, so we can be reached anywhere, at any time, with any kind of marketed information. Nobody understands this better than Bob.

Bob has designed and successfully compiled a guide to understanding and maneuvering the realm of digital marketing. This book takes you through a quick tour of the mobile world, from its beginning to its ever-changing present, before diving into what it takes to transform that marketing medium into much more. It's a page-turner of pure genius. I found myself nodding along to the ideas and exchanges that take place in the text.

SMS text-based messages have the biggest reach. Bob has designed an unarguable discussion about the reasons why this is possible. He says it himself, "What can be simpler than sending a text message?" The only negatives of mobile marketing are the smaller footprints, multiple formats, and regulatory issues, which call for careful design, but Bob provides amazingly comprehensive checklists on all the key factors to optimize.

Relevance Raises Response is the marketing guide to everything mobile, and soon everything marketing *will* be mobile. Bob has constructed a navigational map to maneuver around the bumps in the road for mobile marketers at a time when they are going to most need it. Bob touches on every aspect that mobile devices are revolutionizing for marketing—SMS text-based messaging, social media advertising, mobile-optimized websites, software applications—and he has elaborated on each with a mind that is immersed in the culture of digital media. Bob's book is what this industry needs—an updated, experience-driven text that is proven successful by his own strategies and business success.

Bob's book is an ideal reference for any mobile marketing pro!

Michael Cowpland, PhD
CEO, Zim Corporation
Founder, Corel, Mitel Networks

There has never been a time in the history of communication like the time we live in now. Today, you can instantly be connected to almost anyone, anywhere, at any time. Time zones, countries, and even language barriers are no longer roadblocks. We literally carry the world in our pockets and purses with ever-smarter smartphones, tablets, and watches. With so much available at the touch of a screen, how can you and your business stay relevant to your customers and continue to build your brand? What does this mean to you and your business? How can you harness this tremendous power of information and commerce?

With so many options and so much noise in any marketplace, mobile marketing has to be a key part of everything you do for your company, your personal brand, and your customers. Amazon, the number one retailer online, has seen a steady trend of commerce, with well over half of their business coming from mobile devices. There is no question that this trend will only continue to grow.

Bob Bentz saw this trend long before anyone else, and so his advice and perspective has much more depth and context. He understands how the industry was formed and developed.

There isn't a more knowledgeable expert than Bob. You will also appreciate his humor and direct approach. He has a way of keeping you engaged and moving through the concepts and tools that makes this not only an informative read but also fun and enjoyable.

What Bob Bentz will teach you in this wonderful book, *Relevance Raises Response*, is *exactly* how to use that incredible power to "Engage and Acquire With Mobile Marketing." It will make you think. It will challenge your perception of the status quo of mobile and how to use it in your marketing strategies. It is, without question, the core of what you need to know about mobile marketing and sales.

In my own business, there has never been a doubt to the power of mobile marketing. As part of our branding as best-selling authors and workplace consultants, we write articles for LinkedIn. The mobile app and marketing that comes with it has boosted our profile and credibility in ways traditional marketing never could. Our articles are even appearing on smartwatches now. With each article published, we see our followership increase. Every time we have had an idea or concept go viral, it has been the mobile apps that have driven the trend. This is no longer a revolution; this is the way we live, work, and buy. Understanding not only its power but also exactly how to do it will be critical for your business and the building of your personal brand.

This book will help you understand the history of mobile marketing, as well as give you a priceless road map on how you can use mobile to build your business. As the world of marketing gets more and more complicated and fragmented, this knowledge will serve you and your clients well.

Enjoy the book. Study its contents. Implement the strategies and grow your business.

Chester Elton
"Apostle of Appreciation"
Best-Selling Author
Founder, The Culture Works

PREFACE

Yeah, I Know This is Only the Preface, but Trust Me,
You Need to Read This!

STILL NEED CONVINCING?

There was a time when businesses had to convince clients that mobile was something that they should be concerned with. Those times are now long gone, and mobile marketing business proposals are no longer dotted with statistics of just how big mobile is or will soon become.

People have bought in. They get it.

MOBILE GOES MAINSTREAM

The Internet became mainstream two decades ago. Today, mobile is just a logical extension of the Internet medium. The evidence of mobile's emergence became apparent during the 2008 presidential election. Barack Obama could have announced his running mate, Joe Biden, on his web page, but instead, he chose to do it via mobile SMS text messaging. With that announcement came the confirmation that the United States was embracing a new technology—a technology that his opponent, John McCain, did not know much about.

My companies have always embraced the latest technology and the way people use it. There was a time when the slogan at our company was, "Your Message on the Move." It made perfect sense in the early 2000s, when the idea of mobile marketing was to reach consumers when they were "on the go." And, while we still want to reach consumers on the go, mobile is much more than that today. We not only want to reach people when they are out and about, but we also want to reach them on their couch, in their homes, and in their offices, because that is where most mobile is being consumed. Mobile marketing is no longer just about reaching consumers who are waiting at the bus stop.

People around the world are fixated on their mobile phones. They check their smartphones 150 times per day on average.[4] Mobile has become their constant companion.

GIVE ME THE STATS

For fantasy football coaches and baseball managers, statistics are everything. Sure, you may cheer for your favorite team, but when it comes to the other teams in the league, you really only care about the stats. In fact, in professional sports today, the statistics are often more important than the outcome of the game itself.

You won't find a lot of statistics in this book. That's not because mobile statistics aren't important—in fact, they are incredibly important—but statistics only serve to make the book outdated before its time. Just read some of the other books on mobile marketing that are only a year or two old—they're already ancient history!

But don't be concerned. By purchasing this book, you'll never be behind the times on statistics in the fast-changing world of mobile marketing. As an adjunct at the University of Denver, there is an intrinsic need to continually update the statistics that correlate with this book for the graduate level class that I teach. Links to all of the updated statistics and information can be found at the website RelevanceRaisesResponse.com. Here, you can obtain the same statistics that the students are using in my class...without the tuition fees.

I JUST WANT TO LOOK AT THE PICTURES

Sorry, but pictures are another thing that you won't find in this book. That's not because I don't believe that a picture paints a thousand words. It's because pictures, just like statistics, tend to leave a book outdated quickly, especially when those pictures involve mobile phones that are so quickly changing in appearance.

REAL-WORLD EXPERIENCE

This book won't contain a lot of academia and philosophizing. Although I am an adjunct faculty member at a university, I don't consider myself to be an academic. Therefore, you won't have to read about lots of mobile generalities and theories.

Brands and businesses already understand the importance of mobile by now; they just need to know how to do it properly. That's where this book will come in handy. What you'll get here is real-world, proven strategies from an author that lives mobile marketing every day. It's my passion. It's my livelihood.

How to implement your own mobile strategy is what I hope you will glean from the pages that follow.

—**Bob Bentz**

CHAPTER 1

INTRODUCTION TO MOBILE

The mobile phone is our lifeline. It is our gateway to the world. It is our digital DNA.

YOUR DIGITAL DNA

*I*n the 21st century, a phenomenon occurred in the United States and the world. A mobile phone began appearing in nearly every pocket and every purse of every person old enough to own one. Never before in the history of technology had one device become the centerpiece of our lives.

The cell phone you own today is your digital DNA. If you grew up in Denver, but have since moved to Austin, you have probably continued to maintain that 303 area code number, despite the fact that you live in the 512 area code now. As long as you pay your bills, you will likely die with the same mobile phone number that you have today, regardless of where you move or how many different devices you own.

Mobile phones are so very personal that even spouses do not share them. Most people would consider it an invasion of privacy if their spouse looked at their text messages without asking first. When your phone rings, it plays your favorite ringtone that you selected. Only you control what apps you put on your phone. Only you know the passwords to open them. Your mobile phone is YOU! Nothing you own is more personal.

In 1975, advertising legend David Ogilvy coined the phrase "Don't Leave Home Without It" for American Express. This was long before the mobile phone was popular, but Ogilvy's phrase probably typifies the mobile phone better than it ever did the credit card. Leave your mobile at home and you will likely be looking for the next place you can safely do a U-turn to go back to pick it up. If you forget your wallet, that just means you'll be eating at Panera for lunch and using Apple Pay. The wallet can wait; the mobile can't. Your phone is your lifeline. It is your gateway to the world.

YOUR MESSAGE ON THE MOVE

In 2007, an advertising agency came up with a catchy slogan for our business to describe its mobile marketing services: *Your Message on the Move.*

At the time, that slogan did a great job of portraying the potential that mobile marketing brought to the advertiser. A brand did not have to just reach consumers on their landline at home when they were watching television, reading the newspaper (remember them?), or on their desktop computer in the office. Now, it could reach consumers when they were out and about...and near the store. It could reach consumers on their terms and it could reach them 24/7.

But something changed along the way. Now, mobile no longer just characterizes reaching people that are on the move, because mobile has become the ordinary, not the extraordinary. Today, mobile is consumed everywhere, even on the couch at home— something that was not commonplace in 2007.

2010—THE YEAR OF MOBILE

During the early 2000s, there was a lot of discussion of the "year of mobile." Article after article touted the upcoming year would be that coveted year when mobile marketing became a "can't live without" promotional strategy. And, at the completion of the year, authors seemed convinced that the next year would definitely bring the elusive year of mobile.

Of course, the premise that one particular year could be the turning point for an industry that evolves incredibly quickly is ludicrous in the first place, but let's take a shot at this one anyway. And, to discuss mobile, it makes sense to discuss the two most influential companies in the business—Apple and Google.

In 2007, Apple developed the first iPhone. It was a game changer. Mobile was no longer just about making a cellular phone call.

Apple's new creation changed the way we thought of mobile, and the mobile phone evolved into what it is today—a multidimensional communications tool. But of course, smartphone penetration took awhile to really catch on and have enough mass appeal to be a significant factor for a marketing strategy.

In 2010, Eric Schmidt, executive chairman of Google (now called Alphabet Inc.), announced at the Mobile World Congress that his company would develop for mobile devices first, and everything else, including the then-ubiquitous desktop computer, would be secondary. This was the start of the buzzword "mobile-first" as a philosophy for doing business. Today, mobile is the single most important medium of communication in the world. Mobile has gone from a nice thing to have to a must-have for forward-thinking businesses.

So when was the "year of mobile"? In my mind, it was 2010, because that was the introduction of the moniker "mobile-first." Today, sagacious businesses know that a mobile-first strategy is the single best way to succeed long term.

CUTTING THE LANDLINE CORD

Men over 35: remember as a young teenager when you wanted to call a girl? It was one of the most stressful things you could do! Not because you had to talk to the girl, but because her dad might just pick up the landline phone and you'd have to talk to him! Things are sure a lot easier for boys today, now that mobile allows them to have one-to-one communication with the girl and no fear that her dad might pick up the phone. It is just one of the many unsung bonuses that we now take for granted with mobile.

The rise of mobile has been inversely linked to the demise of the once-dominant landline phone in the home. Consumers are continuing to abandon their landlines in rapid response to the dominance of the mobile phone. There was a time, however, when you couldn't fathom living without a landline in your home. In fact, landlines peaked in the developed world in 2001, when 57 of every 100 inhabitants had a landline. Among the entire world, landline penetration peaked in 2005, when there were 20 landlines for every 100 people in the world.[5]

There were numerous reasons why people began cutting their landline phones in favor of going exclusively mobile. The recession of the 2000s certainly did not help the landline industry, as consumers began looking for places that they could save a buck. The landline was redundant technology and many were cut, helping households save about $600 per year for a device that was becoming increasingly less relevant in the modern world.

The wireless carriers had something to do with it, too. With stiff competition in the mobile industry, carriers began offering unlimited plans in an attempt to attract new customers. No mobile calling minute limits struck another blow to the landline providers.

Then, there were VoIP (voice over Internet protocol) services. VoIP allowed for free phone calls to be made on the Internet. New Jersey–based Vonage debuted in 2001, with a significant television-advertising budget to grow its users. Consumers couldn't seem to avoid Vonage's advertising on the Internet, as digital advertising at the time was incredibly cheap. Skype was another VoIP protocol service that consumers latched onto. Founded by entrepreneurs in Denmark, Sweden, and Estonia in 2003, it was originally named "Sky Peer-to-Peer" and leveraged the same peer-to-peer networking idea that Kazaa had established a few years earlier. Skype had amassed 683 million users when it was sold to Microsoft in 2011 for $8.5 billion.

Improved cell service was another reason that the landline became increasingly obsolete. In areas where reception was inconsistent, the introduction of home microcell towers greatly improved mobile service. These cell phone enhancements plugged into high speed Internet service to give near-perfect reception, even in homes where the traditional mobile reception was poor.

Finally, one of the major reasons for keeping a landline, emergency services, seemed less important when mobile carriers began implementing 911 services as required by a Federal Communications Commission (FCC) mandate.

When AT&T petitioned the FCC to exit the TDM (time division multiplexing) business in 2012, it seemed as though the end had come to the once-mighty home landline. One could hardly imagine how AT&T would leave the home landline business that had once made it the largest company in the world, but AT&T had no more interest in commodity home landline sales and running calls via copper wires through a PBX (private branch exchange). It was dying technology that no longer produced much revenue. AT&T knew its future was in wireless, not wired landlines.

Landline use is clearly going away, but it hasn't gone the way of the dodo bird quite yet. According to a report from the National Center for Health Statistics[6], households headed by men are more likely than those headed by women to have cut the landline cord. Poorer households, and those living in poverty, are also more likely than high-income households to be cell phone–only households.

Some like the convenience of the landline. It's in the same place all the time, so you do not have to look for it; you'll always know where it is. Others like the tradition of having a landline in the house. And you cannot mistakenly put the landline on silent when you are expecting an important phone call.

Cell phone technology simply is not as perfect as landline technology. With landlines, you do not need to keep the phone charged; the fixed phone is self-charging. Therefore, it will work in a power outage. Voice quality is almost always perfect. International calls are cheaper, and you do not need to buy a special international plan. Perhaps the best reason of all to continue to keep your landline service is that it really is not costing you anything anymore. Many service providers, such as Comcast, offer bundled services that provide households with cable TV, Internet, and landline service for a single package price. Bundled services are especially popular in the Northeast, where landline penetration is, not surprisingly, the highest in the United States.

If you are concerned about dropping your landline service because you do not want to miss an important phone call, there is a solution that you can consider. While you cannot port a landline number to Google Voice, you can port a landline number to a mobile carrier. Once you have done this, you can then port your number a second time from the mobile carrier to Google Voice. Then, if you get an occasional important phone call on your old landline number, you can receive it on your Google Voice account. This will eliminate any concerns of losing your long-time landline number.

HISTORY OF THE MOBILE PHONE

The first mobile call was placed in St. Louis on June 17, 1946, from a telephone installed in an automobile. That was the first car phone.

In 1947, AT&T introduced cell phone service between New York and Boston. The phones were known as push-to-talk telephones. The project was approved by the FCC, but it was a massive failure due to too much interference.

William Rae Young was a Bell Labs engineer who first suggested what ultimately became the concept behind the modern-day cellular mobile phone system. It was Young's idea to create the hexagonal cell concept through cities so that every mobile phone user would be able to communicate from at least one cell tower through the telephone system. The system did not receive widespread adoption due to its required size and exorbitant cost. Only a few of the mega-rich citizens (in addition to James Bond) actually used them. While Young had what was ultimately the best idea for mobile service, it was 1971 before AT&T formally proposed Young's hexagonal cells idea to the FCC.

In the early 1970s, Motorola and Bell Labs were in a race to produce the first handheld mobile phone. That race ended when Martin Cooper, general manager of Motorola's Communications Systems Division, made the first modern mobile phone call from handheld equipment on April 3, 1973. A patent for the technology was granted on October 17, 1973.

Cooper's fame has certainly increased in recent years. He has appeared in a series of Mazda commercials and has been interviewed by *60 Minutes*. Cooper's Mazda 3 commercial appeared in Super Bowl XLVIII when Seattle thrashed Denver 43–8. "When Martin Cooper invented the mobile phone in 1973, connectivity took a mighty leap forward," the ad states. No doubt. Cooper's initial phone call was the ultimate "in your face." He called the offices of Bell Labs and Dr. Joel Engel. In the commercial, the landline recipient of the phone call is in an office, and the actor playing Cooper says, "Guess what we just did?"

"People want to talk to other people - not a house, or an office, or a car," said Cooper. "Given a choice, people will demand the freedom to communicate wherever they are, unfettered by the infamous copper wire. It is that freedom we sought to vividly demonstrate in 1973."

"As I walked down the street while talking on the phone, sophisticated New Yorkers gaped at the sight of someone actually moving around while making a phone call," added Cooper. "Remember that in 1973, there weren't cordless telephones, let alone cellular phones. I made numerous calls, including one where I crossed the street while talking to a New York radio reporter - probably one of the more dangerous things I have ever done in my life."[7]

The first mobile phone that Cooper used was known as "the brick" and it weighed in at a hefty 30 ounces! Ten years later, in 1983, Motorola introduced a slimmed down, less wieldy version of the brick. The 16-ounce, 13-inch-tall DynaTAC 8000x phone took

10 hours to charge and, when fully powered, offered a mere 30 minutes of actual talk time. The DynaTAC cost $3,995. In the movie *Wall Street*, famed actor Michael Douglas uses a DynaTAC cell phone.

Motorola rolled out the MicroTAC flip phone in 1989. It was the first commercially available flip phone. To this day, the flip phone remains the best mobile phone for prevention of the infamous butt dial. For this reason, the flip phone continues to have loyal users still hanging on to their feature (non-smartphone) phone.

In 1990, mobile phones reached critical mass as subscribers topped one million for the first time ever in the United States, encouraging producers to create new, user-friendlier phone styles. The first truly pocket-sized flip phone appeared in 1996 when the Motorola StarTAC hit the market. The StarTAC was a clamshell-style phone that weighed just 3.1 ounces and was very futuristic for its time. In fact, it was allegedly inspired by the popular science fiction television show *Star Trek*.

The Nokia 9000 Communicator was a highly innovative release in 1997. It actually included a keyboard on the phone and could send and receive faxes. It had an LCD screen and could also render web graphics in monochrome. The monochrome screen eventually gave rise to the ability for customers to customize their screens with unique graphics such as the Playboy rabbit head—then the best-selling monochrome graphic. Nokia also brought us a new pastime in 1998—playing Snake on our mobile phone. Has there ever been a more basic, yet addictive, mobile phone game?

Cameras are a very important part of today's mobile technology. Have you ever noticed that nobody sees UFOs anymore, now that we have cameras with us all the time? Including a camera on a mobile phone became a reality in 2000 when the Sharp JSH04 was introduced in Japan. It was also the first phone to allow MMS (multimedia messaging service). MMS allowed users to take pictures and send them to friends—a common feature that we take for granted today. The first USA phones with built-in cameras were the Nokia 7650 and the Sanyo SCP-5300, introduced in 2002. The Nokia model had a 176x208 pixel color display. Compare that to the iPhone 6, which has eight megapixels in its camera.

Canadian company Research in Motion also introduced a new phone in 2002. It was an innovator with the introduction of its BlackBerry 5810 model. This was the first mobile phone that integrated data devices. For the first time, consumers could now have their e-mail and personal digital calendar with them at all times. The Palm Treo 180 and Microsoft Pocket PC soon followed, going after the same market—the on-the-go businessperson. The BlackBerry was life-changing for business people, perhaps in a bad way, because they would never again be completely away from the office. It was the perfect business phone. The BlackBerry made people completely connected to the office—and to the boss—like never before.

With mobile technology, however, you are never the leader for very long unless you are constantly innovating and consistently creating a better product than the one you offered just a few months ago. As innovative as the BlackBerry was, there was something even bigger on the horizon. Motorola hit pay dirt in 2004 with the introduction of its slim RAZR phone. The RAZR was just 0.54 inches thin and appealed to the public's demand for smaller devices. Motorola sold over 130 million RAZR phones. It had a nice run, but was eventually replaced by touchscreen technology.

Prior to 2007, most people used feature phones that operated on the Symbian operating system. These phones allowed you to talk, text, and browse the web, but they did not allow for much customization. Consumers were reliant on the apps that came preloaded on the phones. There was a race in industries like the ringtone business to get "on the deck," which was completely controlled at the carrier's discretion. In 2007 Apple began marketing the iPhone, the biggest game changer of them all. The iPhone was the world's first touchscreen smartphone and was incredibly easy to navigate for the non-technical user. Its screen resolution and touchscreen interface were showstoppers. The iPhone quickly showed just how clunky BlackBerry and other previous smartphones were. Moreover, the iPhone was revolutionary in the sense that the software could be opened to the development community to customize it with innovative apps. These apps could utilize the built-in functions of the phone, such as the camera or the GPS, to offer a smooth and streamlined user experience. Apple's iOS was the first operating system to offer downloadable apps.

Apple did not get everything right with its debut smartphone, however. For instance, it missed simple copy and paste technology on its introductory iPhone offering, but with hardware and software updates, it was able to fix and improve its product every year.

Initially, if you wanted an iPhone, you had to use Cingular (now AT&T Wireless) as your carrier. The iPhone enabled Cingular to close the gap on market leader Verizon and helped it earn hundreds of thousands of new subscribers, especially coveted upscale consumers who could afford the high price tag of iPhone. In addition to traditional phone service, Cingular was also able to sell large amounts of data plans to its new customers.

Google purchased Android in 2005; in November of 2007, it unveiled its Google Android operating system. Its HTC Dream phone was introduced in October of 2008. As opposed to iPhone, Android was released across many handset manufacturers and was not exclusive to any one carrier. Because of this, Android attracted consumers that wanted a smartphone but did not want to change providers. Android systems were also cheaper than iPhones, thus opening up the ability to own smartphones to a larger group of customers.

As smartphones gained market share, businesses began to take notice. Their business websites needed to be optimized for the smaller screen of the phone, since consumers were now accessing the Internet on mobile in large numbers. And with two major competitors in the operating system market, publishers needed to develop apps for both the iTunes and Android marketplaces. They also needed to develop apps for BlackBerry, but most publishers soon dropped development when BlackBerry failed to innovate beyond its initial corporate mobile e-mail success and began losing subscribers.

The playing field leveled once again in 2011 with Verizon's announcement that it had finally reached an agreement with Apple to sell the iPhone. The move upended the balance of power in the industry and ended AT&T's exclusive hold on the incredibly popular device that had fueled much of the company's growth. Sprint also joined the iPhone party in 2011 and T-Mobile got on board in 2013.

Apple shook the mobile world yet again in 2010 when it introduced the iPad. The iPad used mobile technology, but made it optional to be able to make a phone call from it. The iPad was a mobile device that was used more like a desktop computer than a smartphone. It paved the way for much of the mobile mind shift. Competitors began scrambling to compete with Apple. Dell, Samsung, Motorola, BlackBerry, Vizio, Toshiba, and Hewlett-Packard all introduced mobile tablets within a few months of the iPad's debut. Within a year, there were over eighty tablets on the market.

Ever since the smartphone appeared, there's been a general trend toward thinner and larger screen sizes. At the same time, the size of the tablet has been shrinking. The two devices compromised, and the mashup became a "phablet"—a five-to-seven-inch screen size first attributed to the unveiling of the Galaxy Note in 2011. Phablet sales surged in 2015 with the introduction of Apple's iPhone 6 Plus.

Another important development has been the wearables market. Google Glass, introduced in 2013, was essentially a smartphone with a head mount. Apple Watch, introduced in 2015, can text, support apps, use Apple Pay, track your fitness, and control your television. Oh yeah, it can also make a phone call.

You'll Always Remember Your First

Over the years, phones have changed dramatically. They have gone from weighing more than three pounds to weighing less than three ounces. They've lost their antennas. They've changed their keyboards, colors, and functions. But you'll always remember your first mobile phone, even if it seems like a dinosaur today.

The things our mobile phones do today are things that not even Captain Kirk thought about on *Star Trek*. Our phone has replaced our landline and enabled us to be untethered yet still communicative. The mobile phone has replaced our camera, our stereo, our gaming system, our alarm clock, and even our movie screen. The newest mobile phones do even more. The Galaxy S4, for instance, can detect temperature and humidity from our environment. Improved health is on the horizon with mobile as well. We have already seen the popularity of the Fitbit and the Health icon on the iPhone. Fitbit users challenge friends to stay in shape by competing for who takes the most steps in a day or climbs the most stairs. iPhones keep track of their owners' movements and cause them to go back to grab their mobile phones when walking from their office desks to the restroom so that they get "credit" for those steps. Future phones will help save lives. They will monitor your heart rate and perhaps even forewarn you of an impending heart attack or stroke. The mobile phone has come a long way from when you thought it was cool to play Snake on it.

SPINNING CONNECTIONS TO WI-FI

Early connections from mobile phones were similar to dial-up technology on the desktop years before: they were painfully slow. But, like everything else in the mobile industry, innovations were fast and furious. Analog cellular networks, known as 1G, were the most widely deployed system in North America after Dr. Martin Cooper's invention. It was known as 1G due to its being the first generation of cell phone technology.

Early GSM (Global System for Mobile Communication) networks started seeing significant deployment beginning in 1991. GSM technology, first utilized in Europe, put customer information on a removable SIM card. This enabled customers to easily swap the SIM card between phones to enable service. These second-generation mobile phone systems used digital transmission—an improvement over 1G's analog. 2G phone networks supported faster mobile phone-to-network connections for a higher quality of voice transmission. The improved technology in chip design also allowed companies to significantly reduce the size of the "brick" phones that were required with 1G technology.

2G's introduction opened the door for the most popular of all data services—SMS (short message service), or text messaging. The first phone-to-phone text message was sent in Finland in 1993. But 2G did not stop there. 2G also enabled the first downloadable content to mobile phones—ringtones. The first use of ringtone technology was by Finnish company Radiolinja in 1998. Internet service first debuted on 2G mobile phones in 1999 by NTT DoCoMo in Japan.

As mobile phones entered the 21st century, consumers began demanding more and more data services, especially improved Internet access. Enter mobile broadband, known as 3G. 3G supported data applications with much higher speeds (up to 144 kilobits per second). The high-speed connections significantly transformed the industry. The first commercial 3G network debuted in 2001, also by NTT DoCoMo. Much of the innovations in mobile phone technology came from Asia. In 2002, code-division multiple access (CDMA) technology was released in South Korea. In 2003, the technology expanded to Italy and Great Britain, thanks to its success in Asia.

In the United States, the first commercial 3G network was deployed by Monet Mobile Networks using CDMA2000 technology, but it soon after shut down. Verizon launched the first popular use of 3G in July of 2002, also using a version of the CDMA2000 technology. Rollout for 3G was slow, as it required a significant investment by mobile carriers to upgrade to the new technology. By the end of 2007, however, there were 190 3G cell phone networks in 40 countries around the world. 3G technology was ideal for the advent and ultimate proliferation of the smartphone. 3G enabled cell phones to be connected at much faster data rates, which led to an explosion in app offerings. Streaming video and music to 3G handsets was another major innovation.

Native IP Networks, or 4G services, were introduced in 2009. One of the fundamental differences between 4G phones and their predecessors was that they were IP-based, meaning that the phones were able to transmit data using the same architecture of the standard Internet Protocol. 4G phones were assigned their own unique IP addresses, which increased the overall capabilities for the devices. With 4G, maximum upload speeds increased to 50 Mbps, a whopping 10 times faster than 3G service. 4G also provided mobile broadband Internet access. For example, laptops were able to use wireless modems to connect to a mobile phone's 4G network. In addition, 4G's increased speed supported live video over the cellular network. With 4G, the consumer is "always on," with enhancements like GPS location services. We are currently still utilizing 4G networks.

MARKETING TO MOBILE DEVICES

First, there was television, and then the desktop computer. Today, cunning marketers are embracing the "third screen" of mobile and turning it into a marketing juggernaut, to the point where mobile will soon become the "first screen." Along with the increased performance of enhanced devices and connections comes an opportunity for businesses to engage and acquire new customers and users.

At one time, mobile marketing was practically synonymous with SMS text message marketing; that was all marketers really knew. But today, there is so much more to consider regarding what can be done with mobile marketing. Mobile marketing does not mean just one thing anymore in a mobile-first environment. As the evolution continues, the rapid introduction of more mobile marketing possibilities will create even more efficient ways of reaching the mobile consumer. It may seem like mobile has come a long way, but the industry is still in its infancy, and if you have been involved in it for more than five years, then you are a veteran.

Today, mobile marketing is one of the most powerful ways to reach people. It enables you to reach a laser-targeted audience in a relevant way and engage them on their most personal of devices. Relevant marketing means engagement marketing. It is about creating a relationship with your customer or prospect by delivering content that is both relevant and personal. Mobile marketing is no longer just a trend; it is a vital way for businesses and organizations to engage existing customers and acquire new ones. Mobile marketing is modern-day marketing. Very soon, the term "mobile marketing" will sound as ancient as the daily newspaper or prime-time television. We'll all know then that mobile marketing has matured because we will drop the term "mobile" and simply call it marketing.

Want to learn more about mobile marketing? See updated statistics and other important information at RelevanceRaisesResponse.com.

Chapter 2

ADVANTAGES OF MOBILE

Mobile is the closest a brand can get to its customer.

THERE IS NO PRIME TIME ANYMORE

*I*n the 1980s, television advertising was a juggernaut. There were only three major networks, a handful of independents that didn't have many viewers, some cable networks—like MTV—that took ads from taxidermists, and then there was this start-up called Fox that had the absolute worst programming you could ever imagine. But even if you were a big local advertiser, there was one thing that eluded you—prime time! Sure, you could advertise on *Good Morning America*, *The Sally Jessy Raphael Show*, and even the local news, but shows like *60 Minutes* were reserved for just the big dogs. You couldn't afford it.

Until recently, there was still a misconception among small businesses that mobile was like television prime time. Facebook changed all that with its easy-to-use Boost Post advertising feature. Since many small businesses already use Facebook for the essentially free advertising that comes from organic business page posts, entrepreneurs have been boosting posts for as little as $5, thus putting them on the same marketing playing field as Lexus or even Dollar Shave Club.

Moreover, local businesses can now use geotargeted mobile advertising to pay for advertisements that will only show up in their local trading area—an area that may be as small as a single zip code. There is no waste as one might have with traditional media. Add to that the unsurpassed demographic, psychographic, and interest enhancements that mobile provides for laser-focused targeted advertising and you have quite a successful medium for local business promotions.

Most importantly, local advertisers are not at any disadvantage compared to larger, nationally known brands, because there is no prime time when it comes to mobile advertising. With the exception of sleeping time, the audience for mobile marketing and mobile engagement is essentially the same 24 hours a day. Think about it. You check your phone when you wake up in the morning, through the workday, in the evenings, and even late at night.

A mobile advertisement at 9 A.M. is worth the same as a mobile advertisement or TV ad at 9 P.M. in prime time. You reach essentially the same number of people and you receive similar engagement and acquisition. It's like a mini–Super Bowl every day. For local small business advertisers wise enough to be using mobile marketing, you can now play in prime time with the big dogs.

ADVANTAGES OF MOBILE MARKETING

When it comes to mobile marketing, true engagement is when you connect with a consumer in such a way that it makes an impact and enables your business to generate a conversion or acquire a new customer. There are many engagement-enhancing advantages to mobile that can't be found with traditional marketing.

Mass Reach

Much of the talk about mobile marketing is regarding its tremendous ability to provide laser-focused targeting. And, while there is no doubt that targeting is one of its best weapons, the high penetration and mass market that mobile brings cannot be undervalued. Do you know anybody who does not own a mobile phone anymore? Chances are, even your grandparents text and check their Facebook accounts on their mobile phones.

Instant Results

The days of brand building *Mad Men*–style by Don Draper are over. While building brand recognition is still an important part of a marketing campaign, businesses want—and often insist on— immediate results. Mobile provides those immediate results. It is direct response marketing. A flash sale is a good example. Need to clear some inventory now? An SMS text message, app push message (message sent to those who have downloaded an app), or spontaneous mobile advertising campaign can do just that. Include an embedded link or tap-through, and an e-commerce sale can be made on the spot.

Always Reachable

Mobile users are said to be "always on," meaning that they can be reached 24 hours a day, seven days a week, 365 days a year. Consumers do not have to tune in to a radio or television show to see your message because mobile is everywhere. Just look at the statistics of how many of people have their mobile phones within reach all day, even while sleeping. Now, it is probably not a good idea to be sending an SMS text message or app push message in the middle of the night, but you get the idea. Your target market is available and does not have to do anything to receive your mobile message.

Always Shopping

With mobile, consumers are always shopping. It is no longer a requirement to go to the mall or be in front of QVC on the television. At the bus stop? No problem. Consumers can be shopping on their mobile phones. They do not have to *go* shopping, because they are *always* shopping.

The traditional sales funnel has been replaced by the mobile shopping funnel. The consumer may have come to the brick-and-mortar store to buy the product, but the shopping process began weeks before by researching on mobile. Portability, connectivity, and affordability give the smartphone a privileged place in driving e-commerce. Smartphones are often used on the go and, in many cases, they assist in a purchase that does not necessarily terminate on the device itself, but in the physical store.

Your customers have become untethered connected consumers. They are information seekers who are price and feature savvy, because so much information is readily available literally at their fingertips.

Creative Media

Banner blindness is a phenomenon in digital and mobile marketing that is a real concern. It is why creativity takes on such importance when advertising on mobile. Mobile users are in a hurry. They often aren't at home relaxing. Therefore, your message needs to make a quick and immediate impact.

Too often, however, brands are using mobile as an add-on to their existing marketing plans and saving their most creative work for traditional media; they think of mobile marketing as nothing more than sending bland text messages every so often. The good news is that mobile marketing offers a cornucopia of rich media and features that increase user engagement with your content and can make your message stand out from the din of promotions that are commonplace in today's world. Even a simple text message ad, for instance, can be creative with the right copy. If you want to send a picture along with your text message, use MMS and show how great that dress would actually look on the customer. Think of rich media as a highly customizable experience that is only limited by your own imagination. You can embed audio or video in the message. You might even include animation. Ads can resize, move, or pop up. Consider a mini-game, such as a scratch-off or matching game, to engage consumers.

Rich media should enable the consumer to remain on the page, at least initially. It should also respond in some way to the actions taken by the customer, with the end result being an engagement rate that is up to eight times greater than with traditional banner advertising.[8]

Easy

Doing mobile marketing at a high level isn't easy, but it is not difficult to get into the game initially. Even a local pizza shop can get involved. You do not have to be Papa John's to do mobile. There are numerous do-it-yourself SMS text message marketing sites on the web that can help a business facilitate its initial entry into the world of mobile marketing. And, what can be simpler than sending a text message? Most are very user friendly and even the least tech-savvy marketers can be pros in about 10 minutes.

Social media is also mostly mobile today. And features such as Facebook's Boost Post are fairly simple to learn how to use. Boost Post is not the best way to do Facebook advertising, but if you want to do something quickly and easily, it can work without much effort, so a small business can continue to concentrate on its critical day-to-day operations.

Timely

With traditional media, you usually can't say exactly when your message will run. If you are buying midday advertising on radio, for example, you are buying a 10 A.M. to 3 P.M. block. If you are a restaurant attempting to create more lunchtime business, advertising at the end of the time period is probably not going to help you much, at least on the day that the advertisement runs. Not so with mobile. With an SMS text message or an app push message—or a mobile advertising campaign for that matter—you can stipulate exactly when you want those messages to run. Subway sends all of its text messages at 11 A.M. to reach those opt in consumers on the job or in the office to remind them to consider a Subway sandwich for lunch.

Stands Out

Mobile marketing is a decade old, but it is still very much in its infancy. Show your audience that you are doing mobile effectively and your business will stand out from the pack. It shows you are on your game, innovative, and the type of business that consumers want to work with.

Viral

An added perk of mobile is its virality. This is a bonus market that you do not get with any traditional media. When was the last time you clipped a coupon and sent it to your son at college? With social media, a consumer can easily share your advertising message with a friend. Maybe the person you reached isn't looking for a new job, but she has a friend who is. She can tag your recruiting ad with her friend's name, and your marketing has just reached a targeted consumer who needs your service now.

The same thing happens with SMS text message marketing. It is easy to take the message you received and share it with a friend. And it works! A national restaurant chain once discovered that 21 percent of those that redeemed their mobile coupons were not even part of the original opt in list of customers.[9]

Personal

The mobile phone is a very personal device. Borrow somebody else's phone and change something on it, and you'll feel their ire.

Marketers can customize their mobile messages to each individual. For example, there may be different SMS messages for different target groups. A business might personalize the message to also mention the recipient by name, which increases engagement and response rates. A restaurant, for example, may know that it is mostly males, ages 13–24, who eat its cheesesteaks, so the message to teenage boys and young men is to promote cheesesteaks. Targeting moms 35–44 is a different story; they will be concerned with a healthy, family-friendly alternative, such as a salad. Mobile enables you to provide the message that the consumer is most likely to respond to based on his or her own demographics and personal preferences.

Customer Lists

One of the greatest benefits of mobile marketing is that every lead or opt in that it generates becomes a part of your business's database. That list is yours and only yours, and it becomes very valuable data indeed. Data accumulated by your own customers is dubbed "small data." Combined with the "big data" from a third-party provider, those lists can pack a powerful punch.

Nothing builds a list better than SMS text message marketing. Since SMS is opt in marketing—as opposed to e-mail marketing, which is opt out marketing—your customers are asking for you to market to them in a medium that is far more likely to be seen and read. How often does that happen with traditional marketing?

Two-Way Communication

With what other medium can you get an immediate response from the customer or prospect? Send a broadcast SMS text message to your opt in audience or send an app push message and you'll get immediate feedback. Is the customer interested in the offer? You'll know right away by reply messages and soon after by purchases or in-store lift. Mobile offers instant deliverability and high response rates, whether it is through alerts, information, advertisements, or mobile coupons. There's no waiting, because you put the message in the hands of your audience wherever they are. Good business and good business communication is always a two-way street, and mobile permits instantaneous engagement like no other medium.

The two-way communication feature of mobile enables your business or organization to instantly collect valuable opinions on your offering. You can choose to interact with just one or a few of your audience members, or you can choose to interact with all of them at once. Two-way communication ensures that your audience completely understands your message. You're also communicating with them in the method that they have chosen and prefer. Such communication turns them into long-term buyers and brand promoters.

Trackable

Philadelphia retail legend John Wanamaker once said, "Half the money I spend on advertising is wasted; the trouble is I do not know which half." Wanamaker would love mobile because he would know exactly which half of his advertising is working and which half is being wasted.

The attribution ability of mobile marketing is a huge advantage over the traditional advertising that Wanamaker used in the 1800s and early 1900s, and it is a huge advantage over traditional mediums used today, such as television, radio, and print. With mobile, results are completely measurable. Businesses can appraise the same things that traditional mediums can measure, such as reach, frequency, and gross impressions, but with mobile, there are so many more impactful statistics that can be measured. With a mobile marketing campaign, for instance, a business can examine multiple key performance indicators, such as click-through rate, leads, opt ins, opt outs, in-store lift, sales, and more.

Optimizable

The detailed analytics provided by mobile marketing campaigns enable savvy marketers to maximize results. Since every aspect of the mobile marketing strategy is being analyzed on a real-time basis, results can be optimized with A/B testing of all elements of the campaign. A/B testing compares two marketing elements to determine which one performs best. Marketers can experiment with a tremendous amount of variables on a website to optimize results. Such variables include design, graphics, copy, offers, and every other element of both desktop and mobile websites. A/B testing will be discussed in greater detail in a future chapter.

Lookalike Audiences

After considerable A/B testing, your business is going to find its perfect message and the perfect target audience. Once it has, your business is going to reap the rewards of that effort. But the beauty of mobile is that it does not have to end once you saturate that formula. With proper use of lookalike audience profiling, you can expand your market wider and wider, given the sheer mass that mobile provides to marketers. Lookalike audiences are targets that are likely interested in your product because of their similarities to the initial successful target group. Facebook has perfected this feature. With Facebook, you can even upload a customer list and it will find lookalike audiences that match that customer list, enabling you to efficiently promote to that newly defined audience.

You may think that you know your audience, but an algorithmic approach to identifying that market is a tremendously more successful way to target new customers. Think about it. Your friends are your friends because they are likely similar to you in many ways. Mobile enables you to effectively identify such groups in order to maximize your return on investment (ROI) by marketing to those most likely to become fans or purchasers of your product or service.

Demographic Targeting

With mobile, there is no need to cast a wide net like the one provided by radio, print, or television and hope that a prospect swims in. That is because you can target your ideal prospect based on gender, age, and other demographics, such as income level, job, parental status, household size, and education. Sure, if your prospect is reading *Wall Street Journal*, it is probably pretty safe to generalize and suspect that you are reaching an upscale person involved in business, but there is certainly no guarantee. You could be reaching a student reading for a graduate-level communication class. Television does a very poor job of targeting the right audience as well. Sending feminine hygiene product advertisements to men isn't going to help your sales any, so why pay to reach them? With mobile, you don't have to.

Geotargeting

If there is just one feature that makes mobile such an outstanding marketing medium, it is geotargeting. With geotargeting, a business can reach only those consumers who are within the range of their retail store. That means no waste!

Imagine you live in a large city such as Wanamaker's Philadelphia. The Philly metro area includes not only the city and its Pennsylvania suburbs, but also southern New Jersey, nearly all of Delaware, and parts of northeastern Maryland. If you are in the western suburbs and your business has a trading radius of just five miles, why would you use traditional media and reach people in South Jersey?

Let's say a couple from San Diego is visiting Las Vegas on business or vacation. They would not normally receive advertisements from or be familiar with Las Vegas area businesses, but with geotargeting, your restaurant can serve them advertisements when they are down the street checking Facebook or navigating their way around the city with the Waze app.

Interest Targeting

Interest targeting is also something that mobile does very well, and it is a key factor as to why mobile marketing is such a powerful tool. Nowhere is that more evident than when it comes to social media marketing. Take Facebook, for example. Facebook is tracking not only what you have posted on its own site but also wherever you go on the Internet. Ever see those icon buttons to "Like" an article on Facebook? Whether you Like that article or not, Facebook logs you on the page that you are reading and registers that you have an interest in that subject. Interest tracking like that offered on social media enables you to laser-focus your marketing to just those people who are superfans of your subject matter.

Multimedia

A business may have a mobile-first strategy, but a mobile-only strategy remains risky and extreme. The fact is that all marketing works, even print; it is just a matter of getting the right media mix to maximize your ROI. Usually, that media mix includes elements of traditional media, such as print, broadcast, and out-of-home (billboards, bus shelters, and the increasingly ubiquitous screens that surround us every day), coupled with digital Internet and mobile marketing.

Within mobile marketing itself, the mantras are "cross-device marketing" and "omnichannel marketing," meaning that the same creative and selling message should reach the customer in an attempt to drive conversions, regardless of which device (smartphone, phablet, tablet, or desktop) that consumer is using. Cross-device marketing attempts to identify the same user across multiple devices so that the same brand message can reach that consumer multiple times.

At the end of the day, mobile is no different than traditional media in attempting to get maximum reach for the advertiser with the largest possible frequency. That is why your message has to be the same, regardless of the type of device or mobile media that is being used. Couple that with the same message through traditional media, and you have the recipe for a successful campaign—a true omnichannel marketing strategy.

Value

Think back to your college economics class and the concept of supply and demand. At this point, not all advertisers "get" mobile. If they did, they'd cut back on their print advertising even more than they already have, because the advertising dollars spent on mobile does not nearly match the time spent with the medium. Bottom line: mobile simply isn't getting its fair share of the advertising pie.

What that means is that the supply of mobile exceeds demand. And that means there are real bargains available in the mobile advertising world. This will not last forever, but for now, mobile remains underrepresented in most promotional budgets.

PUSH VERSUS PULL MARKETING

Traditional marketing normally uses a push strategy. Drive-time radio ads, prime-time television ads, coupons, attractive packaging, point-of-sale (POS) displays, direct mail catalogs, and a salesperson making a direct phone call to a prospect are all examples of push marketing. This type of advertising casts a wide net in the hopes that some of the right fish will swim in. It does not necessarily try to build relationships with prospects, but more likely will simply try to push products to them.

Push marketing, sometimes called outbound marketing, creates quick demand for a product and hopes to make immediate sales to pay for the large advertising expenses. The negative to push marketing is that sales are often fleeting and do not continue if a high promotion budget isn't always in place. With push marketing, the consumer needs to be consistently engaged to have success for a long period.

Take the example of McDonald's. Its Dollar Menu strategy is an example of a push strategy. McDonald's hopes to entice the consumer with POS offers at discount pricing, both on television and when they are at the restaurant.

It's no surprise that the opposite of a push marketing strategy is a pull marketing strategy. Pull marketing is any technique used by a company to generate interest in a product and pull them into a relationship with the brand. Modern pull marketing techniques use a variety of media to create interest in a product or company and then encourage consumers to seek out the product on their own. A pull marketing strategy is especially popular on the Internet because of the viral effect of social media. There have been several successful clothing products featured on ABC's *Shark Tank*, for example, that used a pull strategy. These products succeeded initially by making all of their revenue by strictly promoting with free organic posts on Pinterest that generated interest in the fashions.

Companies that produce goods or services can use pull marketing strategies to raise awareness of a product before it is readily available or before the company has made a large production run. This enables the company to gauge interest in the product prior to producing a lot of expensive inventory, because the last thing a business wants is to see its product unsold and in the bargain bin at the Dollar Store.

A pull marketing strategy, also known as inbound marketing, is customer focused and will most likely evolve over time based on considerable market research. Effective target market analysis is necessary to determine the most ideal customer, the one who will seek out the product. The message needs to be especially powerful, because you are asking customers to find and purchase the product on their own.

Blog posts, press releases, white papers, infographics, e-books, e-mail marketing, social media, pay-per-click marketing, search engine optimization, and public speaking at a trade show are all examples of pull marketing strategies. Such marketing tactics are used at the top of the sales funnel to attract new qualified prospects that will eventually become revenue sources for the business.

The Pusher

In the early days of Madison Avenue, a push marketing strategy was the norm. Advertisers wanted to reach as many people as possible with their advertising budgets. And, with only three television networks and powerful, dominant city newspapers, it was easy to reach large numbers of Americans with a single advertisement.

Today, however, it is getting much more difficult to use push strategies exclusively. Television viewers have an abundance of television channels to choose from, and daily newspapers do not have anywhere near the same circulation that they once did. Adding to the complexity is the fact that consumers often do not watch television in real time, preferring instead to skip through advertisements via DVRs.

Some consumers are even offended if a brand pushes messages to them. This has led to legislation controlling push marketing messages. Remember the telemarketing business? It once employed over three million Americans whose jobs were to call you at your home, interrupt you, and try to sell you something. Now, there is a Do Not Call list that prevents telemarketers from legally calling you at home without previous permission. That is, unless they are simply overseas, using inexpensive VoIP technology, and do not bother to adhere to the Do Not Call regulations.

SMS marketing is no different. Push the consumer a text message without their previous permission and you'll feel the wrath of the consumer and may find yourself defending a class action lawsuit for TCPA (Telephone Consumer Protection Act) violations.

If you are in sales, you know how difficult it is to even reach a prospect on the telephone anymore, especially if your call is unsolicited. People don't seem to answer the phone with regularity, and when they see the caller ID, they definitely do not answer it. Pushing a sales message via a cold call is still effective, but it is becoming increasingly difficult, and many young sales professionals simply do not want to do it.

With the onslaught of advertising messages that consumers experience all day, it is no wonder that they are developing a natural aversion to push marketing strategies. Consumers don't want to have a message pushed at them, especially when they do not have an interest in the product in the first place.

We're Pulling for You

In the case of mobile marketing, it is not a very good idea to use push marketing exclusively, because the mobile device is so personal that most users will find it too intrusive. It is the intimate nature of the mobile device that makes marketing far more effective when a pull strategy is used. When a customer responds to a pull message, he is saying, "I want to engage with your message and I want to be part of your brand." Only if the customer agrees can a true one-to-one relationship be created between brand and customer. A subtle approach is going to work more often than an aggressive one. Mobile marketing is no different than the dating world—there needs to be interest on both sides, and being too forward initially is certainly not going to improve your chances.

Pull marketing is what is used in most promotions that utilize mobile marketing. It is the more modern marketing concept and is certainly more powerful in developing a relationship with the consumer. Since we know how personal the mobile device is, a pull strategy is probably the only type of mobile marketing that will consistently work.

Of course, there is value to all marketing, including push marketing campaigns. If it didn't work, the television industry would be out of business, and that is far from happening. The smartest marketing strategy is the one used by mobile in a typical SMS marketing campaign. The advertisement generates interest in the product. Then, the consumer sends a keyword to a short code to opt in—a pull strategy, since the consumer initiated the relationship. Once a verifiable opt in is received, the business can continue to send "push" broadcast text messages to the opt in database.

SMALL BUSINESS POWERHOUSE

There has never been a medium more ideally suited for small business marketing than mobile. For small businesses, it is not so much about amassing large amounts of fans and followers; rather, it is more about actively engaging with their best customers. Since small businesses have fewer customers, it is arguably easier for them to directly connect with their most loyal ones. A small business can segment them more efficiently based on learned preferences and therefore provide more customized offers. Such personal offers often allow customers to become brand ambassadors who will promote the business, such as sharing a social media post. A small business needs to take advantage of the viral effect—an area where mobile naturally excels.

Small businesses have small advertising budgets, and they can't afford to waste a single dollar. What the small business person puts into advertising is money he does not take home to his family, so it must be effective and provide immediate ROI.

A local business also has a small trading area, normally just a few zip codes or a radius of a few miles from the retail location. The beauty of mobile for the small business owner is the geolocation aspect that only mobile can deliver. With traditional media, there is always going to be waste, because rarely can print or broadcast target such a finite geographic area as effectively as mobile can. Add the demographic targeting and the interest targeting that mobile can deliver and you have a perfect storm for the ideal promotional vehicle for small businesses.

But the single best feature of mobile may be that you can activate it and stop it whenever you want. Rainy day at the golf course? Stop the mobile advertising and save your budget for a sunny day. (Unless you sell umbrellas—then your marketing team can kick your targeted ads into overdrive!) Have extra product that you need to unload? Message your customer base and let them know. Stopping and starting your advertising campaign isn't a possibility with traditional media. Print advertising is already scheduled. You can't call the TV or radio station and ask them not to run the advertisement just because the weather looks grim.

Although mobile can be highly effective in creating brand awareness, in most cases, mobile marketing is direct response marketing. With direct response, you should get immediate, trackable results, so you'll know if the advertising is working or not. If it is not, cancel it and start it again on another day with a new strategy, new product offering, and new creative.

KEY PERFORMANCE INDICATORS (KPIS)

No matter what you do in life, you need to set goals for yourself. Mobile is no different, only instead of calling them goals, we call them key performance indicators, or KPIs. A KPI is a metric used to determine the success of a business (or a business's specific effort) by assessing a particular critical factor. There are many different end-result KPIs to consider. Obvious ones might be increased sales, increased memberships, or similar. But often increased sales figures, especially for luxury items with a lengthy path to purchase, are not immediately available, and even if they are, they may not be an effect of the mobile marketing promotion. Therefore, early-term KPIs are often considered so that the business can get a more immediate evaluation of the effectiveness of the campaign.

Choosing the right KPIs relies on a good understanding of which factors the organization needs to evaluate. Such KPIs will likely vary based on the department doing the evaluating. What is important to marketing, for instance, may not be as important to the sales or finance departments. Effective KPIs may not be financially related, even though increased sales is often the ultimate, and most obvious, outcome of an effective marketing strategy.

Key performance indicators work best if they are

- timely and able to be measured frequently;

- simple and easy for all involved to understand;

- team based so that all departments are pulling together for success and there is no finger-pointing later;

- based on factors that have had significant impact in the past;

- acted upon and approved by senior management;

- able to be evaluated and analyzed to lead to future success.

Choosing the right KPIs for your organization is paramount to evaluating the success of a mobile effort. Too often, businesses blindly adopt KPIs that others in the industry like to evaluate and base the success of their program on those. An example of a KPI that is often improperly used in mobile is tap-through rate. Tap-through rate can be an important KPI, but if the marketing message is misunderstood or exaggerated, it can result in a terrific tap-through rate but poor sales conversion. In addition, a tap-through on a mommy blog may not be as valuable as one on a *Huffington Post* article.

Be sure that your organization starts with the basics and understands both the goals of the promotion and how it plans on achieving them. The process should be an iterative one that involves feedback from multiple department managers and those implementing the details of the campaign. Then the overall goals need to be understood by all employees who are involved in the process of attempting to reach a particular KPI goal.

With mobile marketing, there are many different KPIs that you can consider based on the type of effort that you are employing. Here is a rundown of some of the metrics you can assess and subsequently use to optimize your marketing's efficacy and engagement:

- Active users—usually judged based on daily or monthly active users. These are your best customers and the ones you need to learn more about so that you can continue to improve on the product.

- Ad revenue—total advertising revenue that a publisher has collected from its app or mobile web product.

- App downloads—how many consumers have downloaded the app.

- App revenue—gross sales from the app and/or its upgrades, such as in-app purchases after a free app download.

- App reviews—the rating (typically one to five stars) and commentary consumers give regarding their experience with an app. The quantity and quality of reviews matter, so call out some favors when your app first hits the stores.

- App store rank—where your app stands in relation to all other apps in the marketplace. The higher you rank in the app stores' download lists, the more likely you are to get continued downloads. This is why it is so important to get off to a quick start when you first submit the app.

- Call tracking—number of calls generated. This is often measured by companies using a unique phone number to track call statistics.

- Click-through rate—of the consumers that have seen your offer, the rate of those that clicked (or, more appropriately in the mobile world, *tapped*) through to the landing page of the offer. This is a metric to be careful of focusing too closely on, because some bad actors in the mobile ad space will inflate this measurement with bots and other unwanted traffic.

- Completion rate—the ratio of mobile video viewers who watched until the end of a video to those who began the video.

- Conversion rate—the percentage of users who have done the action that you are soliciting, such as made a purchase or registered information.

- Cost per acquisition (CPA)—the cost to obtain a specific action from a user, such as an app download, text message opt in, or sale.

- Cost per click (CPC)—the cost to generate a click-through.

- Cost per install (CPI)—the cost to drive the installation of the app.

- Cost per lead (CPL)—the cost to generate a lead.

- Customer satisfaction scores—whether or not a customer was pleased with a product, usually derived from follow-up messaging.

- Delivery rate—the percentage of text messages that were successfully delivered.

- Failure rate—usually an SMS KPI, the number of messages that were unable to be delivered.

- Frequency—the number of times the average person has seen your marketing message. Frequency is certainly not unique to mobile marketing and can be used to compare the effectiveness of a mobile campaign versus a traditional advertising campaign.

- Gross impressions—the total number of times the message has been seen, regardless of whether the same person saw it multiple times. Reach times frequency equals gross impressions.

- Hits—the number of service requests handled by the Internet server. This is the most basic KPI and has probably been around the longest. In the dot-com boom days, hits, not revenue, were the source of the oftentimes ridiculous valuations of companies. Today, however, it is not a very effective KPI to consider, but at least the boss will understand it without an explanation.

- In-app purchases—total sales made in the app.

- Items in cart—average number of products being purchased per order. This is often called "basket size" in the brick-and-mortar world.

- Keyword tracking—monitoring whether or not words specific to your product or service are bringing consumers to your website via search engines. A great way to track the effectiveness of different promotions for your SMS campaign is to use different inbound keywords for each medium.

- Leads—the number of consumers that have indicated interest in a product or service and are now being turned over to sales or marketing for follow up or continued marketing.

- Lifetime value—what a customer is worth to the business over a lifetime. This is usually matched against acquisition costs to determine if the marketing is cost effective.

- Lift—increased store traffic, also called in-store visits.

- Load time—how quickly your mobile website loads. In the app business, it is known as app launch. Cutting even partial seconds off of your load time will lead to significant improvement; people today are not known for being very patient.

- Loyalty programs—statistics on the number of customers engaged in a mobile loyalty program.

- Mobile e-mails—the percentage of promotional e-mails being read on a mobile device.

- Mobile traffic—the percentage of web traffic coming from a mobile device.

- New customers—the number of new customers. It is an obvious one, but you can bet the boss is measuring it.

- Opt ins—how many customers have agreed to receive your SMS marketing messages, also known as list growth.

- Opt out rate—the percentage of opt ins that have replied with STOP to be removed from future text message marketing. If you get a flurry of opt outs, perhaps you are sending too many messages or too many irrelevant messages to your database. This also applies in the social media world, particularly Facebook, where oversaturation of your ads to a given audience, or poorly thought out messaging, can cause customers to block your ads or unfollow your page.

- Organic searches—the percentage of overall traffic on the mobile website that has been generated from search engine clicks.

- Pages per session—average number of pages visited per user in the app or on the mobile website.

- Permissions—the number of people who downloaded the app and also registered their personal information.

- Purchases—how many people have bought your product.

- Push notifications opened—the percentage of app push messages that were actually opened.

- Reach—total number of unique consumers that your message has reached. Along with frequency, this is another statistic that can be compared against traditional media.

- Redemption rate—number of mobile coupons that have been redeemed.

- Retention rate—the percentage of users or buyers that have returned to purchase or use the product.

- Revenue per user (RPU)—revenue divided by total users.

- Session length—the length of time a consumer spends on your app or mobile website. Naturally, a longer session length should indicate greater engagement. If consumers are leaving quickly, they are probably not getting what they thought they would.

- Social shares—the number of times a user has shared information about your company on social media. Social media shares prove the virality of mobile marketing. More shares means more engagement and free promotion for the organization. The business is reaching individuals that it never had to pay for! Plus, the message was so important to the recipient that he's taken the time to promote it on your behalf, and it carries with it his implicit endorsement of your business.

- Subscription rate—the percentage of users that have purchased a subscription. This act proves that an organization has a sustainable business model.

- Tap-through rate—see click-through rate.

- Time between visits—how long it takes consumers to come back on average.

- Time spent—the number of minutes a consumer is on your site. The Interactive Advertising Bureau believes the average time spent watching your mobile video is the most important KPI for the video category.

- Traffic-to-lead ratio—how much traffic it takes to generate a single lead.

- Usage—whether the app is being downloaded and then falling into the app graveyard or being used consistently.

- Win rate—also known as fill rate, this is the amount of mobile advertisements that have been accepted programmatically by publishers (website and app owners) and displayed.

This is certainly not a complete list of mobile marketing KPIs, but it is quite a few. Choosing the right ones in advance of the campaign will allow alignment of all members of the organization and will create a common goal when running your mobile marketing campaign.

While immediate and interim KPIs are certainly an important gauge of the overall success of a campaign, early mobile marketers were too hung up on some of the more short-term ones. Tapping on a mobile ad and downloading an app are certainly important, but it is what happens after the click or app installation that really matters. Lifetime value may be impossible to predict at this early stage of mobile marketing, but in the long run, it is retention, compared to the cost of acquisition, that matters most.

Want to learn more about mobile? See updated statistics and other important information at RelevanceRaisesResponse.com.

Chapter 3

MOBILE-OPTIMIZED WEBSITES

There's a tsunami of traffic moving from desktop to mobile, and marketers must ensure that the user experience of mobile and tablet is as convincing as the desktop experience.

THE DAY MOBILE SEARCH TOOK OVER

*D*ecember 25, 2013, was a big day in the world of mobile. According to Google, it was the first day that the total number of searches on the search engine from mobile exceeded those from desktop.[10] It certainly makes sense that Christmas Day would be the first, given the large amount of new mobile phones given as gifts and the multitude of people who are traveling away from home on the holiday.

Mobile searches have become more the norm than an anomaly; every day sees more mobile searches than desktop searches. Among ethnic groups, African-Americans and Hispanics are more likely than Caucasians to search from mobile.[11] According to the *Path to Purchase Report*, with vertical markets like restaurants, the number is understandably significantly higher when it comes to mobile search.[12] In developing countries like India, where broadband is not popular, mobile access to the Internet is the predominant form of web access and has been for many years.[13]

Mobilegeddon

You have heard of Google. It is kind of becoming a big deal. So when Google speaks, most business owners listen. According to Google, 61 percent of consumers accessing a site that is not mobile friendly will leave for a competitor's site.[14] Those stats are a few years old, so I suspect the real number is even higher today.

Google's goal has always been to deliver the very best results to searchers that it possibly can, so it did not miss the massive mindshift from desktop to mobile search. In an effort to reward sites that provided a positive mobile experience, Google rolled out its mobile-friendly update on April 21, 2015. The update was designed to boost the rankings of mobile-friendly pages—pages that are legible and usable on mobile devices—in mobile search results worldwide. Conversely, pages designed only for large screens would likely experience a significant decrease in rankings in mobile search results. The press dubbed the new update "Mobilegeddon."

Because of the threat of Mobilegeddon, the spring of 2015 saw a lot of businesses scrambling to make sure their websites were finally optimized for mobile. They should have done this years earlier, but, buoyed by Google's threat of lower search rankings, they finally got around to getting it done. Today, thanks in part to Google's Mobilegeddon, mobile and desktop search rankings have never been more different. Different search engine rankings for desktop and mobile have been around for years, but it's clear that Google's mobile-friendly update has made the situation even more dramatic between sites that are mobile optimized and those that are not.

The genie is out of the bottle. Google is not going to abandon its mobile-friendly strategies when there are now more mobile users of its product than desktop users. As long as people continue to search on their smartphones, Google is going to prioritize those searchers in an attempt to give them the very best user experience. Google has even provided a resource so websites can test their mobile friendliness. It is a minimal test at best, but it's a source for finding out what Google thinks. Want to test whether Google thinks your website is optimized for mobile? Try the test here: https://www.google.com/webmasters/tools/mobile-friendly/.

HOW TO OPTIMIZE YOUR WEBSITE FOR MOBILE

Until about 2012, most businesses created a different mobile version of their website. This was a smaller, easy-to-navigate version of the desktop site, often using a different domain, such as: http://m.website.com. The preceding "m." indicated that the user was on a site designed specifically for mobile. When consumers came to the domain from a mobile device, they were directed to the site that was exclusively made for the smaller screen of the mobile phone.

Then things began to change for the lowly mobile-only website. Google Best Practices announced that a business really should be using the same domain for desktop and mobile users. The SEO community began endorsing responsive design as the best way to obtain high search engine rankings on both desktop and mobile. Hence, Google's announcement caused the near-death of the m-dot mobile website. Today, sites are rarely designed using a different URL for mobile phones.

What Technology Should I Use for Mobile Web Development?

To provide a great web experience across multiple devices, marketers basically have two options: build a website using responsive design or create device-specific versions of the website using adaptive design. Technically, however, there are four potential solutions to designing a mobile website:

- Unique mobile site—an m-dot website or a unique site solely for mobile users, although this technique is virtually nonexistent in modern web design.

- Responsive web design (RWD)—a responsive website that fluidly changes to any screen or device size.

- Responsive web design with server side components (RESS)—a site that uses device detection to maximize the efficiency of responsive design.

- Adaptive web design (AWD)—a site where the elements change to fit a predetermined set of screen and device sizes.

A unique mobile site is old-school and most likely not the way to go in over 99 percent of mobile designs. If your business is almost exclusively mobile, perhaps there is a reason to have a unique m-dot mobile site, but it is going to be a very rare instance indeed.

Responsive web design, most commonly designed with HTML5 code, is going to be the likely choice in nearly all new mobile web builds. It can also be designed using CSS3 and JavaScript. Responsive design has the striking advantage of being highly flexible, as it fluidly changes to accommodate any device. RWD works by sending the same code, regardless of device, and then rearranging it on the client side, thus allowing the same webpage to be displayed on any device. It serves the same HTML code on the same URL, whether the user's device is a desktop, tablet, phablet, smartphone, feature phone, or wearable. It can also respond differently based on the screen size of the device. Developers can decide which graphics and content will be used for mobile and tablet users. Text and images can be adjusted based on any browser or screen size. When new devices are added, there is no additional programming required. Most importantly, however, responsive design is Google's recommended design pattern. For many websites, RWD achieves a reasonable balance between mobile-friendliness and ease of implementation.

There are several key design considerations that will make a website look and operate at its best with responsive design:

- Header—The header and masthead should be simple so as to not take away from the key selling points. The logo is the key brand image; an overly horizontal logo may not look great on smaller vertical screens.

- Navigation—Navigation is much trickier on a small screen. Often, designers will use a navigation button shown by three horizontal lines, usually in the upper right corner of the site. This is called a hamburger menu because it looks like a burger surrounded by the bun. Some sites use a left-side navigation that can expand outwardly to cover most of the screen.

- Images—It is impossible to include too many images on the mobile screen. Therefore, designers often use image carousels that allow users to swipe through multiple product images.

- Footer—A footer doesn't take up valuable space like the header, but it's just as important because it is a consumer's last stop on your site. Consumers are used to using the footer as a navigation tool. It should also include the very important "Contact Us" link.

One of the challenges of responsive design is the tablet. The tablet, although technically a mobile device, is most often used more like a desktop computer than a smartphone. With responsive design, developers need to build the code to execute on three primary devices (desktop, tablet, smartphone). The tablet often straddles both of the other devices in its user intent. An admirable trend in responsive design techniques that combats the tablet struggle is to again use a mobile-first approach. In this way, designers create sites with the smallest screens in mind first and then add features and content for larger ones. It is a lot easier to add value to a site when going from smallest to largest screen size than to decide what elements to take away when going from desktop to mobile. Focusing on mobile first means the site will be clean and won't have the bulkiness that often slows a mobile version down.

The main problem with RWD is that, by default, all devices are sent the same size graphics, regardless of screen size. Therefore, low-resolution screens are sent the same images as those sent to high-resolution screens. This is problematic in that the smaller screens cannot show the images at their native resolution and have to "shrink" them to fit. This method can be inefficient and can take up additional data that should be unnecessary.

Responsive web design with server side components is a web development technique that takes RWD to the next level. RESS combines traditional responsive design with server-side detection, allowing RWD to further optimize graphics to fit device specifics. RESS can also enhance the mobile website in other ways. If bandwidth is at a premium, RESS can limit data usage by only serving the most important images. In the same manner, mobile video can only be served if there is a fast connection available. And RESS can avoid Flash on devices that do not support it.

RESS seems to be an obvious enhancement to RWD, so why doesn't everybody use it? The negative to RESS is that feature detection is often difficult. The feature detection code on the site needs to be updated every time a new browser or device hits the market, and that is difficult to keep up with. There are some third-party services that will do this for you, but nevertheless, it's a limiting additional hassle for RESS. If your site uses RESS, it's never going to be completely done, and there will always be additional costs.

There are limitations to responsive design and reflowing the same content on every device. Certainly, there are advantages to offering a unique and customized experience for every device user. This is especially true in the case of e-commerce sites, where making the sale is paramount to the existence of the business, hence the need for adaptive design.

Adaptive design employs dynamic serving that uses the same URL regardless of device, but it generates a different version of HTML based on information the server recognizes about the user's browser. With AWD, a specific experience is sent depending on the type of device. In this case, web developers can customize specific content and adapt it to the device itself. An example might be a wide shot of the crowd at the president's speech being served to a desktop user and a close-up of the president's face being served to a smartphone user. AWD allows developers to design lighter versions of a site so it will load faster, since extraneous items will never make it to the end user. It also allows developers to take advantage of the different unique features of certain smartphones and tablets.

Adaptive design is not all about designing for the device itself. Depending on if a user has a slow or fast connection, a site could serve different resolutions of its images. They are not necessarily custom to each device, but to the bandwidth levels available to the user.

The common thought process is that the obvious choice is always going to be responsive design, but that is not the case. There are instances where adaptive design makes sense as the preferred design method. Because adaptive design is created for the exact specifications of a particular mobile device, it does provide a better overall user experience. This is especially apparent in the case of load times, since content used is formatted specifically for the intended screen size.

An example of a company that would be apt to use adaptive design is an airline or travel site. For a travel-related business, sites need to be highly interactive and engaging; they also need to have multiple options since it is a high-ticket item and closing each deal is paramount to success. With its exciting graphics and complex interactivity, an online casino is another type of site that needs to use adaptive design. With offerings ranging from table games to slot machines to bingo, it is easy to see why extra care must be given to ensure precise compatibility with all devices. Players are there for entertainment, and adaptive design provides the best possible user experience, regardless of the device used.

On the other side of the debate, the biggest concern with adaptive design is that it is very expensive to develop, since some brands may choose a custom development for every desktop and mobile device. Moreover, when new devices are introduced, the programming could start all over again to accommodate the new entries. An additional concern with adaptive design is that some older devices may still be in the market, and they may not be supported by the original design. Because of these concerns and the ongoing commitment to updating, adaptive design is never going to be the solution for everybody.

Finally, there is the issue of Google's preferred method. You need not be concerned of lost rankings if you use adaptive design instead of responsive. If an AWD site maintains canonical links to desktop content, it shouldn't be a problem for a site's organic rankings. (A canonical link element is supplemental HTML code that helps webmasters prevent duplicate content issues. Duplicate content is a negative for search engine optimization, and a canonical link works to indicate the "preferred" version of a web page.)

Have you seen a website that you like, and are wondering what design style they used? Here's how to determine if the site has used responsive design or adaptive design. With responsive design, the web design does not respond to the device itself, because in most cases it simply doesn't care about the device type. Instead, responsive design responds to the screen resolution. To test this, look at a site on a desktop and change the size of the window by grabbing one of the corners and expanding or contracting it. When the window size is changed, the website will also change its size and shape to fit the smaller or larger screen of the browser. Some of the elements of the site may shift to accommodate the change in screen size, but all of the elements will remain on the screen regardless. This is an example of a responsive design site.

An adaptive design site will act differently. Go to a travel site, such as Southwest.com, and do the same thing. Grab the window in the corner and drag it to the middle of the screen to shrink the screen size. Instead of seeing the elements of the site moving around based on the new site size, you will see some of the images simply being covered up. If this is the case, it is an adaptive design site.

The technology used for a website's design is going to vary based on the specific needs of the brand. Choosing the right method is important because the site is going to remain active until its next overhaul. Regardless of which approach is best for your particular needs, the important thing is that you provide an improved mobile user experience and gain the search engine rankings, and sales, that your business deserves.

Principles of Mobile Site Design

It is actually more difficult to create a mobile version of a website than it is to create a desktop version because there is so much less real estate to work with. Following these guidelines will help provide your mobile customers with a satisfying user experience:

Home Page

- Call to action—This is the single most important element of your website. It is the action that you want the consumer to take. Therefore, make sure that it's easy for your users to find it. Put the call-to-action graphics and buttons in obvious places where they cannot be missed.

- Menus—Mobile users have a lot less patience than desktop users. They do not want to scroll through a long list of options to find what they want. Present the fewest number of menu options possible and make the categories obvious and distinct to make it easier for mobile visitors to navigate.

- Navigation—Users should be able to access the most important content in one click from the home page. This usually involves using the three-line "hamburger" button in the upper right. A back button should be at both the top and the bottom of each page.

- Home page access—Make sure that it is always easy to get back to the home page without having to hit the back button multiple times. Be sure that the top banner logo allows users to retreat back to the home page.

- Video—A lot of text on the home page of a mobile site is not a great first impression. It's better to include a video to engage users right away.

- Sale promotions—It is tempting to hit users with prominent display of sale items on the home page, and this is fine, so long as the short-term promotions do not interfere with the navigation or, most importantly, the call to action.

Site Search

- Site search boxes—Especially if your site is a large e-commerce or information site, visitors will want to be able to search within your site search box. Make sure it is prominent, visible, and at the top of the page.

- Misspellings—It is certainly more difficult to type a search item into a search box on a mobile phone. Make it easier on your customers by adding misspellings and autocomplete.

- Queries—To get better search results, ask as many questions up front as possible. For instance, a shoe site might ask for sizes, since showing shoes that are not available in a particular size probably is not going to do the customer much good.

Registration

- Delayed registration—It is often annoying when you walk into a retail store and the clerk immediately asks you what you are looking for. In most cases, you just want to look around first. Same with your website. Don't ask them to register before engaging them with the product they are interested in. Registration is a turnoff.

- Guest checkout—Permit guests on the site. As much as you might want the user's information, some simply do not want to give it to you, and if you demand it, you'll likely get false information anyway. Let them purchase without registering. After using the guest registration and making the purchase, ask them again to register, but this time give the user a good reason why they should register, such as receiving e-mail discounts.

- Convenient checkout—Remember a returning visitor's information to make it more convenient when checking out.

- Tap-to-call—Some aspects of the checkout process might be confusing to some users. Others may be nervous about providing their personal data online. Therefore, you should always allow for a tap-to-call help button during the checkout process. If your business is too small to allow for 24/7 live operators, at least provide a recorded IVR (interactive voice response) program to get leads to call back the next business day.

- Tap-to-text—This is the same as tap-to-call, although simply touching a button will enable the customer to send a text message to the business.

- Tap-to-chat—This will initiate an interactive chat service with your business.

- Allow conversion on another device—It can be difficult to fill out long forms on the small screen of the mobile phone. If a prospect becomes annoyed with all the tiny blanks she has to fill in, she may abandon the form. Allow prospects to be sent information via e-mail so they can finish the process and convert to a customer when they are on a desktop.

Forms

- Short forms—Ask only for the information that is absolutely needed and nothing more. You can collect more details later.

- Efficient forms—Make your forms simple to complete. When entering the zip code, for instance, the form should autofill the city and state to reduce the amount of fields required. Put the zip code form before the city and state to save time. Do the same in Canada, but remember that Canadians use alphanumeric postal codes instead.

- Information entry—If the field requires numbers, such as a phone number or zip code, automatically shift the user's mobile phone to the numeric keyboard.

- Toggles—A toggle is easier to navigate than a dropdown. Users will prefer using them.

- Calendar—People often do not know what the date is, but they usually know what day of the week it is. Offering a visual calendar for events and travel sites make it a lot easier on the mobile user and will help them make fewer mistakes on date selections. Global users will appreciate this since much of the world puts the date first and the month second, as opposed to North America, where the month always comes before the date.

- Labels within text boxes—Your site will be dealing with many different mobile screen sizes. A mobile user can easily get confused, often not knowing whether they should input copy in the box above or below the label, for instance. That's why you cannot fail if you have the labels inside of the boxes.

- Automatic cursor—When the form is filled, automatically have the cursor jump to the next field box. Of course, you cannot do this for a name or address, but you can do it for phone numbers and zip codes, where there are always a standard number of digits.

Usability

- Tests—It is critical to test, test, and test more. Don't just use the people in your office; they are probably too close to the product to find errors that outsiders may find. There are online services that will enable you to test on a range of devices without having to purchase all of the devices.

- Pinch and zoom—A good mobile site should never require the user to pinch and zoom to see items.

- Expandable images—While a good site will avoid pinch and zoom, it's great to offer expandable images, especially on e-commerce sites.

- Portrait and landscape—Whatever is used on your home page should be used throughout the site. Don't make users turn their phones between portrait and landscape!

- Windows—Users should never have to open new windows on mobile. It is a pain for them and may cause you to lose the sale.

- Desktop site—Some users may prefer using the desktop site over the mobile site for whatever reason. Do not deny them the ability to use the desktop site, but do not label it "full site" either. If you label it "full site," users tend to choose it, fearing that they are missing out on something, and then they get frustrated because it does not look great on mobile. Use the term "desktop site" in the footer to denote the site. And do not always link back to the home page of the desktop site; it's better to link back to the most relevant page on the desktop.

Technical Checklist

- Configuration—Make sure that your configurations are correct and that you are taking mobile users to the mobile site and desktop users to the desktop version. This sounds basic, but it happens.

- Landing pages—Landing pages often work best on mobile where the theme can be exactly based on the mobile advertisement or source of the click-through. These are discussed in more detail later.

- Analytics—Ensure that your analytics tools are tracking both mobile and desktop separately.

Things You Must Include on Your Mobile Website

- Tap-to-call—Your contact page should include a tap-to-call button so that mobile visitors can easily touch their smartphones to outdial to your business. It is best to put the company phone number at the top of the mobile web page so that it is easy to find. Include the brothers of tap-to-call, tap-to-text and tap-to-chat.

- Hours—Mobile users more than likely want to visit your business at the moment they're searching. Let them know when you are available.

- Map—If you are a brick-and-mortar store, make it easy for consumers to find you. This involves including a Google Map or something similar on your mobile website.

- Address—For those not interested in using a map, be sure to include the business's physical address in the footer where it can be found easily. This also helps with local SEO.

- Social media buttons—If your company is actively promoting itself on social media, include the social media buttons on the mobile website. It may also lead to additional Likes and follows.

What to Avoid

- Small type size—There is a tendency among designers to save space by using small type size. This takes away from usability. Use fourteen- to sixteen-point size fonts, especially for important calls to action.

- Slow loading items—With increased use of high speed Internet and Wi-Fi, it's becoming somewhat less important to avoid slow-loading items on the mobile version of your website, but it's still best practice to always try to decrease load times. Large graphics and long videos are examples of things to minimize. Want to test if your mobile website is slow? Go here: https://developers.google.com/speed/pagespeed/insights/.

- Unplayable content—Flash, for instance, is not widely supported on mobile devices. Users that cannot access some content will become frustrated and dissatisfied. HTML5 will provide a good standard for all users.

- Interstitials—Screen real estate on mobile devices is precious, so any interstitial has a negative impact on the user's experience by covering up the content that the user came for in the first place. Interstitials for app downloads or registration forms are the biggest culprits. Moreover, it's also not always easy to get rid of the interstitial, thus adding additional angst. Further, in November of 2015, Google announced that sites with large interstitial advertisements that cover the entire page will be subject to penalties as part of its algorithm to promote mobile-friendly websites.

- Long forms—Users won't fill them out. They are a big pain to do on a smartphone.

Take the Thumb Test

When it comes to mobile navigation, I like to simplify things. I call it the thumb test. Open up a website on your mobile phone and navigate through it using only your thumb. Now, imagine that you are a large man with really big thumbs. (If it were me, I'd be Dwayne "The Rock" Johnson.)

Were you able to easily get to where you needed to go? How many "fat-finger" clicks did you make? If you can navigate a site like The Rock would need to, then you have developed an awesome mobile site. Buttons should be at least 45 pixels to ensure easy tapping.

Mobile Landing Pages

Not having mobile-optimized landing pages often leads to poor results, because a desktop landing page can be too busy for the short attention spans of mobile users. A mobile landing page has only a few seconds to load or users will abandon. It needs to grab their attention quickly and engage them so they'll act on your offer. Draw your audience in by utilizing the following tools:

- Design—Use a single column design. Nothing else makes sense for mobile landing pages. Scrolling should only be vertical, never horizontal.

- Color—Keep it to a single color scheme. Be sure that the text copy has a strong contrast versus the background.

- Margins—It is easy to bump something on the small screen of a mobile landing page. Make sure that any clickable link has significant margins (non-tappable areas) around it to prevent as many fat-finger taps as possible.

- Above the fold—The fold is the point where the mobile website content shows but further content is not visible. Imagine it as the Mason–Dixon line of the mobile web.

The user must scroll down to see anything below the fold line. If you must have a fold, keep the most relevant information above the fold.

- Logo—A logo won't make the sale, but it helps with credibility.

- Address—If the brand is not well known, an address can offer additional credibility so the customer knows this is a business with a physical location rather than some potential Internet scam.

- Copyright—Adding a copyright tells the consumer that they need not continue shopping for a better price, because the product is exclusive.

- Headlines—Mobile landing page headlines need to be short, very short. Keep them to four words or fewer if possible. Matching your landing page header to the banner or pay-per-click advertising that the consumer tapped is best practice.

- Copy—Plan to keep it short. When you are done writing your landing page copy, go back and edit it again to keep only as much copy as is absolutely necessary. Use bullets and short sentences.

- Graphics—It is a small screen, so do not try to squeeze too many pictures onto it. If users need to pinch and squeeze at all, you have done a bad job. Everything they need to see must be seen instantly. Use carousels if you have several images you want to show. If you must use stock photos, make sure they do not look like stock photos. Spend a little extra to get good ones; the picture is the most important thing on the site.

- Call to action—Think of the call to action as an elevator pitch, and the person with you is only riding up one floor.

The call to action must be clear, immediate, and strong enough to make the viewer want to act on it quickly. It should be a different color than the rest of the page so that it stands out—orange works best. If it's confusing at all, the user will certainly say no.

- Additional navigation—Don't take away from the call to action. It may be tempting to include additional website navigation in case they want to buy something else, but doing so clouds the offer and makes the landing page too heavy. Keep focused on the goal of making a conversion and follow up with additional information only after the sale has been made.

- Forms—It is very difficult to fill out forms on a smartphone. Keep them simple and short. Ask for as few items as possible. The key is to get users to submit the minimum information required to be considered a lead, such as e-mail and name. If you must get more information, break the registration form into two parts. If there is information that is not required, but would be nice to have, ask for it only after the conversion has been made. Offer an added incentive to get the consumer to complete the form.

- Drop-down menus—Rather than asking the customer to fill out a long form, consider using a drop-down menu with prearranged answers for added ease.

- Social logins—Customers can easily obtain their general information by linking to a social media account, which is simpler than filling out a lengthy form for basic contact information. Social logins can streamline the overall process.

- Load times—Second to shorter forms, load times are the most significant thing a landing page can do for improved results. Don't use Flash or plugins that may be incompatible with your customer's phone. Don't use resized features as they will suck up additional, unnecessary bytes. Keep the size of the landing page to less than 20 KB. Ask your programmer if writing the code in HTML5 will speed things up. Keep in mind that just because your site loads in less than five seconds on 4G doesn't mean that the consumer using 3G will stick around long enough to see the landing page load.

- Tap-to-call—The single best thing a business can get is a phone call. Make sure that you tap-enable the landing page by including it in the HTML, and make sure you have staff available to actually answer the call!

  o Include the country code if the promotion is available outside the home country of the business.

  o Put a little phone icon next to the number to make it stand out.

  o Include a call to action, like "Call Now," in the copy.

  o Be sure to list the phone number in case the user wants to call from a different phone or landline, write it down to call later, or give to a friend.

  o Use an actual phone number on the button instead of "tap to call"; some businesses report up to a 20 percent increase in calls if the actual phone number is used instead of a button. This is increasingly important if your business is local and can use a local area code, because people do prefer dealing with a local company.

  o If the office has limited business hours, consider hiring a company that can answer the calls after normal business hours.

- Thank-you page—After a visitor converts, send them to a conversion page and follow up with an e-mail to the customer. Use the follow-up e-mail to gather more information or attempt to sell an additional item.

- Social sharing—Ask your visitor to share the content with a simple-to-use social sharing button. It is an added viral bonus for your business when consumers share your product with their like-minded friends.

- Localize—If you know the user's location, your business can localize the landing page to indicate something specific about the offer or direct the user to the nearest store location.

- Submissions—Create an XML sitemap for your mobile site and submit it to Google and Bing.

- A/B testing—There's one final place where you need to excel with landing pages, and that is with adequate testing. Don't go with what you like, go with what the statistics tell you to go with.

Responsive E-Mail Design

Another important element of responsive design is incorporating a business's e-mail marketing as well as the company website. The result will enable e-mail content to be viewed seamlessly on multiple screen sizes. The best converting e-mails are colorful and visually appealing. Unnecessary elements are removed. Text is readable on the smaller screen of the mobile device and the call to action is clear.

Here are some best practices for e-mail designs:

- Size—Keep the e-mail to a single column layout and less than 600 pixels wide.

- Copy size—Apple recommends that font size be 13 pixels for copy.

- Buttons—Apple's recommendation is 44 pixels height and width.

- Color—A high-contrasting color combination will pop and get the best response.

- Images—Use fewer images and only use the best ones. Try to use more vertical images instead of horizontal ones. Format them so that if they are touched, they lead to the call-to-action landing page. Use local, recognizable pictures if possible. Include happy people, babies, and puppies whenever possible.

- Alt tags—Some e-mail recipients will have providers that automatically block all graphics. An alt tag allows them to at least know what they are missing, and it may encourage them to allow graphics to appear in the future.

- Above the fold—The most critical elements of the e-mail need to be delivered above the fold.

- Navigation—Simplify the navigation. Include only the most important elements.

- No Flash or Java—Most won't work in HTML e-mails that are read on mobile.

- Plain text option—Some people won't download pictures, so get your message across using just text if required. Allow recipients to accept a text-only version of the e-mail.

To gauge if your e-mail marketing is working, the following metrics can be tested:

- Delivery rate—the number of e-mails that were delivered and not rejected by the recipient's server. Delivery rate does not include messages that were spammed out by the recipient, because the sender would have no knowledge of this.

- Bounced messages—messages that were rejected. Hard bounces are those messages that are rejected because the recipient e-mail is no longer active or because the server has blocked the sender. This is why it is so important for a sending domain to maintain a positive reputation. Soft bounces are messages that are rejected for other reasons, usually because the e-mail is heavier than the allowable size limit that the recipient's server permits.

- Open rate—the percentage of messages that were opened. Actual read rates are going to be lower than open rates, because an e-mail may have been opened, but there is no way to gauge that it was actually read.

- Tap-through rate—the percentage of recipients that tap through to a landing page. For an e-commerce site, this is perhaps the single most important statistic. A secondary statistic would be to measure the cost per tap-through.

- Unsubscribe rate—the amount of users who choose to stop receiving your e-mails. Sending too many e-mails or sending irrelevant e-mails will certainly increase the number of recipients that choose to opt out through the unsubscribe button.

THE ABCS OF WEBSITE TESTING

David Ogilvy once said, "Never stop testing and your advertising will never stop improving." That's certainly true when it comes to web design. With website development, most businesses think that when their site is done, it's done for a few years, save a few blog posts and personnel changes here and there. But websites need optimizing too. That's where the concept of testing comes in. There are numerous things that you can test on your web page, including but not limited to the copy, images, offer, call to action, buttons, color, navigation, layout, login, program flow, checkout process, messages, and upsells. Even subtle changes can make profound differences in results.

A/B testing, also known as split testing, is the marketing term for randomized testing with two variants, such as landing pages, home pages, or checkout processes. With A/B testing, a control variable A is pitted against an experimental variable B. The purpose is to test, with statistical accuracy, the outcome of a hypothesis that will possibly contribute to better results. With A/B testing, a business is not flying blind. Instead, it is letting the results of the A/B test drive choices and decisions involved with creating the best possible website.

With website design, the process of testing various elements on a web page or website is done in the hopes that making changes will lead to better conversion rates among randomly sampled, but similar, visitors to the site. An example might be testing whether offering free shipping or a BOGO (buy one, get one free) offer gets more business. Or it may be a more subtle change, such as whether a green button or an orange button generates more sales. Such a change may seem insignificant, but some e-commerce retailers have seen double-digit differences in conversion based on slight changes to design elements.

Testing must be statistically accurate (aim for a 95 percent or higher accuracy level by having enough visitors to the site before drawing any conclusions) and will hopefully lead to a large and noticeable discrepancy between the elements being tested. In most cases, the results will simply eliminate some of the hypotheses from the mix, as the results are statistically insignificant. When there is no impact from the changes made, this is known as a null hypothesis, and the outcome is that any such alterations do not change the results for better or worse.

Testing via the A/B method is simple and will get results quickly since there are only two choices available. By keeping the variables small, a large amount of tests won't need to be done, and results will be available quickly. If a site doesn't get a significant amount of traffic, A/B testing is likely the only way to make certain that a test is statistically accurate. Because A/B testing results are pretty straightforward, they're a great way to justify to the boss the benefits of continuing to put effort and expense into an already completed website.

Testing on web conversion has come a long way in the past few years. Many sites now perform multivariate testing, which is a far more sophisticated form of testing than the two elements of an A/B test. Multivariate testing allows marketers to simultaneously test various elements within a website in order to effectively understand the relative impact of each element, or combination of elements, to its ultimate conversion. Testing multiple elements of a website at the same time is sometimes called full factorial testing.

Multivariate testing is more complex, but also more desirable, because the business doesn't have to continually perform A/B tests to find the ultimate winning formula. Instead, multivariate testing compares multiple variables to produce results with various combinations. With multivariate testing, the website owner can test several variations of each element of the site in order to see what changes have the most positive impact on conversions. Instead of doing 10 A/B tests sequentially, the marketer can do just a single multivariate test that will lead to quicker results and better prediction of outcomes.

Multivariate testing is not recommended for sites that do not get a lot of traffic, because it is difficult to be statistically accurate given the multitude of variable combinations. Without sufficient traffic, what you'll be left with is a confusing set of statistics, many of which do not make any logical sense.

One of the difficulties with multivariate testing is that there is often a disconnect between a marketer's inherent skills and his background in mathematics. Most marketers, unfortunately, do not have an advanced mathematics degree or even a knack for it; it's simply not in their creative DNA. Thankfully, there are numerous tools on the Internet that can help a web designer perform multivariate testing in a way that ensures accurate results. One free tool that you can use is Google's Content Experiments, which is part of Google Analytics. With Content Experiments, you can test up to 10 pages at once to determine which one results in the greatest conversion rate. Content Experiments uses multivariate testing on an A/B/N model. In statistics, "n" denotes a variable between one and any number. A/B/N testing enables a business to test three or more site variations at a time. High traffic sites can use A/B/N testing to analyze a broader set of variations in a faster period of time. Content Experiments delivers separate URLs to all visitors so that statistics can be tracked on a single web page's various combinations of elements.

With Google's Content Experiments, you can

- compare how different web pages or app screens perform using a random sample of your users;
- define what percentage of your users are included in the experiment;
- choose which objective you'd like to test;
- get updates by e-mail about your experiment's progress.

In summary, with A/B testing, you are essentially testing two different versions of a web page to see which one works better. With multivariate testing, you are varying several elements on a single web page to see which combination works best. As for which testing method to use, A/B testing is almost always going to be superior for small businesses and multivariate for large sites and big businesses.

Regardless of whether you utilize A/B or multivariate testing, here is the step-by-step process that a business should use:

1. Define KPIs—What will constitute a success? What do you want to achieve through the testing? Ultimately, that is probably going to be more conversions or greater sales. Add some micro-conversions to the mix as well. (Micro-conversions are smaller steps the testing will gauge, such as testing different buttons or different copy.)

2. Identify bottlenecks—Where are customers abandoning in the conversion process? This is the first place a business will want to look for improvements.

3. Hypothesis—Determine a few different solutions to the bottleneck. For example, if consumers are abandoning too often on the checkout page, try different payment solutions or consider adding PayPal as an alternative to credit card processing. Estimate the cost of any new product investment or labor costs in making the required changes to see if the anticipated value of the change makes the effort and corresponding cost worthwhile.

4. Implement and wait—Patience usually is not the boss's greatest virtue, especially when she is seeing a reduction in revenue due to testing. The changes that are being implemented usually result in one step back to make two

steps forward. Wait until you have enough visitors for the testing to be statistically accurate. Dispose of the really poor changes early; they are not going to turn around. Keep accurate statistics along the way with details of when specific changes have been made.

5. Final results—Now that you have tested many different variables, start enjoying the larger number of conversions.

6. Never stop testing—Sit back and enjoy the improved results on your website for a while, but never stop thinking of ways to improve it. Your work in marketing research is never done. Continue looking for new, often very subtle ways, to improve the performance of the business. Always remember Ogilvy's quote included at the beginning of this section.

In conclusion, multiple mobile devices certainly have not made A/B or multivariate testing any easier for marketers. Test results need to be tracked on desktop, tablet, phablet, smartphone, and feature phone. Tests may work out great on one device but not at all on another. It is one of the biggest challenges today with testing, especially if your site uses responsive design. If there is a significant difference in results over various devices, you may need to consider using adaptive design instead.

CONTENT MANAGEMENT SYSTEMS

It is far easier today to create and update websites for a business. That is due in part to the excellent content management systems (CMS) that are available through tools such as WordPress. A CMS, sometimes referred to as a web management system, uses a content management application that allows marketing or administrative employees that may not know hypertext markup language (HTML) to manage and modify the content of the site without involving the webmaster or an engineer. The content delivery application uses the new information to update the website itself each time that the content is changed.

The obvious CMS systems are the templates created by tools such as WordPress, but there are far more sophisticated enterprise-level CMS systems as well. CMS software such as Joomla! or Drupal keeps track of all of the content on the business website and serves the appropriate answers to users. CMS software can do a lot of different things, such as make all content searchable or keep track of an individual user's permissions. It also can make it easy to create polls, picture galleries, podcasts, and forums.

MOBILE SEARCH

In the beginning of this chapter, Christmas Day 2013 was recognized as a landmark day in the evolution of mobile search. Fast-forward a year and a half to May 5, 2015, when Google announced that more than half of the inquiries on its search engine every day were coming from mobile smartphones and feature phones, even when removing tablets from the mobile equation.[15] That's how quickly mobile search has become the norm, and it shows no signs of lessening.

There are essentially two primary reasons why a person searches on mobile. When a consumer is on the go, he is usually searching for something local, because there is an immediate need for something. This type of search is the reason that local search optimization is such an important part of a brick-and-mortar business's mobile marketing plan. On the other hand, more than half of all searches in the home now come from mobile, thus defeating the premise that mobile search is only done on the move. In fact, people search on mobile because it is often the handiest device when a new product or service is needed. Because of this, mobile search is an important information gathering point at the top of the sales research funnel, even though the ultimate purchase might be credited to a desktop computer.

Mobile Search Engine Optimization (SEO)

If your marketing plan doesn't include mobile, then your marketing plan is not finished. The same can be said of search engine optimization (SEO). While many of the elements that are critical in search engine optimization for desktop are the same as mobile, there are some definite differences when optimizing a website for mobile.

First, it is important to note that search engine ranking for mobile is considerably more important than it is for desktop. Mobile searchers are in more of a hurry and less interested in researching. Therefore, tap-through rates on mobile are far more likely to be in the first few search result positions than with desktop. Moreover, it is far less likely that the mobile searcher will visit page two of search results, thus making it highly unlikely that a consumer will find a listing that doesn't make the first page.

Mobile search engine optimization consists of improving site design, site structure, page speed, and other variables to make sure a site is properly servicing mobile searchers. In general, the same basic principles that deliver high rankings for desktop searches will also work for mobile searches.

Below are some notable differences for mobile SEO from traditional desktop SEO:

- Keyword searches—Keywords should usually be shorter, as smartphone users are less likely to enter long-tail keywords. Try the Google AdWords Keyword Planner or something similar to find short keywords that are akin to your primary keywords.

- Long-tail keywords—When choosing long-tail keywords for expensive products on a mobile site, think of what the initial search will be for. Often, an initial search for a luxury or expensive product is done on mobile at the top of the funnel and the actual purchase is later deferred to desktop.

- Design for each keyword—One of the advantages to using adaptive design instead of responsive design is that you can design a mobile version of your site for each keyword, as well as for each device.

- Avoid bounces—A good user experience is critical. Google will rank your site based on how many bounces (those that leave the site immediately) it gets and how often consumers return to the site.

  o Thumb test—If you cannot navigate your site using your thumb, then it's likely not a good user experience, and you won't get the repeat use that Google wants to see. Given the smaller size of the mobile phone, your mobile site needs to be simple to navigate.

  o Site design for mobile—Don't ever use pop-ups, Flash, or other technology that is not completely mobile compatible.

- Page speed—Load time is especially important with mobile, since consumers are often searching where they do not have access to Wi-Fi. Users have no patience when it comes to the web. Check your website speed on Google PageSpeed Insights to see how your site ranks speed-wise versus others.

  o Use file compression tools to reduce the size of your CSS, HTML, and JavaScript files.

  o Optimize the background code by removing commas, spaces, and unnecessary notes.

  o Eliminate redirect pages.

  o Leverage browser caching so that return visitors will

have quicker loading pages.

o   Improve server response time by fixing problem areas, such as database queries.

o   Optimize images to make sure they are properly sized.

o   Use a "less is more" approach to mobile web design to ensure quick load time.

- Video—Searchers love video, so include video wherever you can. But consider putting video on a page unto itself so it loads quickly.

- Geotargeted copy—Geotarget your site to mobile. Think about how people search for local businesses. Out-of-town people, for instance, might search for "family restaurant near Disney World." Or they may rely on their GPS and search for "gym near the Hilton." Others yet may rely on voice search through Siri. Consider adding such keywords to your prominent responsive design site pages that target mobile search.

- Local citations—Be sure to register your business with sites that are primarily made for local mobile search, such as Yelp and TripAdvisor. There are a host of such local sites, and there are many great lists online that you can work from. Registering your business on all of them will have a great impact on your business.

- Address—Be sure to use the same business address on all of your local citations. For example, if your business is on First Avenue, choose whether you're going to write it as 1st Ave, First Ave, 1st Avenue, etc., and stick with it. Be consistent so that you get local "credit" for all local listings.

- Google My Business—Make sure you have your business listed at Google My Business, previously known as Google Places.

- Tap-to-call—Put your phone number on every page and make it tap-to-call, so if the consumer simply touches it, they will dial your business. Think pizza takeout.

Local Search

Local search and mobile search are nearly synonymous. Mobile is the here and now and the future of search, especially when searching locally. Thanks to mobile local search, we can quickly and easily find things around us, and we are doing so in massive numbers.

Remember how we used to find local businesses? It required the Yellow Pages, a map, and a landline phone. If you got lost, you needed to look for a payphone to find directions to the business. By today's standards, it was hardly a convenient solution.

Today, consumers are searching on mobile with keywords like nearby, closest, and near me. According to Google, searches using the term "near me" increased 34-fold from 2011 to 2015. Over 80 percent of searches using these keyword terms come from mobile devices.[16] Considering that half of all on-the-go searches have local intent, it should come as no surprise that "restaurants near me" is the most popular search at all times during the weekend.

When a consumer searches for "restaurants near me," it is known as a mobile moment. A mobile moment is a chance for a business to win by giving good information that will lead to a sale, and the great news is that there are hundreds of games every day for the local small business. Mobile moments can happen in many situations. It may be at a retail store, where the customer is researching a product or looking to see if there is a better price online. It may be a visitor in a new city wanting to find a gym. Perhaps it is a mom wanting to know where to get a new softball glove for her daughter's t-ball team.

Here are some things you can do to enhance the chances of your business getting found in local search results:

- City and state—Add your city and state everywhere. Add it to the title tags, header tags, URL, alt tags, meta description, and, of course, to the content itself.

- Maps—Always include a map. It makes sense to use a Google Map, since Google is the search engine where a site would most like to rank.

- Local citations—A business will want to be listed on as many sites as possible. It will also, however, want to avoid duplicate listings on any site, especially Google. Often, multiple people will submit a listing for a particular business, and this confuses Google. If there is more than one listing for a single business, ranking power will be divided among the duplicate listings. Moz Local will give a summary of all of the listings and then the work can be done to fix them.

- Consistent listings—Businesses move to new locations often, and this can create inconsistent NAP+W (name, address, phone + website) listings. Moreover, inconsistent listings can occur if one listing says "Rd." and the other says "Road." These may seem like minor things, but they can have a significant impact on local search rankings.

- Reviews—Link to your Google Plus page and set up a page on the business website where users can find a convenient link to reviews.

- Schema markup—Schema markup helps the search engine recognize what the page is all about. Using schema code to let search engines know about a business location can be very valuable to local rankings.

No one strategy or tactic is correct for every business and, when it comes to local or mobile SEO, there is never a guarantee that Google or other search engines will rank your site higher. But if you can gain organic rankings, they will stay with your business for a long time; they are the best type of promotion you can have, because they have no direct hard costs except for the effort you put into them.

Want to learn more about web development for mobile? See updated statistics and other important information at RelevanceRaisesResponse.com.

Chapter 4

TEXT MESSAGE MARKETING

SMS text message marketing is the workhorse of mobile marketing. It is the pillar that holds up the mobile marketing building. If you can only do one thing in mobile marketing, it should be text message marketing.

WHY TEXT MESSAGE MARKETING?

Next to making a website mobile friendly, SMS text message marketing is the single most important thing you can do to get started with a comprehensive mobile marketing strategy. It is inexpensive and offers the single best return on investment of any mobile marketing tactic that you will employ. Implementation is easy because it is a universal application that works the same on all phones; in fact, even the most basic of cell phones can use SMS. Whether you are a national retailer or a local pizza shop, there is a place for text message marketing in your marketing plan. There are more mobile phones in the world than human beings,[17] and only SMS reaches more than half of those humans. Not apps, not Facebook, not Instagram, not Snapchat, not WhatsApp. Only SMS.

Text messaging is ubiquitous. It is the one and only Tyrannosaurus Rex in mobile. Text messaging is the feature that consumers use the most on their mobile phones. In fact, more Americans text than actually talk (remember talking?) on their mobile phones.[18] No account registration or installation is required. And, best of all, text messages, as opposed to e-mails, are opened and read by nearly all that receive them.

If you are marketing via mobile, it all starts with a mobile-optimized website and SMS marketing. Neither are particularly sexy today, but SMS messaging is at the basic foundation of most ongoing, successful mobile marketing campaigns.

Here's why SMS text message marketing is so very powerful:

- One-to-one communication—Mobile is about personalization because it is the most personal device that we own. A text message from a business can be targeted in that the message speaks directly to the consumer; it is a personal connection.

- Mass communication—It is the mobile solution that can reach nearly 100 percent of your target market. A business can reach out and touch all of its best customers with the tap of a button.

- Opt in marketing—As opposed to e-mail marketing, which is opt out marketing, SMS marketing is opt in marketing. Consumers must give permission for the business or organization to send them text messages. That means consumers feel so strongly about your brand that they are saying they WANT to receive your advertisements.

- Instantaneous—The message does not need to be planned well in advance and can react to the situation at that very moment. Messages are sent and received in a matter of seconds. Think an unplanned flash sale.

- Timely—Unlike traditional media, an SMS campaign can be intimately controlled, down to the exact date and time when the customer is most likely to buy. For a restaurant, that might be just before lunchtime. For an urban discounter, it may be paydays on the 15th and the 30th of the month.

- Trackable—Mobile, by its nature, is highly trackable, as opposed to traditional media. Results from all SMS promotions can be tracked with unique identifiers or promo codes.

- Optimization—By using A/B testing, a savvy marketer can test multiple promotions in order to find the best offer and best creative for the best target audience.

- Loyalty—Text messaging offers the ability to increase loyalty and reward best customers by letting consumers be part of a business's VIP club. It enables a business to instantly communicate with its customer base.

- Virality—A consumer can easily forward a text message to a friend who might want your offer. This is advertising that a business benefits from but does not have to pay for (the best kind of advertising).

- Lift—SMS marketing can significantly increase foot traffic at a retail store. This is especially true during traditionally slow days. A restaurant, for example, can use SMS to attract diners on Mondays and Tuesdays, when business is usually slow.

SMS Versus E-Mail Marketing

Perhaps the single most important statistic in text message marketing is this one: **97 percent of mobile subscribers will read a text message, even a promotional one, within 15 minutes of receipt.**[19] Compare that to e-mail marketing, where only about 19 percent of all messages are opened.[20]

It is not hard to imagine. Our e-mails are chock-a-block full of spam every day. Even the best spam filters in the world can't keep our inboxes clean. You're going to get junk e-mails—a lot of them—and there is not much that can be done about it. Fortunately, there still are not a lot of spam text messages reaching mobile phones, at least in direct comparison to e-mails. Sure, the occasional one slips in there, but for the most part, the stricter rules protecting our mobile phone text messages appear to be working.

Tap-through rate is another area where SMS excels versus e-mails. There are varying studies on this, but the general conclusion is that the tap-through rate on text message embedded links is as much as five times greater than e-mails'.[21]

UNDERSTANDING TEXT MESSAGE MARKETING

There are many elements that go into a text message marketing campaign. Understanding each of them is important to creating an effective, ongoing SMS campaign that will produce results. Before we dive into those, let's look at how SMS works.

Standard text messaging means that there is no cost to the consumer to receive the text message, except for the fact that it may contribute one additional message to the consumer's monthly text message plan. Since most consumers now have unlimited text message plans, the fact that one message is added to the monthly plan has become rather insignificant.

Standard text messaging through a short code uses Short Message Peer-to-Peer (SMPP) technology. SMPP is an open, industry-standard protocol for sending SMS data over the Internet. A different technology is also available for sending messages through Simple Mail Transfer Protocol (SMTP). SMTP is an Internet standard for electronic mail (e-mail) transmission. Since every mobile phone has a corresponding e-mail address, you could send messages to the inboxes of a cell phone via e-mail protocol and not traditional text message protocol. The advantage to SMTP is cost savings. SMTP was once an offering of most online text message marketing companies but is seldom seen or used anymore since the cost of sending SMS has declined so much in recent years. If you'd like to find out the email address associated with a mobile phone, you can find a list of all of the carrier emails at *The Text Message Blog* (www.TextMessageBlog.mobi).

There is one other type of text messaging that is available, but it is very rarely used. It is called Free To End User (FTEU), and it means that the text message received will not be counted towards a consumer's monthly allotment of messages. To provide FTEU messages, the business incurs any additional costs from the text messages. The primary users of FTEU texts are the carriers themselves, who often send promotional text messages to their customers.

Now that we've covered text messaging basics, let's look at some of the elements of text message marketing.

Opt ins

Text message marketing is opt in marketing, meaning that you must have permission from your consumers before sending them a promotional text message. While getting permission may seem like a daunting task at first, it is precisely why SMS text message marketing is so darn effective.

Permission-based marketing with SMS was once much easier to validate. There was a time when a business could send somebody a promotional text message if it had a previous relationship with that consumer. In other words, a tire retailer might have compiled a list of phone numbers from previous customers. While it could not legally send a text to all of the residents of the city, it could send a text message to those customers that had purchased tires in the past.

That all changed in the USA on October 16, 2013, when new TCPA laws came into effect. They caused companies to change the way business was done with text message marketing and, in many cases, required a new, more stringent opt in from consumers. Because not all previous opt in consumers chose to re-opt in, the new laws dramatically reduced the size of many companies' opt in databases.

Today, in addition to numerous other requirements, you have to have "prior express written consent" to qualify a consumer as a legitimate opt in to your database. This applies to any program that is considered to be under telemarketing rules. These rules require a clear and conspicuous disclosure informing the user that

- by opting in, the user authorizes the seller to deliver, or cause to be delivered to the user, marketing messages using an automatic telephone dialing system;

- the user is not required to opt in, directly or indirectly, as a condition of purchasing any property, goods, or services.[22]

Text messages can only be pushed to consumers after they have consented via some kind of action that creates a verifiable opt in. Now, this does not mean you have to have a signed paper for all of your opt ins (although that is a legitimate qualifier). There are several legitimate opt in methods that provide verifiable express written consent:

- entering a mobile phone number on a web page
- signing up through a web widget
- signing a document or providing an electronic signature
- sending an interactive text message to a phone number with the appropriate keyword
- opting in over the phone via IVR technology

After opting in via a website form, the business must then send a text message to the consumer verifying the opt in. This is the only way to be sure that the phone number registered online is from the same person that desired to opt in. The reply message must contain the brand name or product description, customer care contact information, opt out instructions, product quantity or recurring message disclosure, and the "message and data rates may apply" disclosure. That is a lot to get into a 160-character message! In some instances, such as a sweepstakes entry or vote program, the reply message may not be legally necessary, but it makes sense to send it anyway. Otherwise, the consumer may think the interactive text message program did not work properly and will continue to text again and again. Since each text message costs the business money, it is advantageous to offer the reply message to avoid multiple text messages from a single customer.

In most cases, a company obtains a legitimate opt in via an interactive text message promotion. In other words, the consumer responds to a text message like this:

Text RESULTS to 84444

(Disclaimer—84444 is a short code owned by the author's company. The text message sample promotion listed above is to opt in to receive text message tips.)

Once the consumer has opted in to your database via a pull method interactive text message promotion, you can then send them broadcast text messages. The push broadcast portion of the equation is usually the big moneymaker in terms of increased engagement and long-term business.

Obtaining the initial opt in is the most important element of an SMS program because without it, the database won't have enough volume to have a significant impact on sales. Calls to action for an opt in must be clear and accurate and not use any deceptive means. Also, when a consumer opts in for a particular SMS program, she is only opting in for a single program. It is not permitted for that opt in to be used for multiple programs, even if they are using the same shared short code. In other words, just because a consumer opted in to the database of the deli, it does not mean that the oil change business down the street can use the phone number in its database. Never are consumers providing a blanket opt in. They are providing only a single opt in for one business only.

Beware. When a business gets involved in mobile marketing, purchasing a database of "already opted-in numbers" from list brokers using aggressive sales techniques to jump-start your SMS campaign may be enticing. Don't do it. As noted above, an opt in is for one business only and is not transferable. Therefore, there really is not any way for a database to have legitimate opt ins where the consumer has indicated that they want unlimited promotional text messages from multiple businesses. In text message marketing, everybody starts at zero.

In some cases, a double opt in process may be better for the business. A double opt in is where the consumer must reply in the affirmative to two text messages to become part of the database. It is often used in the case of a sweepstakes, because of the preponderance of legal requirements for such programs. In the case of a sweepstakes, an initial reply message may be confirming the contest entry, and the second reply message may be to ask for a reply message of "Y" or "YES" to become part of the recurring text program. Mere participation in a contest is not a legitimate opt in unless that opt in is announced and then confirmed within the reply text message.

Opt outs

There is a fine line between your best customer—one that registers for your database—and one that opts out of that database. Opt outs are a key performance indicator that businesses should keep track of to make sure that consumers are not choosing to leave the database too often. Sure, there might be a legitimate reason why the consumer wants to opt out, like moving from the area, but in most cases, an opt out is the result of sending too many text messages or not sending text messages that are of great enough value.

It is easy for a consumer to opt out of the database. They can simply reply to a text message with STOP, END, CANCEL, QUIT, or UNSUBSCRIBE. If subsequent text, punctuation, or capitalization is added to the opt out message, the provider must still accept it. In Canada, the French equivalent of these words is also required. STOP, however, is the reply that is most often used by a consumer to opt out of a database in the USA.

Recurring message programs are also required to promote opt out instructions on the initial opt in response and on a monthly basis once the program is in use. Some businesses take this to the extreme and include an opt out message in every broadcast text. This is not required and should not be done, because the more that a business promotes the opt out, the greater the likelihood that the database will shrink. Once the consumer chooses to opt out, the business can send a message confirming the opt out but cannot send any future messages, or it will be in violation of the law. It is also required that opt out information be displayed in bold type on advertisements.

A basic requirement of any online SMS services that a business might use is an automatic feature that removes a consumer once they have chosen to opt out by sending STOP. In other instances, a consumer might contact the business directly and ask to be removed, in which case the business must manually remove the customer's phone number from the database.

An acceptable opt out rate for a typical retail store or restaurant is less than 5 percent per year, and a good one is less than 3 percent per year. One word of caution: in my experience, I found that consumers are more likely to opt out on the weekends, so be careful to monitor this closely if your business likes to send weekend text messages.

Keywords

An SMS keyword is the word that a consumer sends to a phone number, usually to receive immediate information back and often to opt in to a database to be marketed to in the future. In the previous example (Text RESULTS to 84444), the keyword is "results." The customer puts the short code number (84444) in the space where she would normally insert the phone number. Then, the customer inserts "results" in the area where she would normally insert the message.

Choosing a keyword is one of the most important steps in your text message marketing strategy, because the keyword offers branding for your product offering. A business should choose a keyword that follows these tips:

- brands the business or promotion

- is easy to remember, so as to gain the viral pass-along effect from customers and employees

- is just one word to avoid problems with autocorrect

- is easy to spell

- is not an acronym

- does not include numbers

- is as short as possible

- is not some "clever" spelling of a keyword

The primary keyword that a business will want to reserve is its own name. This keyword will be the master keyword that is used continually for generating opt ins. This permanent keyword should be printed everywhere—on business cards, literature, t-shirts, outdoor signage, menus, and anywhere else that makes sense. If the business name is difficult to spell, clever, or contains multiple words, it may be best just to go with a single word keyword that best identifies what the business does. If a business wants to understandably reserve its difficult-to-spell brand name as a keyword, it should also consider reserving the potential misspellings of that keyword.

Often, businesses have common names, and the keyword that your business wants may not be available. A second choice may be to pick the primary product that your business sells, but a keyword like "pizza" is likely not going to be available at an online shared short code provider. If the primary keyword a business wants is not available, you can choose an adjective that describes the business, such as "tasty" or "hungry."

In addition to the primary keyword, your business is going to want to use different keywords for various promotions. Some of these promotions may be short-lived, and you will be able to retire those keywords after using them for the short-term promotion. Others may be annual events, and your business will want to retain those keywords in its online accounts, because if they are released, another business may pick them up. The advantage to using new keywords is that it will get your regular customers participating in your texting program again, and you can place those users into a different database, which may be helpful in segmenting for future promotions.

One of the great things about an SMS strategy is the tremendous viral advantage. If a person knows that his friend likes to get coffee at Dunkin' Donuts, he will pass along the keyword and short code to that friend. It is not unusual for a business to get 15–20 percent of its mobile coupon redemptions from viral sharing.[23] But the consumer may not remember to do so if the keyword and short code are not easy to remember, so it is always best to keep things simple and memorable when it comes to choosing a keyword and short code.

Keywords that are compound words or two words are also not good choices. A business might have the best cheesecake in the world, but "cheesecake" is not a very good keyword because some people will spell it as two words (cheese cake), and some will intend to spell it as one word, but autocorrect will "fix" it for them. Automated SMS response systems cannot detect the user's intent, only the exact spelling, so picking the wrong keyword could result in lost opt in opportunities. One memorable SMS promotion was a sweepstakes that gave away a trip to Hawaii. The advertiser chose the keyword "Hawaii." Although a wonderful place, Hawaii is not particularly easy to spell. Moreover, some people include an apostrophe when spelling it. Hawaii was not a good choice as a keyword because of the difficulty in spelling it. Acronyms, such as ATS, don't make for good keywords either because autocorrect will inevitably try to change the acronym into a real word. Avoid numbers in keywords as well. It is confusing to think of texting a number to a number. But more importantly, there is that zero and "oh" thing.

When it comes to texting, consumers often don't recognize what is a letter (O) and what is a number (0)!

Typing on a mobile phone is not easy. There are a lot more misspellings on the smaller screen of the phone than on a desktop computer. Fat-finger misspellings are a common problem on mobile. That is why using a short keyword is far better than a long keyword; there are fewer chances to misspell a keyword with fewer letters.

Another poor idea is using a clever spelling of a word as your keyword. A restaurant called "Finger Lickin' Chickin'" may be a snappy name, but using "chickin" as a keyword is not a good idea because a customer's autocorrect is likely going to correct that word to the proper spelling of chicken.

One of the questions often asked is in regards to capitalization of keywords. Using caps or lowercase letters has no impact on the keyword so don't worry about it. To make the keyword stand out, the best way to write it in your advertisement is to use all capital letters, but if somebody responds in lowercase, the interactive text message will still work properly.

Some keywords are not available to businesses because the phone carriers have reserved them, and thus they are not available on short codes. Keywords such as STOP, HELP, INFO, END, CANCEL, UNSUBSCRIBE, QUIT, and others are taken before the short code is activated in the marketplace.

Short Codes

Short codes (also called "common short codes") are usually 5-digit or 6-digit numbers that consumers can send text messages to. In the example above, the short code is 84444. Short codes are specifically set aside for commercial use only. In the United States, short codes are administered by iconectiv (transitioned from Neustar in 2016) in an arrangement made possible by the Common Short Code Administration of the Cellular Technology Industry Association (CTIA). In Canada, they are administered by the Canadian Wireless

Telecommunications Association (CWTA). USA companies that wish to purchase their own short code, as opposed to using the shared short codes that are widely available from companies online, can see which codes are available by visiting US Short Codes at http://www.USShortCodes.com. In the USA, there are no short codes issued that begin with the leading number 1.

Short codes in the USA can be leased for $500 per month for a randomly assigned short code and $1,000 per month for a vanity short code. A vanity short code is one where the business specifically chooses the short code. With a random short code, the number is assigned by US Short Codes. Payments for short codes are due three months in advance. Canadian companies that wish to promote with short codes will find the available numbers at http://www.txt.ca. The cost is $500 each for the first three months and $350 for each month thereafter. In Canada, a business can choose either a 4-digit or a 5-digit short code, but there are no short codes available with the leading number 4.

Obtaining a dedicated short code in the USA is not easy. There is a difficult application period that normally takes about three months if all goes smoothly. This includes the provider and the aggregator setting up direct testing of the short code by each of the American carriers individually.

Businesses that use short codes directly, or online companies that provide shared short codes, usually do not have a direct relationship with all of the carriers. Instead, they have a relationship with an aggregator. An aggregator has direct connections to the carriers. When a text message is sent, it gets passed on to the aggregator, which then passes it along to the appropriate carrier.

There is a hard cost associated with every text message sent through a short code. It may be small (less than a penny), but it is a legitimate hard cost. There was a time when some short code providers offered unlimited text messaging, but those times seem to have disappeared, despite the downward pressure on the cost of SMS. In addition to the hard cost associated with each text message, several carriers in the USA have surcharges of up to a half cent on text messages both received and sent through a short code. To date, Cricket, MetroPCS, Sprint, T-Mobile, and US Cellular have invoked carrier surcharges per text, and Cricket and MetroPCS each charge an extra $500 when a new short code is activated on their systems. Verizon and AT&T proposed surcharges, but due to pushback from customers, they eventually dropped the idea. With about two-thirds of the American mobile market combined, should Verizon and AT&T add surcharges, it would be catastrophic for the industry. Carrier surcharges are extremely short sighted on the part of the carriers and are partly responsible for the slower growth of short code messaging in recent years.

Although a hassle to obtain, a larger business that has the infrastructure to support the technology and the cost of owning its own short code may want to consider directly obtaining one. The advantages to owning your own short code are

- all keywords being available to your business;
- no concern of the vendor going out of business and thus losing the short code;
- no concern of a customer going rogue and endangering the viability of the shared short code that your business is using;
- the control and ability to develop any unique technology that might be required for your particular business.

Most businesses both large and small, however, choose to outsource the technology to one of the many online companies that offer SMS marketing services. That means that multiple companies will be sharing the same short code. There are some obvious advantages to outsourcing text message marketing to one of the many online providers. Some of the advantages to using a shared short code are

- cost savings, by eliminating the responsibility for the monthly fees associated with leasing a short code;

- the economies of scale that a shared short code has negotiated with its aggregator in regards to the per-SMS cost;

- cost savings in development;

- the technology already being in place;

- a quickness to market, since no technology or testing is involved and there is no waiting period for approval of the short code;

- 24/7 coverage in the case of an outage;

- interaction with a company that has been doing this work for many years and is willing to share its best practices and success stories from direct experience with thousands of SMS promotions.

The most important thing to look for when choosing a short code is memorability. While having a memorable short code may not be that important if a business is using print advertising, it is extremely important if the advertiser is doing broadcast advertising, especially via radio. With broadcasting, the message comes and goes so quickly that the importance of having a memorable short code cannot be overstated. It is very surprising that some USA online vendors had the short-term thinking of saving a mere $500 per month and settling for a random, non-memorable short code.

A second important thing when choosing a short code is being able to use that same short code number all across North America. The economies of the United States and Canada are interlinked and so is the media that they consume. Canada's vast border with the United States is 5,526 miles (8,893 kilometers) long, and over 90 percent of Canadians live within 100 miles (160 kilometers) of this border. Think of border cities like Buffalo and Toronto; Detroit and Windsor; Seattle and Vancouver. In these cities, much of the media consumed is actually from another country. If your advertisement includes the same short code number in both countries, that is a huge advantage!

Now, don't get the wrong idea. Short codes are viable only in the country of origin, so your USA short code won't work on both sides of the USA–Canadian border. But by reserving the same short code number in both the USA and Canada, a business greatly expands its opt ins and the eventual success of its text message marketing strategy.

Long Codes

In some cases, long codes are used for text message marketing. A long code is simply a traditional ten-digit phone number that does many of the same things that a short code number can do, although it isn't really intended for interactive text messaging. Some carriers frown on long codes, in part because they don't make any money from them. Some say that long codes cannot be used for marketing purposes at all, but rarely is there enforcement of this.

The advantages to a business using a long code instead of a short code are clearly cost motivated. In addition, if the business is local, the local area code can be used as part of the long code. Some consumers may be more comfortable sending messages to a phone number with an area code that is identifiable with their hometown.

Disadvantages of a long code are that the number is longer and therefore less memorable. It also probably does not make a lot of sense for a national company to be identifying with a single location's area code. Some say that response time on the autoreply is slower on long codes. Finally, there is the (admittedly remote) threat of a promotion being squashed by the carriers if too many promotional messages are being sent via a long code.

Interactive Text Messages

Often called an autoreply, an interactive text message is the message that is sent to the consumer after the consumer sends a keyword to the short code. Interactive text messages are usually sent to confirm an opt in subscription to a program.

The act of sending the keyword to the short code is known as an MO in the business. This stands for mobile origination, meaning that the consumer originated the interactivity. The autoreply message is known as an MT message, or mobile termination. It signifies the reply message being sent from the business to the consumer.

In some instances, businesses may choose to not send a reply message to a consumer, such as after a sweepstakes entry or voting-program text. This is usually suggested as a cost-savings move, since all short code text messages have an intrinsic cost associated with them, but it is a very bad idea. As stated before, the consumer needs to have the placebo of knowing that her text message has been received. If the consumer does not get the reply verification, she will often continue sending the keyword to the short code. The cost of this messaging, and the carrier surcharges involved, will exceed the cost savings of not offering the reply message.

Building a valuable database of opt ins starts with the initial interactive text message offer. It is critical that the business offer something of significant value to get the consumer to act. That value must be something that can be used immediately. If it has to be free, so be it. One small pizza restaurant offered a free pizza slice and even used the keyword FREEPIZZA in the SMS promotion (a rare instance where a two-word keyword worked well). It may be counterintuitive to offer something for free when the customer is already willing to spend their money at your store, but the lifetime value of the opt in is worth so much more. By participating in the promotion, consumers are giving the business explicit permission to market to them and send them specials and personal communications in the future. That is far more valuable than the cost of a slice.

The interactive text message needs to have a strong call to action. Free pizza is certainly a strong incentive to be redeemed. When a mobile coupon such as this is offered, most marketers will use "show text" in the reply message as the redemption method. When the promotion is from a larger company, such as Domino's, it will use an alphanumeric coupon code in the reply message.

There should also be no doubt from the customer that he or she has opted in to the database. Part of any interactive message that constitutes part of the opt in is confirming the act of opting in. A good way to do that is to reply in part with something like: "Thanks for joining the WTNH VIP text club."

Broadcast Text Messaging

Capturing the mobile phone number of your customer or prospect is very valuable indeed. In fact, one national discount retail business pegged the value of an opt in to be $11 per month in increased sales![24] With an opt in database well in excess of 100,000 phone numbers, you can see how significant this is. Ace Hardware is another company that is very active with SMS marketing. In a published report in *Mobile Commerce Daily*, Ace Hardware pegged its value of an opt in as being $183.60 lifetime!

The key to broadcast text message marketing is to send consumers messages that are of value. That may seem obvious, but here is why it is so important. There is a fine line between your best customer, somebody who likes your company to the point where they have ASKED to receive your advertising, and your worst customer, somebody whom you have sent so many messages to that they have opted out of your text message marketing advertising. The customer is allowing you to access his most personal of devices, so it is imperative that you don't take advantage of that access. Send too many messages that are not pertinent to the consumer and you will likely get an opt out. If you are Ace Hardware, you can see just how much that opt out will cost you!

How often a business should send broadcast text messages is one of the most common questions that experts in the industry get. There is no magical number of broadcast messages that should be sent each month. That really varies based on the product. If you opt in to the San Jose Sharks hockey team text message database, you will see that they indicate you may receive "5msgs/wk." That may seem like a lot when compared to a department store, but keep in mind that fans of a sports team are passionate about that team and won't mind receiving five messages per week. On the other hand, if you are a local pizza restaurant, five messages per week is way too many. A volume of three per month may appear to be a good starting point to go up or down from, but the real question is not how many messages should be sent, but rather how many messages of value can be sent. Before sending any text message, a business should put itself in the customer's shoes and ask if the proposed text message will bring sufficient value to the customer. If the answer is not a clear yes, that broadcast text message effort should be tabled.

One of the major blunders of retailers sending broadcast text messages is assuming that every broadcast message should be a mobile coupon. If all broadcast messages offer discounts, consumers get reliant on them and will not shop at the store unless they have a coupon. Also, if too many are sent, they don't seem special anymore. Marketers need to come up with reminder texts that keep the brand or business in front of its opt in audience without always relying on mobile coupons. For a frozen yogurt store, such a text might be the new flavor that is now available. For a clothing retailer, it could be a hot new fashion that is now available in the store. For a hardware store in a cold-weather climate, it might be a text message announcing that snow blowers are in stock in anticipation of the snowstorm in the upcoming weekend.

DATABASES

The size of the database is certainly important, but so is its segmentation. It probably does not make sense to throw everybody into the same master database. For instance, if a business has multiple locations, it will want to keep separate databases for each store location. This will enable the business to offer different promotions to each database when necessary. Subway does this. It adds the store number to the end of the keyword so that the database is segmented by store location.

If a business has multiple products, it will want to separate consumers by the products they are interested in as well. For example, a sporting goods store will want to maintain different databases for customers that respond to different promotions. This will enable the store to know which customers are interested in golf, tennis, bowling, soccer, football, baseball, softball, camping, or running. If it is a storewide sale, send the same message to all databases; if it is a preseason golf promotion, send it only to the specific golf database. Relevance will raise response.

There are also opportunities to take advantage of weather-related situations by regionalizing databases. For instance, if unusually hot weather is sweeping the southern states, it is a great time to send a text message about frozen yogurt or an air conditioner sale.

Recurring events are another great reason to maintain separate databases. If you collected opt ins for the annual Beerfest, it makes sense to target those users next year and remind them to purchase their tickets early.

Growing the Database

When it comes to text message marketing, the size of the database clearly matters. Obviously, the more people that are reached, the more people that will engage and the more successful the campaigns will be. Many marketers do a good job of growing their database in the early days of their SMS campaigns and then begin concentrating more on the broadcast messages than on continuing to grow the list. The problem with this is that there will be inevitable deterioration of the list as customers opt out due to leaving the area, not having a need for the product, changing phone numbers, or a variety of other reasons. Therefore, a business needs to keep priming the pump with more and more opt in members. Maintaining an effective, ongoing opt in strategy is a key factor to a successful text message marketing program.

When a business begins a text message marketing campaign, it should put the primary keyword and short code everywhere. It should be every place that the business publishes its URL or its main office phone number. There are a host of great ideas of where to put the text message engagement:

- outdoor advertisements
- print advertisements
- direct mail
- TV advertisements
- radio advertisements
- online advertisements
- website
- pop-ups on the website
- online ordering page
- blogs
- digital and mobile advertisements
- social media posts, including YouTube
- social media headers
- e-mails

- e-mail signatures

- business cards

- receipts

- in-store signage

- outside store signage

- promotional products, such as pens

- pizza boxes

- backs of waitress's t-shirts

- tabletops

- bathroom stall advertisements

Another great way to grow a database is with employee participation, especially at a restaurant or retail store where there is significant interaction with the customer. A business can create an internal competition where employee names are used as the keyword for the opt in. Even a small prize can get employees motivated to participate.

Transferring a Database

If a business uses a shared short code from an online vendor, there may come a time when that business wishes to transfer to another provider. One of the things a business must be able to do is to move its database when needed. Some online providers don't permit the business to download the database, making it virtually impossible to ever move it! Thus, your program is held hostage.

If a business chooses to begin working with a new provider, it is required that a notification be sent to the members of the database, notifying them of the impending change of short code. Rules require that this final text message from the previous short code include an opt out message. Opt out messages always are concerning, so it is best to include in the final message from the previous short code that the first text from the new short code will offer a great new mobile coupon incentive.

CRAFTING A GREAT TEXT MESSAGE

Sometimes it is more difficult to write a short message than a long one. Such is the case with text messaging, when you have only 160 characters to work with in the United States and 136 in Canada.

Abbreviations

Abbreviations are acceptable in text message marketing. When text messaging first caught on, they were actually kind of hip and cool. That is no longer the case, however, as consumers are more likely to find them annoying. Write your message as best as you can, shorten it as much as you need to, and then, and only then, should you start inserting abbreviated words.

Embedded Links

Embedded links are actual URLs that are inserted into a text message. They are quite handy to the smartphone user, because he can simply touch them and proceed onto the World Wide Web to easily access the website. The problem with embedded links is that they can often be very long and take up too many characters. There is an easy solution to this problem: use some kind of URL shortener, such as a bit.ly link. It is free and will save valuable characters if the business does not care about the branding that the actual URL offers. Of course, it goes without saying that the link must go to a landing page or website that is properly optimized for mobile.

Tap-to-Call

Same as with an embedded link, a business can also embed a phone number in an SMS message. It becomes an easy tap-to-call for the mobile user, who can simply touch the embedded phone number and make a call to the business or organization. If the business wants to track the number of calls that the SMS message directly generates and quantify the value of the messaging, a unique tracking phone number can be used.

Mobile Coupons

Mobile couponing can be a valuable tool for SMS marketing. Usually, a mobile coupon is redeemed with something like "show text to receive 10 percent off." Of course, it is very possible that a consumer can transfer such a text message to a friend, who can then also use it. A business should be happy about that, even though the friend may not be an opt in member of the SMS service. This actually happens quite often, as evidenced by some of the studies done by Dunkin' Donuts and Subway. Expect that up to 20 percent of those that redeem your mobile coupon may have received it via forwarding from another opt in member.

Mobile coupons are most effective in garnering immediate business, therefore any mobile coupon should have an expiration date on it. A business must create a sense of urgency. In most cases, that expiration date should be a week or less. If it is a "show text" kind of promotion, there is no way to stop the consumer from using it multiple times, so a business should limit the valid time period for the offer. A business can also do even shorter flash sales very cost effectively with SMS. It could offer significant discounts that need to be redeemed by 5 P.M. the same day.

Some business may use a unique promo code with every SMS offer. This allows the business's POS system to track the effectiveness of the campaign, and with larger companies, it is often the only way that the POS system will allow a discount.

Sweepstakes

Of all of the text message programs that you will do, a text-to-win contest will have the greatest amount of participation. Everybody wants to win something for free, and a text message sweepstakes (known as a competition in the UK) is an easy way to enter.

Many marketers make the mistake, however, of believing that simply entering a sweepstakes is means for a verifiable opt in, but that is not the case. A business must still provide the opt in requirements in the sweepstakes response message if that interactive text message has the intent of validating a new opt in to the database.

Text Message Voting

American Idol made text message voting popular long before most Americans were texting. In fact, it gave rise to a much greater recognition of texting in general. Many live events on the national and local level use text message voting because it is a real-time gauge of public opinion. Just like with sweepstakes, voting is a great way to gain more opt ins for your ongoing SMS marketing plans.

Weather-Related Promotions

Businesses can take advantage of weather situations by sending messages based on the upcoming weather. If it is unusually cold, it is a great time to promote winter gear or sell snow blowers.

Text Message Alerts

After the mass shooting tragedy at Virginia Tech in 2007, many universities clamored for a quick way to notify the campus in the case of an emergency. SMS messaging was a quick and obvious way to notify college students en masse. Emergency text message alerts were one of the early categories that produced significant revenues for shared short code providers. Today, most universities don't contract directly with text messaging companies. Rather, they work with safety organizations that offer everything from alarm systems to multimedia messaging, but text messaging remains a part of that all-encompassing emergency notification system.

Alerts are also used for less critical situations. Real-time text message alerts are sent by businesses for office and store closings due to weather and other unanticipated emergencies. Youth sports leagues send them for cancellations and announcements. Real-time alerts make sense, since the vast majority of text messages are read immediately upon receipt.

BOB'S TOP TEXT MESSAGING TIPS

1. Capitalize on the viral effect of texts. Encourage recipients to "FWD to a friend."

2. Personalize your message with the first name of the recipient.

3. Send a free offer to customers on their birthdays. Better yet, send customers a free offer on their half-birthdays. You'll likely be the only one they get.

4. Make sure to count the spaces as part of the 160 characters permitted in the USA and 136 in Canada!

5. Start your message with action verbs like BUY or COME.

6. CAPITALIZE the most important words so they stand out: SALE; FREE; TODAY; ONLY.

7. Your first words need to grab their attention. Use action words at the top of the message to get the recipient to read the entire message.

8. Use words that require immediate action like "limited quantity" and "the first 10 texters."

9. Only use abbreviations when you absolutely must to stay within the required characters. Abbreviations used to be cool, but now they are just annoying.

10. Avoid slang like the plague.

11. Never send a text that is so long that it needs a second message to reach completion. If your message is long, use an embedded link to give more info on a landing page.

12. Send your broadcast messages when customers are most likely to buy, like just before lunchtime. Texting = immediate response.

13. Experiment with different times and days to maximize results.

14. Need to identify store(s)? Use a follow-up text message to ask for the hometown of the consumer.

15. For restaurants, the best text promotions have been "buy one, get one free" and "kids eat free" offers.

16. Don't make every text message a mobile coupon. If you do, customers may wait for them.

17. If you don't discount, provide something else of value to the customer, like some quirky news or information related to your brand.

18. Identify your company. How many times have you received a text and didn't know who sent it? This is a major freshman mistake.

19. Send texts when the game ends and fans are walking to their cars, when customers are looking for the next thing to do. Works great for bars and gentlemen's clubs.

20. Don't try to have two offers in the same text message; there's not enough room.

21. Don't use two-word keywords. Autocorrect will cause havoc if you do.

22. When it comes to keywords, the shorter the better.

23. If Hispanics are your target, also reserve the Spanish equivalent for your keyword.

24. Make customers feel special. Call your text list the "VIP Club" or something similar.

25. Make your text offers exclusive to the texting club. To truly make them special, they should not also be found in your e-mails, social media, or traditional advertising.

26. Make sure every text message carries something of value. The last thing you want is an opt out.

27. Don't repeat offers unless there is a really good reason for doing so. If a text message has been especially successful, that may be a rare instance to use it a second time, but don't make a habit of doing so, or you may increase your opt outs.

28. Nothing offers better immediacy than text messaging. Create an amazing offer that is only good for the next hour. Include details on how to redeem the offer so there is no confusion.

29. All broadcast text messages should be sent between 8 A.M. and 9 P.M., based on the time zone of the consumer, not the business. That is just not a good idea; it is a TCPA rule.

30. Don't send broadcast texts during traditional drive times. We don't need any additional driving distractions.

31. Build your social media presence by linking to your Facebook and Twitter sites.

32. Promote opt ins via social media channels.

33. Share knowledge nuggets that show you are an expert in your field.

34. Send a text message that is nothing but a tease for the next big announcement coming via text.

35. Use texting on the fly to bring in customers during unexpected slow times.

36. Celebrity in the house? Let your opt in list know about it.

37. Beat the competition to hot news. Text the news and a link to your website for complete details.

38. Ask the recipients what they'd like to see in the texts. You'll be surprised at how many great ideas you receive.

39. Track your results with redeemable mobile coupon codes.

40. Always put an end date on mobile coupon offers.

41. Sweepstakes are the most effective way to increase your database of opt ins. Allow your customers to enter your sweepstakes a second time by liking your Facebook page or mentioning you on Twitter. Offer both a grand prize and some consolation prizes to maximize participation.

42. Keep multiple database lists and target your offers based on the origin of those lists.

43. Add your personal keyword and short code to your business cards and content marketing author identifiers. For example, Text BOB to 84444. (*Note: this will give you the author's personal contact information.*)

44. Vanity short codes allow for easier recall and will help encourage the viral aspect of texting.

45. Place an iPad near the cash register and offer a discount for a first-time opt in. Sure, it will cost you in the short term, but in the long term, you will make so much more by having that consumer in your database.

46. Let the consumer know how often you will be texting them. It is not only a rule, it is common courtesy.

47. Give a great reward to new opt ins. New opt ins are the hardest to get, so reward them handsomely.

48. Send thank-you messages to the customers on your opt in list.

49. Never, ever buy a list of "opt ins." There is no such thing. Nobody has signed up to receive unlimited spam texts.

50. Being too salesy can be a turnoff and result in an opt out. Monitor opt outs after every broadcast message to make sure you aren't pushing the wrong consumer buttons.

51. Divide your lists. Do A/B tests with different creative, different offers, different days of the week, and different times of day.

52. You need to let consumers know about the opt out STOP message when they opt in initially and monthly thereafter, but don't overuse mentioning the STOP message, as it will definitely increase opt outs.

53. If you are doing radio advertising, repeat the keyword and short code at least once. Radio listeners are usually doing something else, so the keyword and short code needs to be especially memorable.

54. Be sure the receptionist at the radio station has the text message details, as she will receive calls asking for it.

55. If using an embedded link, be sure to lead the consumers to a mobile-optimized website.

56. Track your results. Keep stats on every broadcast text you do.

57. If you do business in both Canada and the United States, it is best to use the same short code in both countries so you don't have confusion, take up more space in your ads, or need to change creative.

58. Cross-promote with complimentary products and businesses. Encourage your opt ins to sign up for

the other list and vice versa in an effort to grow the database.

59. Always discourage texting while driving.

60. Doing texts for B2B? Send messages just three minutes before the top of the hour, when businesspersons are waiting for meetings to start.

THE KPIS OF SMS

Key performance indicators need to be used to gauge and track the effectiveness of every SMS promotion that a business does. These are common metrics used to evaluate performance. Below are several KPIs to consider for SMS promotions:

- Delivery rate—the percentage of text messages that were received. (By the way, there is no way that you can know how many of your messages were opened or read. Once the text message reaches the consumer, it is unknown whether it is actually opened or not.)

- Tap-through rate—the percentage of consumers that tapped on the embedded link.

- Tap-to-call rate—the number of phone calls made to the embedded phone number.

- Redemption rate—the number of products purchased because of the text message.

- Opt out rate—the number of customers who chose to opt out within a day of the broadcast message being sent.

- Opt in rate—the number of new subscribers registered from the promotion.

- Cost per opt in—the amount of advertising and promotion invested per each new subscriber.

A/B TESTING

It is amazing how small changes can have a profound effect on the success of an SMS campaign. If the database is of significant size, it is best to perform tests on various messages and offers to see which one works best before sending the promotion to the complete database. Here is a list of tests that a business should make for its SMS marketing:

- Copy—Does a casual or business tone work best? What is the optimal length of a text message?
- Database—Which databases work best for your offer?
- Personalization—Does adding the person's name to the message have a positive effect on conversions?
- Call to action—Do subtle changes to the call to action have a profound effect on results?
- Offer—What is the best offer to get the consumer to convert or come into the store?
- Timing—What day and time is best to send broadcast messages?
- SMS versus MMS—Is picture messaging worth the added cost?

OTHER TEXT MESSAGING SERVICES

Premium SMS

Premium SMS offers the ability for operators to charge for a text message. Unfortunately, such services were mostly banned on a national scale in the USA in 2013. The move to end premium SMS service was spearheaded by Vermont Attorney General Bill Sorrell. The move was made in part due to programs where consumers allegedly downloaded software on their mobile phones and unscrupulous premium SMS providers billed them, apparently without their knowledge. This process is known as cramming and is, of course, illegal.

Charitable donations via premium SMS, like the one that First Lady Michelle Obama did after the Haiti hurricanes, are permitted. And, in a move that should surprise nobody, Mr. Sorrell and other politicians are still be able to raise campaign funds via premium SMS.

Premium SMS was originally thought of as a viable alternative to the decline of 900 numbers. It certainly made sense to think that way, given the proliferation of mobile phones and the impact of text messaging. But the service never really caught on in the USA to the same extent that it did in other countries. And, just like with 900 numbers, the initial participants were often bottom-of-the-barrel, late-night-television type services. In the end, premium SMS services ended in the USA because of the carrier's inability to enforce charges due to government regulations that protect the consumer over the provider regardless of which party is at fault. The premium SMS service is still available in Canada and in most countries worldwide, but in the USA, it exists only for nonprofit organizations and political fundraising.

International SMS

International SMS is also known as bulk SMS. Some now refer to it as global SMS. These are messages sent to individuals outside your home country. Remember, short codes are only designed to serve a single country and they don't cross borders. Therefore, any international text messages must be sent from a long code.

Just as with domestic text messaging providers, there are international SMS providers. Most of the companies in the business are from Europe, since it is obviously more important to have international texting capabilities between the numerous countries in the European Union than in the vast United States or Canada.

MMS (Multimedia Messaging Services)

MMS is an advanced form of SMS. With MMS, the message can include sound, pictures, and video, thus allowing for a larger variety of branding essentials and a more engaging experience. It can send a single message or multiple images in a slideshow format. It can also include a GIF or a video of up to 40 seconds in length. It is also not limited to the traditional amount of spaces that SMS is; the text can be unlimited in length.

Pricing for MMS has declined in recent years, just as SMS messaging has, but the cost to send an MMS is still greater than basic text messaging.

An MMS message has the advantage of being able to include a scannable quick response (QR) code within the message itself. A QR code is a black-and-white matrix that can be scanned by the camera on a smartphone to produce a shortcut to a URL, mobile coupon, or some other mobile activity. With a scannable QR code, the consumer can take the message to the store and redeem it immediately. The scannable code can also be launched from a beacon—a Bluetooth-enabled device that is present in a retail store.

Retail clothing stores have been the most effective users of MMS to date, because visualizing fashion is so important. Unlike SMS, where the consumer has to touch an embedded link on their smartphone to see the picture of the clothing, MMS contains the picture within the message itself. With the image included, the business can effectively tie the messaging to the other branding and graphics that are being used in its traditional advertising campaigns.

An excellent MMS message also includes a social media sharing button to take advantage of the virality that only mobile can offer. A simple click of the button and the customer can share the image on her Facebook or Twitter account.

Over-the-Top Instant Messaging Systems

Use of SMS text messaging is flat. Not because people are messaging less, or that businesses are finding text message marketing to be ineffective, but rather because there are very popular alternatives to the staid text message. These alternatives are called over-the-top (OTT) instant messaging systems. OTT systems use Internet-connected smartphones to provide an alternative to traditional text messaging. In the USA, Facebook Messenger is the most prominent of the instant messaging alternatives. Google Hangouts is close behind, then Snapchat and WhatsApp.

Messaging apps are far more popular overseas, where international texting is more common and the cost for SMS is usually higher than in North America. Viber is very popular in Europe and has been making a push to grow its business in the USA. WeChat is hugely popular in China, and LINE is very well known in Japan.

There are good reasons why consumers are opting for OTT messaging over SMS. One of the best reasons is the "read" notification; with SMS, the sender does not know if the recipient has picked up the message or not. Messenger, for instance, notifies the user when the recipient has seen the message. With OTT, users also don't need a cellular connection, only Wi-Fi. And international messaging is the same as domestic messaging—no problem.

The primary negative to a business using OTT messaging is that the market remains fragmented, so the business needs to monitor multiple instant messaging platforms. Moreover, these systems will soon take advertising, so the potential exists for the embarrassing situation where a competitor might be advertising alongside your business's direct conversation with a customer or prospect.

Businesses are taking notice of OTT messaging apps. Hyatt and Sprint now use Facebook Messenger to solve customer service issues in real time. Uber allows Messenger users to order and pay for a vehicle without having to download the Uber app.

OTT services offer a real-time way for businesses to connect with a huge global market. It costs nothing and does not require the upkeep of other social networks that require active content production. It is simply another avenue by which customers can reach the business, and it should be considered, especially if the appeal of your product is to young adults.

Text to Landline

Here's some non-news for you: people like to text. They don't really like to talk on the phone. They often don't even listen to their voicemails anymore. Further, a lot of people are texting businesses and often are unknowingly texting a landline phone. Consumers don't care that your company has a landline and not a cell phone. In fact, if they are a young millennial, it may even be unfathomable that there is a type of phone still in existence that does not receive text messages.

Text to Landline technology allows a business to text-enable its longtime landline phone number. To provision a landline to accept texts, a business must provide a letter of authorization to a Text to Landline provider. Of course, an existing home or office landline telephone can't actually receive a text message and display it. Instead, a business can receive a text message to a landline on a desktop computer and interact with the consumer through it. In short, the SMS capability works as an OTT instant messaging system. This capability is not new; Google Voice has used it for several years.

There are several advantages to using Text to Landline:

- Fewer missed sales opportunities—People are already texting your office landline, but you are not receiving those messages. With Text to Landline, those messages will be captured.

- More sales opportunities—Some consumers don't like talking on the phone, especially to a salesperson. Texting puts a business in touch with more potential customers.

- Convenience—Nothing is more convenient than texting on the mobile phone.

- Customer service—With chat, consumers expect an immediate response. With text, a consumer is willing to wait. Hence, your business does not have to offer 24/7 customer service.

- Maintaining sales leads—Imagine that your salesperson is texting with a prospect on her personal mobile phone. When the salesperson leaves for your competition, that lead is going to the new employer. Congratulations. You just spent money on marketing and prospecting and made a sale for your competition.

- Liability—What if something bad happens to the employee that is using her personal mobile phone to text with customers? Suppose there is a disgruntled customer or one that is stalking your employee. You could potentially be liable for not offering a business solution to the communication.

LEGAL STUFF

There are a myriad of compliance regulations that affect SMS text message marketing. Even if you have the best of intentions, it is difficult to understand and follow all of the regulations. There is also a growing trend of class action lawsuits involving TCPA violations that stem from improper text message marketing.

(Obligatory Legal Statement—Please note that the author is not a qualified attorney and these suggestions are the author's own interpretations of the law. A business should always

obtain its own legal advice when pursuing a mobile marketing strategy involving SMS or any other form of mobile marketing.)

Spam

Text message marketing is highly regulated in the United States by the FCC and the CTIA, and even more highly regulated in Canada, whose CASL (Canada Anti-Spam Laws) are some of the strictest in the world.

It should be noted that the CTIA is an industry association that promotes cellular telecommunications and is not a legal entity. Therefore, violation of a CTIA regulation cannot result in a business getting sued. What usually happens is the CTIA audit process finds violations of its codes and passes them along to the carriers, who may choose to suspend or shut down the service or short code. TCPA guidelines, as created and administered by the FCC, however, are laws that must be followed, or the business runs the risk of its programs being shut down, legal action being taken, and fines being levied.

For our purposes, spam is unwanted and unsolicited messages sent in an electronic format, such as a text message. In a legal sense, spam includes messages sent without prior written consent or messages sent after a user has opted out. SMS spam can not only damage your company's reputation, but it can also be costly, very costly. In the USA, fines can be levied for up to $1,500 per text message. Now, that does not mean per text message promotion, or per person reached, but per actual text message sent in total! In Canada, CASL legislation, enacted on July 1, 2014, calls for fines of up to $1 million for individuals and $10 million for businesses that violate its text message marketing spam regulations.

The fact is, as long as a business only markets to people that have opted in to receive the marketing messages, the business will be fine. Seems pretty simple until one sees the large amount of legal considerations that must be followed.

Content

Some types of content are banned from SMS marketing by short codes. The most notable content that is banned in North America is adult entertainment, although it is quite commonplace in the United Kingdom and most of Europe, where the primary carriers are directly involved in the adult entertainment industry. Also banned are endorsements of violence, profanity, hate messages, and discussion of illegal drugs.

Promotion of controlled substances may be subject to additional review by carriers. There have been some interesting interpretations of the rules in regards to marijuana since its legalization for recreational use in some states. In some cases, carriers have banned promotions and even stopped serving certain short codes that accepted business from legal marijuana dispensaries in states like Colorado. Service providers must receive explicit carrier approval before launching such programs.

Any programs that include the marketing of alcohol and tobacco must also include robust age verification confirmations. This includes an electronic confirmation of age and identity at opt in, or the promotions must be restricted to age-verified locations, such as at POS systems in bars.

Sweepstakes and contests may also be subject to additional review by carriers, and all sweepstakes must support a no-cost entry method. A large company will likely seek legal guidance on any sweepstakes program anyway, so it should also receive guidance on the SMS entry portion as well.

Guiding Principles

The CTIA requires that all short code programs comply with a basic code of conduct and that services promote the best possible user experience. This is based on four basic principles in the USA:

- Clear calls to action—Customers must be aware of exactly what they are signing up to receive.

- Clear opt in mechanisms—Customers must consent clearly to opt in to all recurring message programs.

- Opt in confirmation messages—A confirmation message must always be sent to customers. If the program is a recurring message program, clear opt out instructions must also be provided.

- Opt out acknowledgment—Service providers must acknowledge and act on all opt out requests.

Opt in Required Language

Usually, a business will set up an initial interactive text message program for consumers to opt in to the database. This requires notification in the response message if the business is planning to send future broadcast text messages to the customer.

In the United States, a valid response message should look something like this:

Buy lg, get med free. Pizza City. Now part of our VIP club, 3 msgs/mo. Reply STOP to stop, HELP for help. Msg&data rates may apply. T&C: http://linktoterms.com

Note that the response legal language is significant and is going to take up over half of the 160 permitted characters, so you won't have a lot of space left for the actual reply message that the customer really seeks.

If the purpose of the interactive text message program is for a one-time-only reply message, it does not require the legalese above. An example of such a program would be a sweepstakes entry, where the business does not plan on marketing to the users in the future. In such a case, there is no need to offer the legal requirements, since there will not be future SMS contact from the business. This kind of defeats many of the reasons for doing an interactive text campaign, but there are certain times when it is simply a one-time situation.

Additional Opt out Requirements

Service providers must scan MO message logs regularly to identify opt out attempts that were not successful, and the provider must agree to terminate those subscriptions regardless of whether the subscribers used the correct opt out methods. If a business is using a shared short code, this will likely be done by the short code messaging provider, since the business using the service will likely not have access to such information.

Advertising Requirements

Several things are required in an advertisement promoting an SMS marketing program. In the list below, the initial item is the requirement and the second item is a sample message:

- The offer—This is the call to action and what the consumer will get if they participate in the interactive short code program.
  - o Buy a large pizza, get a medium for free.
- The text promotion—It is best written with the keyword in all capitals.
  - o Text RESULTS to 84444
- Message and data rates—This legalese was a requirement even before the updated 2013 TCPA

regulations. It advises consumers that they will be charged for a text message on their mobile plans.

- o Message and data rates may apply.
- Recurring program opt in (if necessary)—Advise the customer as to how often they will receive recurring messages and notify them that the messages will come from an automatic telephone dialing system.
  - o By participating, you consent to receive up to four messages a month, sent by an automatic telephone system.
- Consent of purchase—Customers can't be forced to subscribe to text message programs as part of the purchase process. This disclosure must be "clear and conspicuous."
  - o Consent is not a condition of purchase.
- Opt out—Instruct consumers on how to opt out. It is recommended to be in bold for print advertisements.
  - o **Text STOP to stop.**
- Terms & Conditions and Privacy Policy—This is a URL that links to the terms and conditions plus the privacy policy of the business.
  - o T&C/Privacy: www.yourURL.com/terms

The terms and conditions and privacy policy information is contained on a URL on the web page of the brand or business. It is linked from the advertisement and also from the text reply message. The web page must include all of the information above plus the HELP information and the business contact information. The HELP information is "Text HELP for help."

Violation Notices

If an SMS program is found to be in violation, the service provider will be notified based on the following severities descriptions:

- 0—In this case, the violation is so severe that immediate termination of the short code is possible. Promoting illicit content is an example of this severe violation.

- 1—In this case, serious consumer harm may have occurred and the provider has up to five business days to cure the problem. An unsolicited message being delivered is an example of a level 1 violation.

- 2—In this case, moderate consumer harm may have occurred and the provider has up to five business days to cure the problem. Not mentioning that messages are recurring is an example of a level 2 violation.

Record Keeping

Remember that written consent is required for all legal opt ins. To protect your business, keep records of opt ins and the methodology of their attainment for up to six months. Service providers assume the responsibility for managing information about deactivated and recycled phone numbers, and such information must be processed within three business days of receipt. If a customer ports her phone number from one carrier to another, a new opt in will be required. Records that should be kept include copies of advertisements and copies of the MO and MT messages sent from and to all SMS subscribers.

How to Protect Yourself against a Lawsuit

In the United States, violations of the TCPA regulations have been growing rapidly over the past few years. Most of the class action cases have targeted larger companies, where the expense of class actions is amortized over a large pool of the public that may have been violated. Several thousand class action lawsuits are being filed each year. In Canada, CASL has specifically stated that it will be seeking out small companies that have also violated its regulations. Moreover, it is working in cooperation with the FCC in the United States to bring justice to those companies attempting to hide behind the fact that they are in another country.

A large business should work with counsel prior to getting involved in a marketing campaign that utilizes mobile. Common sense probably is not going to be enough to prevent a suit, because not all of the TCPA rules seem to be based on common sense; it is important that a business know the actual law. Just because a business is using a third party does not exempt it from knowing and adhering to the laws. At least in the USA, action would likely be more valuable against a large national brand than an ad agency or a small business providing texting technology.

Of course, the best way to win a legal case is to make sure that your business never gets involved in the first place.

Disclaimer

The legal requirements in this publication are constantly changing, and those listed here are simply an overview of the industry as of the date of publication. For the most part, the only rules addressed are those in the United States and Canada; other countries likely have their own regulations of the industry.

Any business involved in any type of customer messaging should seek its own legal advice and not rely on this book as anything more than general information. To do otherwise would not be using prudent business practices.

It should also be noted again that the author is not a qualified attorney and any discussion in this book is merely the author's interpretation of the rules. A business must obtain its own legal advice.

Special Note—The author's company is the owner of the 84444 short code in both the United States and Canada. The author's company is also the owner of The Text Message Blog.

Want to learn more about SMS text message marketing? See updated statistics and other important information at RelevanceRaisesResponse.com.

Chapter 5

SOCIAL MEDIA

Every social media network is different. A business needs to select the proper image and social media strategy for each of its networks. Acting the part is half the battle.

BENEFITS OF A MOBILE SOCIAL MEDIA STRATEGY

A decade ago, when MySpace was the dominant social media platform, social media would not have been included in a mobile marketing strategy. But today things are much different, because social media is performed almost entirely on the mobile device.

Think about the social media sites that people use. Instagram and Snapchat have always been nearly exclusively mobile. Twitter is not far behind. Sites like Facebook are becoming increasingly more mobile every year, with almost 90 percent of all accesses now coming from a mobile phone.[25] Perhaps the only bastion of social desktop anymore is the staid business social media site LinkedIn, and even it is moving more to mobile access every year.

There are many reasons why a business should utilize social media:

- Cost—If it is free, it is me. There is no cash up front to get started with social media. If the business is a start-up, social media is likely the only advertising that it can afford. Being broke makes you become a better marketer. Where else can a business promote its products essentially for free? Sure, time is money, and it will take time to get started with social media, but there are not any direct hard costs.

- Branding—Name recognition remains an important part of any business's sales, and consistent social media marketing can certainly help with branding.

- Relationships—Like all of mobile, social media enables businesses to have a one-to-one relationship with the customer. A customer that follows or Likes a business will continue to consistently receive its marketing messages and be able to interact directly with the business.

- Customer service—Social media provides an easy and effective way to offer client feedback and solve problems. It is surely more efficient than waiting on hold for the next available operator.

- SEO—Most professional SEOs would disagree with the idea that a social media post has any direct impact on search engine rankings. But the real benefit is the added exposure that could lead to something that does, such as a link generated from an authority site. In addition, social media sites are indexed by Google, so it is possible to get multiple listings in the search engine ranking pages (SERPs) with an effective social media post.

- Sales—Although selling on social media needs to be subtle, it can and will happen when the consumer does not realize he is being sold to.

- Personal contacts—Many people have a philosophy of not mixing business with pleasure, so friends often do not know what each other does exactly. The beauty of social media is that it exposes a businessperson's friends to their company, and that may ultimately lead to a referral sale that would not have otherwise happened.

But there are certainly downsides to social media marketing as well:

- Commitment—It takes about six months before any tangible results can be recognized, because you need to build followers and stay in front of them for a while before they will buy. Many impatient and busy small businesses give up before there can be any significant results.

- Time (Too Little)—It takes time every week to post to social media sites. If there is not a person dedicated to doing the posts and answering the inquiries, it is not even worth starting. Not answering questions can be a bigger negative than not having a social media presence in the first place. The commitment needs to be immediately consistent and ongoing.

- Time (Too Much)—It is sometimes difficult to find the proper balance in everything a businessperson can do in life. Prioritization is key. Social media marketing itself likely will not be a game changer for a business; instead, it will be a solid supplement. For a small business, the danger is spending too much time on social media. It is incredibly addictive, but remember that there is a business to run! Social media is only a part of a business's overall online marketing strategy, not the majority of it.

- Mistakes—Sending the wrong message on social media can actually hurt sales. So it may not always be a great idea to have the intern handle it.

Engagement

When it comes to social media, the KPI to measure is not the number of messages that a business sends but the number of engagements that a business receives. And when it comes to engagement, shares are what really matter the most.

Sure, a business wants Likes, +1s, thumbs up, and positive comments, but what it really wants is shares or retweets. Shares mean that followers are going out on a limb, with their own reputations on the line, to promote the content. Shares are also the way to benefit from the viral aspect of social media that can reach its zenith when that content is trending. Ultimately, however, that engagement needs to translate to the intended call to action, whether that be increased registrations, sales, or whatever other parameter for judging its effectiveness is in place.

ANALYZING THE SOCIAL MEDIA NETWORKS

One of the best shows on television is *Shark Tank*, and the best shark on the show is Daymond John. Imagine how well FUBU would have done had it had social media to promote its products in its early days instead of resorting to guerrilla marketing efforts, such as painting the FUBU logo on inner-city security gates.

Daymond John recently gave his description of the various social media networks in an interview with *Target Marketing Magazine*. John described FUBU on LinkedIn as the "party you go to with the suit, or maybe the tuxedo, on and you network...On Instagram, FUBU would be the hipster with the cool visuals. On Snapchat, it would be the really young, energetic kids...On Twitter, FUBU would be kind of like the regular party you go to...And on Facebook, you would have this whole family reunion type of presentation."[26]

Every social media network is different. A business needs to select the proper image and social media strategy for each of its networks. Acting the part is half the battle.

Facebook

Facebook was founded in 2004 as a closed collegiate site, similar to Hot or Not, by Mark Zuckerberg with several of his fellow Harvard college students. You probably already knew that from the movie *The Social Network*. Facebook is more than 10 times larger than the biggest TV station in the world,[27] so obviously Facebook needs to be an important part of the social media plans of any business.

To get started with Facebook, a business needs to begin a business page. The business page and the corresponding product pages should be completely filled out, keyword rich, and have engaging content. Like all social media, the cover photo should be eye-catching and should change often, the company's logo should be used as the profile picture of the business page, and the business details and contact information should be included in the "about" section.

In addition to the main Facebook business page, the site allows for additional sub-pages to be placed on the site, referred to as custom tabs. These reside in the same location as the generic tabs already on the site such as "about," "photos," and "more." Adding custom tabs to your business page makes a lot of sense, because search engines do index these pages, and the possibility exists for them to be ranked highly so that your business has multiple product or brand pages in the SERPs. Facebook tab pages will appear to be a separate web page with a unique URL. HTML coding is required to build the page, so some marketers may need to turn to programmers to complete the job.

When a business first gets started with a Facebook business page, it will likely want to invite targeted people to Like the page. This invitation should not be sent until there are at least a few good posts on the business page, since people will not bother to Like a page that is devoid of any substantial content. It should be noted that, unlike friend connections, Facebook business page Likes are one-way, meaning that the person Liking the page will see the business posts, but the business page will not show the posts of the individual who Liked the page. Moreover, unlike personal pages, Facebook business pages permit an unlimited amount of fans to be able to Like it.

Retailer Steve Madden is known as the first brand to take advantage of the Facebook Like button.[28] The shoe retailer's innovation allowed for any shopper on its mobile site to tap the Like button, and then the Like was automatically posted to the person's Facebook page. The result was that all of the shopper's friends could now see it, and thus Steve Madden took advantage of the virality that social media offers.

There are seemingly endless applications available on Facebook; take advantage of as many as possible to enhance search engine rankings. Search engines actively index Facebook business pages, so it is very possible that a business can have multiple listings for a particular keyword search on Google. Multiple search engine listings on page one is like stuffing the ballot box, getting an extra out in baseball, or getting a free mulligan in golf. Ranking a Facebook business page in addition to a company business page is just one more way to gain interest from a prospect.

Facebook used to be an easy and free way to promote a business, but there's no such thing as a free ride on Facebook anymore. In an effort to sell more advertising and limit business posts on personal pages, very few of the organic (unpaid) posts a business makes end up on the News Feed of its followers. Facebook has gotten so massive that if it served all of the posts, especially those from businesses, people would be absolutely swamped by them. Hence, it serves posts mostly to those who have engaged with the business content previously via Likes and shares. Facebook used to call the process of deciding who gets what posts "EdgeRank," but it has since dropped that moniker and now just does it without a fancy name.

If a business is disappointed with the declining reach of its business posts, Facebook also offers a very convenient Boost paid post option. With Boost, the organic post will appear in the News Feeds of targeted users. It is incredibly easy to use but is not always the best way to promote a Facebook post. More on that comparison with paid "dark" posts in the advertising chapter.

Like everywhere on the web, video gets more attention than images. Facebook has long recognized the importance of video, and CEO Mark Zuckerberg has participated in numerous speeches about video and mobile and the important role that video will play in Facebook's current and future marketing strategies. Video offers a great opportunity for brands to engage their followers. Embedded videos on Facebook play automatically in users' News Feeds (unless they adjust their accounts otherwise) and they generate the highest engagement rate of all posts.

Millions of people gathered in one place is the perfect opportunity for a business to increase branding, raise awareness, and grow a community of loyal followers. The enormity of Facebook's audience (it is the most popular social media network in the world) makes it a must-have for reaching all demographics. Don't be fooled by naysayers who say young adults are not using Facebook anymore. Teens and millennials may be using other social media sites too, but Facebook is still an important place to find all age groups.

Instagram

Instagram was founded in October of 2010 as a mobile app by Kevin Systrom and Mike Krieger. Systrom worked previously at Odeo, the precursor to Twitter, and he also spent time at Google; Brazilian Krieger is the technical lead of Instagram. In April of 2012 Facebook paid a lens-cracking $1 billion for Instagram. Not bad for 551 days of work.

There is much talk about the competition for youth and millennial users on Instagram versus Facebook. When one learns that Facebook owns Instagram, it takes away a lot of the competition angle and explains why Zuckerberg appears to not be so concerned about the migration of teens and young adults from Facebook to Instagram.

The major advantage of Instagram over Facebook is engagement. Engagement on Instagram is significantly higher than on Facebook—and all other major social media platforms, for that matter—because of the younger skew and the lack of increasingly annoying political view posts. On Instagram, users seem interested in every photographic post, whether it is from their friend or a celebrity crush. Business posts on Instagram are also very subtle. One company that does a great job with showing its product on Instagram is Forever 21. It shows its fashions on girl-next-door models in pictures that drive traffic to its retail stores.

Like with all social media accounts, choosing a handle on Instagram is very important. When a business searches to find its name, it may discover that it is already taken. In response, Instagram will provide the requested name with a series of meaningless numbers after it, such as "MainLinePizza3253." Rather than take them up on the meaningless numbers, choose the business name plus a period and then a location or product name, such as "MainLinePizza.WaynePA." This is superior for branding and also for SEO purposes. The business profile on Instagram is short, so use as many keywords as possible and disregard unneeded connection words. A clickable link to the business website should also be included.

Instagram is a social media site that is almost exclusively mobile. One can view Instagram on a web browser, but it clearly wasn't designed for desktop use, and using it on a desktop is downright clunky. In fact, it is not even possible to upload a picture or begin a new account from a desktop.

Instagram allows for a business to show its creativity on a platform with less noisy chatter. It is less crowded than Facebook and is based almost exclusively on pictures, not text. Although there are significant opportunities for using text, it almost seems useless, since the picture does most of the talking; the text exists mostly for finding new followers. Instagram offers 2,000 characters in the description, most of which are never used by the majority of users. For a business, however, it makes sense to take advantage of the copy that is available. By using more keywords and more hashtags in the description, the post will be much easier for new prospective customers to find.

Hashtags are especially important on Instagram to stand out from the dearth of images and to get found by new potential followers. Many people search by hashtag on Instagram, so it is imperative to use pertinent ones during the posting process. When a user begins to post a hashtag, Instagram offers hashtag suggestions and the number of posts in each hashtag; this is a great way to select hashtags with the largest possible audience. Another important use of hashtags for a business account is to find and attract key influencers in the same vertical market. A key influencer is a well-known person in an industry who has the power to influence others because of his position or knowledge.

Another important way to gain followers on Instagram is to target the competitors of the business. Finding out who is following a competing business is easy. All that needs to be done is to go to the competitor's Instagram account and click on "followers." Then, target those customers to your business account. If you follow those targeted people, they are likely to follow you back.

Instagram makes it easy to provide multiple posts on other social media networks. For instance, when a post is added to Instagram, it automatically asks if the user wants to share it with Facebook, Twitter, and other social media accounts. Geographic tagging is also part of Instagram, and it should be used on all posts, especially those made by a local business, in order to increase local sales.

A brand wishing to target millennials should certainly be very active on Instagram. Millennials, especially females, love to use Instagram because it is mobile-first (only), simple, and does not have all of the nonsense found on Facebook. With Instagram, nobody seems to have an agenda, and that's refreshing. And because simplicity has been an important part of Instagram since its inception, content on Instagram is more sharable and easier to understand. It is visual storytelling at its best. One does not have to read the description to understand what is going on, because a picture says a thousand words. A brand that can craft an ongoing conversation with its audience on Instagram will have tremendous success.

Twitter

The little blue bird of Twitter is seemingly everywhere. Just watch the local or national news and you will see the Twitter accounts of the journalists next to their names. Everybody seems to want to promote a Twitter account and gain more followers.

More than any other social media network, Twitter requires significant commitment. While the posts (tweets) are short and simple to create, it is the social media site that requires the most posts to have a significant impact. The tweets come and go so quickly among the massive amount occurring that if your message is not seen in the moment, it will likely not be seen at all.

Twitter, founded in 2006, is a lot like headline writing, which is clearly the most important, but often most difficult, part of any article. Many of the same things that make text messaging effective also make Twitter effective. For instance, it is okay to use capitals so long as it does not seem like the tweet is screaming. Tweets, as opposed to text messages, do allow for posts to take advantage of spacing. In other words, a tweet can provide a list of items, each on its own line, which provides more real estate and easier reading for followers. The added spacing does not consume any precious characters in Twitter's character limit.

Tweets work best when they are concise, use short words, and get to the point. It is tempting to want to fill all 140 characters, but even that is too long for some readers. Shorter tweets get greater read rates and allow for multiple retweets with comments being added. Nowhere is sharing more important than on Twitter. Retweets should be a goal for every tweet that a business sends. Retweets mean an endorsement of the thought exposes an entirely new audience to a brand.

Hashtags are extremely important on Twitter, given the vast amount of tweets on the site. People can search for specific hashtag keywords and possibly discover the one your business used. This leads to increased interaction and more followers.

Pictures are also extremely important on Twitter, since the Twitter user is often moving quickly while on the site. A picture will grab their attention and increase retweets. Read rates are significantly higher on tweets with images, so there's really no excuse to not include pictures. One little-used tactic is to put up to four pictures on a single tweet. To do this, simply click the camera icon several times and keep adding pictures.

Twitter also allows for DMs, or direct messages, that are ideal for a one-to-one conversation between brand and customer. Simply click on the "messages" tab and enter the name or handle of the person you want to message, and it will go directly to, and only to, that user. If the consumer begins a DM with a business, it becomes a great way to offer customer service if the account is being regularly monitored, as may be the case at a very large business with a distinct customer service department. Southwest (@SouthwestAir) is an example of a company that does a great job of customer service via DMs on its Twitter account.

If you want to publicly reply to a tweet, post the twitter handle (such as my handle, @BobBentz) at the beginning of a tweet. This tweet will be seen only by users who follow both you and the person you're replying to. If the goal is to give a shout-out to an account that anyone can see, put any character prior to the handle at the beginning of the message so that the tweet looks something like this: -@BobBentz. In this method, all of your followers will see the message. Or, if you have the extra characters, you can rephrase your tweet so that the handle isn't at the beginning: Thanks @BobBentz for the great Twitter info! This will be public too.

A Twitter List is a grouping of like-minded accounts on Twitter. There are lists of users interested in fantasy football, SEO, social media, or the Philadelphia Phillies. Being included on lists can increase the popularity of tweets and get the message to like-minded individuals. If you see a list that you'd like to be part of, simply ask to be included.

Twitter skews older than Instagram but younger than Facebook. It has slightly more men than women. Brands and individuals cohabit side by side on Twitter. It will require the largest time investment of any social media site and will take the longest to see results, but it should be considered part of any serious social media strategy.

LinkedIn

Anybody in business, and especially in sales, knows that getting in touch with a prospect is becoming increasingly difficult. Busy people get so many e-mails, and they simply do not answer calls like they used to, a problem that has been compounded by the use of caller ID. Then, there are those gatekeepers—the impenetrable guard dogs of important executives that a business wants to reach.

LinkedIn is a marketing person's best friend, because LinkedIn, and only LinkedIn, breaks down the barriers erected by the gatekeepers. With LinkedIn, marketers can reach key prospects through personal messages that will not be prescreened by gatekeepers. By using a personal invite and offering something of value with no strings attached, it is possible to forge a relationship. Even important people like to have their egos stroked, so compliment the prospect on her impressive career and offer her something of value, like a free SEO analysis of her business's website. That will get her attention. Once expertise is established, perhaps through published articles on LinkedIn, it is time for a more meaningful conversation.

On LinkedIn, there are no followers or friends, only connections. Such is the businesslike nature of the site. A veteran in the social media business, founded in 2002, LinkedIn does not have the flippant persona of other social media sites. That is why it is imperative that a personal or business LinkedIn account remain focused on business and not the occasional joke or personal post. This is not the place for a funny cat video.

LinkedIn allows individual accounts to network with like-minded individuals through its LinkedIn Groups. LinkedIn allows a user to join up to 50 groups, and there's no reason not to take advantage of all 50. Most individuals join industry associations, and while that is certainly important, it makes much more sense to join groups of individuals in a targeted vertical market. After all, a business is not going to sell to its competitors. Don't forget to join alumni groups; these are often the best sources of new business, especially those from large and loyal universities. LinkedIn has recently changed all of its groups to private groups. This means that only group members will be permitted to read and comment within the groups. LinkedIn has also blocked search engines from crawling the discussions; it believes that this move will provide a more trusted private space for like-minded people to communicate. Moreover, its statistics show that private groups generate greater engagement.

One of the features of LinkedIn is its publishing platform, a mini-blogging platform included with every LinkedIn account. When it first debuted, its reach was terrific, but now that more people are using it for useless posts, it has become more difficult to reach through the din and get a large amount of reads. Some experts think that a LinkedIn user can repurpose existing content from a company blog and place it on LinkedIn's publishing platform. While that may be the case, it is always best to at least rewrite the copy to avoid any duplicate content issues.

In addition to personal pages, LinkedIn offers a great way to publish company pages as well. LinkedIn Company Pages are a great way to market a business to interested people. To obtain a company page, a business must first have an existing personal LinkedIn account from which to establish it. After it is established, an individual can name other administrators to the LinkedIn Company Page.

One of the best features of the company page is that LinkedIn allows a business to have up to 10 product-specific Showcase Pages, formerly known as Product Pages. According to LinkedIn, "Showcase Pages are extensions of your Company Page, designed for spotlighting a brand, business unit, or initiative." With showcase pages, a business can have a dedicated page, each with its own unique URL, for each aspect of its business with its own message to share. Showcase pages enable a business to provide additional content and posts to boost social media presence. It also gives LinkedIn members a chance to follow the parts of the business that they value most.

Status updates, whether for your personal or company page, are shown on the home page of your connections. They should be made regularly so that connections know what is going on with your business and so they will think of your business when its products or services are needed. It is a great way to keep in touch with customers and prospects with company news and innovations. Businesses can also use this section to gain publicity for blog posts on the company website.

One of the things that can really help either a personal or business page on LinkedIn is positive endorsements. Like any social media, positive endorsements can have a great influence on purchase decisions. Ask trusted colleagues and customers to write a personal endorsement for you or your business.

LinkedIn's place in a social media strategy is obvious. Since it is the only major competitor in the business realm, it is a must-use social media site for nearly all businesses, but definitely all businesses that sell on a B2B basis. Its audience is wealthier and older than most social media sites, and that audience can be highly targeted. With LinkedIn, a business does not need to be humble; positioning a business or individual as an expert is the way that will attract new sales. It offers opportunities to network every day with like-minded individuals. An active LinkedIn business account will expand connections to a far greater extent than Facebook or Twitter.

YouTube

YouTube, founded in 2005, is the second-largest search engine in the country, behind only its owner, Google, who acquired it in 2006. That alone should be enough information to convince a business that it needs to be active on YouTube.

The first thing that needs to be done is create a YouTube Channel for the business. It should have a consistent look with the company website and the business's other social media profiles. In its never-ending ambition to confuse us, YouTube requires that the business channel be aligned with the same Google Plus identity. Keep the content exclusive to the business itself; do not mix your son's free-kick goal and post-goal victory airplane dance in his 10U soccer game on the business channel.

There is no doubt about the importance of video when it comes to mobile marketing. The best thing about YouTube is that a Hollywood-level production is not always necessary. People will indeed watch a smartphone video of a single talking head, but the better you can make it, the more that people will watch it. Consider some easy video editing tools. After the raw footage is shot, a business can use tools such as iMovie, Windows Movie Maker, or YouTube's own video editing tools to add additional flair and viewability.

YouTube offers an array of helpful tools on the site that allow your business to apply annotations, embedded links, or call-to-action overlays. It also allows you to link to other pertinent videos in your business channel. Channel sections enable a business to group its videos in various segments so that when one video ends, the next most relevant video begins.

It is beneficial to add a standard intro and outro to the videos that are posted on YouTube. This could be a company logo or jingle used as a branding mechanism. If the business does not have the in-house talent to develop them, many decent ones can be found on Fiverr (www.fiverr.com) for as little as five bucks. These short clips will add a sense of professionalism and continuity to the videos.

YouTube allows for a thumbnail of the video to be the home page of the video when it is displayed. It selects three different moments in the video and allows the operator to choose one of them as the static resting image for the video. One way to trick YouTube into allowing a business logo to be in the thumbnail is to keep the company logo up for a longer-than-normal time at the end of the video, so that the logo becomes one of the three likely thumbnail choices.

Videos on YouTube should always take SEO into consideration. YouTube gives the user a large amount of characters to use in the description, and using keywords in that description can really help with SEO. In fact, keyword density can be higher with YouTube than on a traditional web page. There also is the ability to upload a transcript to the video description, which is especially beneficial for deaf customers or customers who are watching a video in a place where they can't allow the sound to play. This is something that is likely already produced, so it is just another way to use the content that is already available.

There is also the opportunity to allow for social sharing and embedding of the video on other sites. In most cases, it makes sense to permit this, but it does involve ticking a particular setting to ensure that it is available. One of the bonuses of allowing other sites to embed the video is that if users click on the YouTube logo, it will refer them back to the business's YouTube page for playing of the video.

One outstanding feature of YouTube is its analytics. The analytics overview page gives a lot of interesting information that can help in the marketing of the videos, including total number of views for each video and the source of the click-through to find the videos.

YouTube has become a must-use site for any brand that has video to share, regardless of the target market. The only reason a business will not use it is if it doesn't have any videos to share. Given the ease of creating videos on smartphones today, it is difficult to imagine a business not having any videos to share with its audience.

142 | Bob Bentz

Pinterest

Pinterest, founded in 2010, is a female-dominated social media site that emphasizes fashion, cooking, and crafting. With Pinterest, the picture tells the story, not the copy. Perhaps more than any other social media site, it is the color and creativity of the images that will grab the user's attention.

Users on Pinterest upload photographic "pins" to "boards," which are the groupings of the theme's images, such as pinning dresses to a senior prom board. Individuals share images to the boards and so do businesses; the difference is that businesses are hoping the user will click through to its website in hopes of driving traffic and sales to their company.

Whoever handles the Pinterest business account should download the convenient "Pin It" button for their browser. This way, when the employee sees a picture that they wish to share, it is as easy as two clicks, and it is pinned to a board on the company account.

On Pinterest, the marketing is subtle. In fact, a brand on Pinterest can tell its story without ever even using any marketing lingo. If a consumer sees something she is interested in, she will likely click on it and repin it to her own page. It often becomes a shopping cart of things that the individual would like to own. What can be better for a confused man to know what to buy for his wife or girlfriend than finding her online wish list?

The special sauce with Pinterest is the longevity of its pins. It is the anti-Twitter when it comes to longevity. When a person repins a post on Pinterest, it moves right back up into the timeline again and again. Pinterest pins have the longest shelf life of any social media site content. They will often drive traffic to a business website for years because of this reincarnation feature. A business needs to be careful of this, since pins do not automatically fade into the sunset. If a product has been discontinued, the pin will also need to be discontinued to avoid any consumer disappointment.

Business pages are now available on Pinterest, but they are relatively new. Hence, a business might have been using a personal page and now has the opportunity to change it to a business page. There is not much difference between a personal page and a business page, but it certainly makes sense to make the easy switch to a business board if only to take advantage of the demographic analytics that are available to verified business pages.

One tool that business pinners might want to consider adding is rich pins. With rich pins, advertisers can include extra information right on the pin itself. There are six types of rich pins:

- App pins allow users to download your app without ever leaving Pinterest. (For now, this works with iOS apps only.)

- Place pins take travelers to the next level by including a map, address, and phone number.

- Article pins help pinners locate stories they'll find important by adding a headline, author, and story description.

- Product pins make it easy for people to buy items by including real-time pricing, availability, and where to make a purchase.

- Recipe pins show ingredients, cooking times, and serving info.

- Movie pins give pinners a quick glance at films by including ratings, cast members, and reviews.[29]

More than any other social media network, there seems to be numerous businesses, especially in women's apparel, taking advantage of Pinterest's unique ability to drive traffic to company websites. In fact, many brands have created entire businesses based on free promotions on Pinterest. As we mentioned before, there have been numerous examples of this on *Shark Tank*, where businesses in the fashion industry have racked up multimillion dollar sales thanks to organic pins that had no out-of-pocket costs. Pinterest offers a unique opportunity for brands to sell on social media, especially to young females who are ardent shoppers. It is a powerful tool for driving sales.

Google Plus

Google Plus is like the first-round draft pick that ended up being a bench player. There were high hopes for it when it came out in 2011 to be a competitor to Facebook, but users have simply not embraced it anywhere near to the extent that they have embraced other social media sites, and its future is, quite frankly, in doubt.

Unfortunately for Google, it started pushing its social media products to us long after we already had a close relationship with its search engine and e-mail products. To catch up, Google automatically created Google Plus accounts for many online businesses, but those businesses simply haven't discovered or claimed their business pages yet. Therefore, there are a lot of inactive business accounts on Google Plus. If you have not yet created a Google Plus account, check to make sure Google didn't do it for you first, so that you avoid having a duplicate listing.

If Google hasn't already created a Google Plus page for your business, go to Google My Business and start one. Whoever is creating the Google Plus business page should use a generic e-mail address for your business. Use something like marketing@ thebusiness.com rather than a person's personal e-mail account. What often happens is that the person handling the social media account leaves the employment of the business, and then nobody knows the credentials, so future users have to change the e-mail associated with the account.

As much as you may like to, Google Plus should not be ignored. After all, Google is behind the site. Therefore, it is pretty safe to say that Google is paying attention to the posts, indexing them, and helping to deliver search engine results through content marketing. Even if a business does not plan on using Google Plus for finding prospects or building brand loyalty, it should consider using it anyway if only for the SEO value that it clearly provides. In fact, each post has a unique URL that is sure to give your corporate website an added SEO boost.

One of the best features of Google Plus is its circles. With Facebook, all contacts are lumped together. This is not the case with Google Plus. By organizing contacts into various circles, it is easy to promote content to a specific contact category. A business, for example, may have different messages to send to end customers than to value-adding resellers or vendors.

Hashtags are also handled a little differently on Google Plus. When the post is created, any hashtags used are added to the upper right of the post itself. If no hashtags are placed in the post, Google adds them in the top right anyway. In some cases, the suggested hashtags should be accepted, and in other cases, they may not make sense. If the user clicks on those hashtags, then she will see other posts that utilize the same hashtag.

Google Plus communities are a great place to interact with like-minded individuals in your area of expertise. They also offer the convenience of easily moving to Google Hangouts for live discussions of interest for the community. Google Hangouts allow video conversations with up to 10 people at a time. Another feature is Google Hangouts on Air, which allows a large amount of people to view a business presentation.

Another great feature of Google Plus that is different than other social media sites is that it is not cluttered with advertisements. Therefore, there's less competition between organic business posts and paid advertisements.

In the end, a business needs to decide whether they definitely need a Google Plus account. No business needs an extra social media account to deal with, but the SEO value that a Google Plus account can provide probably makes it a necessary evil.

Vine

If there ever was a social media network built on diminishing attention margins, it's Vine, established in 2013. Vine is a short-form video sharing service built by Twitter. It is very easy to share six-second looping videos from a mobile phone to the network. The videos on Vine auto play. A business will be able to see how many loops it receives, and those loops can rack up quickly. And since it is only a six-second commitment, Vine is a great place for videos to go viral.

There is no advertising on Vine other than the business accounts that put out organic posts, so there's very little competition for attention. Moreover, since nearly all of Vine's activity is on mobile (it didn't even get Vine.com, but rather Vine.co for its URL), the short-form videos take up the complete screen of the smartphone, so they can't be missed.

Other than loop counts, a business will not get much in the form of analytics, so it is difficult to judge if a business is reaching the right consumers. Fortunately, there are third-party sources that can track Vine stats, such as Simply Measured.

Vine is, not surprisingly, best used when targeting teens and young adults, and skews slightly female. Also, when a business posts on Vine, it can easily flow to the business's Twitter account as well. If a business's social media marketing strategy includes Twitter, Vine is a natural extension to it.

Snapchat

Snapchat, founded in 2011, offers a way for users to share images quickly to a select group of friends or followers. Snaps are the pictures that are posted and sent to followers. The unique feature of Snapchat is that, based on the length that the publisher has set for it, the pictures quickly disappear in one to ten seconds—at least on the site itself. On Snapchat, the posts disappear, but snaps can be saved on the recipient's phone in the same fashion that they can save a screenshot. Therefore, be careful what you send. The evidence may not really disappear!

Snapchat Stories has really fueled the recent growth of Snapchat. It provides for multiple pictures to be strung together to show a story of what the user did that day. Then, there's the ultimate social sharing tool, Live Story, which allows multiple users attending a single event to share their combined pictures to the site.

Snapchat is a refreshing alternative to other social media sites and is also a place where the audience is highly engaged, perhaps the most highly engaged of all social media sites. The "now you see it, now you don't" messaging app offers an air of exclusivity to teens, college students, and young adults. It is a place where Mom and Dad will not find them, and they can share what is happening without parents and neighbors peering in on the juicy details of their lives.

For brands targeting teens and young adults, they need to go where those consumers are, and they certainly are at Snapchat, which has become a go-to social media site for 13–24-year-olds. The decline in time that teens spend using Facebook is in part thanks to them moving to the Snapchat platform. Snapchat is not for every brand, but advertisers need to fish where the fish are. If a business is targeting this young demographic, there's no better place to find them than on Snapchat.

Tumblr

Tumblr, founded in 2007, is a microblogging platform that utilizes short-form blogging posts. It was acquired by Yahoo in 2013. It is easy to use, and it's easy to publish short thoughts like on Twitter, graphics like on Instagram, and copy like on a blog. Businesses and brands love that they can create full-blown CMS sites on it.

When a brand registers at Tumblr, it does not maintain any copyrights to the content. That is why you see a lot of Tumblr photos on a Google search available for immediate reposting to a viewer's blog or site. That may be seen as a positive in that images can be remarketed, or it may be seen as a negative in not knowing where the brand will eventually show up.

Tumblr has done a better job of targeting young adults and teens than it has of getting the proper spelling of its URL. It translates well to young adults of both sexes and lends itself well to images, GIFs, and videos. It could be a short-form alternative to a company's traditional blog site.

Vimeo

Video-sharing site Vimeo is very similar to YouTube in its technology, but very different in its user base. While YouTube seems to have every kind of amateur point-and-shoot video, Vimeo, established in 2004, generally has higher-quality content. If YouTube is like the high-school play, then Vimeo is like Broadway.

The Vimeo audience is made up of college-educated, high-income, creative individuals, and definitely skews male. The site has a vibrant community of filmmakers and video professionals, so if that group is part of your target market, it is a site your business should be associated with. If your business is going to promote on Vimeo, make sure that your videos are not being shot with an iPhone and have a bit of creativity and professionalism to them. This will be a highly critical audience.

Quora

Quora is a question-and-answer social media website that began in 2009. If worked consistently, it can certainly position a brand or company as an expert in the field. Such a business can be a trusted resource should the user need the product or service. If the product is relatively new and there are a lot of questions about it, Quora is a good place for a brand to share its expertise. A few years ago, for example, it was quite a lively site for questions regarding SMS text message marketing and the legal aspects of the then-new industry.

One of the great features of Quora is that a user does not have to always check it. If there are questions in a business's noted areas of expertise, it will send an alert e-mail of that question and request that the user post a response.

Quora is best used by companies and businesses where there is a lot of confusion among potential buyers. Its demographics are definitely male and 25–34. Most of the users of Quora seem to be entrepreneurs and small businesses. If this is your target market, being active on Quora can be a nice secondary addition to your social media strategy, since you will likely be talking directly to end users.

Ello

Established in 2014, Ello is one of the newest social media networks. It was launched along with a large amount of press as being the alternative to the advertising-infested Facebook, since Ello's special sauce is no paid advertisements. Ello says, "We believe a social network can be a tool for empowerment. Not a tool to deceive, coerce, and manipulate – but a place to connect, create, and celebrate life."

On Ello, users can post content just as they would on the other social media networks. They can share and comment on posts just like with Facebook. If a business or person wants to join Ello, it has to enter an e-mail address and wait for an official invite from Ello, since it is an invitation-only site. (Don't worry, they even accepted me.) It is also app based and does not seem to care much about desktop access at all, since its URL is Ello.co instead of Ello.com.

Ello is great if your target market is one that values privacy. Remember why people are there in the first place—privacy and lack of advertisements—and keep any business posts extremely subtle so as to not alienate users. If your business targets early adopters or unique individuals, it may be just the right network for it, but do not base your entire social media marketing efforts on Ello. There simply isn't enough mass there yet.

SlideShare

If the question "name a social media site" was on *Family Feud*, SlideShare would certainly not be the first one that came to mind. But, given that this chapter is about marketing a business with social media, it certainly makes sense to include it. SlideShare, founded in 2006, works the same as more popular social media sites. The business creates its own site, then continues to supplement it with new presentations. It is best not to put your most recent presentations on SlideShare for competitors to copy, but putting up ones that are a few months out of style can be a great source of leads. A business should also make sure that it does not include any pictures that might come under scrutiny of online copyright trollers or presentations that might have been made to specific prospects or contain special pricing.

If your business is not using SlideShare, it should be. It is a great repository for older PowerPoint presentations. As opposed to YouTube, SlideShare does not include audio, so the slides included must be descriptive. Since they do not have the salesperson's voiceover, some additional copy may need to be added to the slides or the description. The business may also wish to have a more descriptive title page, since this is the only thing users will see when deciding if they want to view it. Posts on SlideShare tend to do extremely well in the search engine rankings and can bring a business leads and significant link juice from an authority domain.

SlideShare works best for B2B offerings and for large-ticket B2C offerings. It sits in the same row as LinkedIn as being purely a business site, so only serious entries need apply. If your business is looking for a secondary B2B outlet where it can tell a more complete story, SlideShare is a good choice.

OTHER SOCIAL MEDIA SITES

Certainly, the above section not an all-encompassing list of social media sites, but it does list the most important ones. Every business is unique, however, so it is not a one-size-fits-all list. Work with as many social media sites as your business has time for and look for ones that may be especially important to your specific industry. Sports-related products, for instance, have access to a lot of social media sites that are sports specific. There are specialty social media sites in the restaurant industry as well.

Photo-Sharing Sites

Images are an important part of content creation and an area that all businesses need to be careful of, given the legal ramifications of using a photograph that is copyrighted. Just because a picture is online does not mean that somebody else can use it. It is not necessarily in the public domain. That is where photo-sharing sites can be helpful for a business. Not only can businesses often obtain images for free, they can also post images for others to use. Some sites allow a business to post photos for free and make them available to others so long as attribution is given. When a business allows others to use its images, it creates an opportunity for valuable backlinks. Some of the best photo-sharing sites include Flickr, Dreamstime, iStock, Shutterstock, and Picasa.

Social Bookmarking and News-Sharing Sites

Internet users have been bookmarking their favorite sites for many years. Social bookmarking sites are simply a way to do so and save those bookmarks on a public website rather than a personal computer. Of course, the difference is that, with social bookmarking sites, those posts are shared with others who can then recommend the articles and sites as well.

Doing social bookmarking for blog articles and business websites is easy, and not a lot of effort is required beyond signing up for an account. Since most popular social bookmarking sites are indexed by Google, it is a great way to build traffic and search engine rankings. Social bookmarking sites rank items by the number of people that have recommended them. Generally, users search for articles using hashtags. The best social bookmarking sites are StumbleUpon and Delicious, although the major search engines also offer this service through Google Bookmarks, Bing Toolbar, and Yahoo Toolbar.

The difference between social bookmarking sites and news-sharing sites is timeliness. News-sharing services focus on what's trending now. Similar to social bookmarking sites, users recommend content and then readers vote on that content. Getting a lot of votes means appearing on the much-coveted home page. When using news-sharing sites, a business's search terms should be utilized in the tags and copy for the submission. If done correctly, news-sharing sites can have a very positive effect on search engine rankings. The most popular news-sharing sites are Reddit and Digg.

Reddit, founded in 2005, is a content-generated website where content is submitted by individuals and voted up or down on by the community. Posts are grouped by subreddits, where users submit content by category. It does not allow for business accounts per se, but there are many there, based on a quick perusal of usernames. Reddit is best if a business's target is tech-minded, young-adult males.

Digg, founded in 2004, was the early leader in this niche, but it has lost some momentum to its primary competitor, Reddit. It bills itself as "What the Internet is Talking About Right Now." Members of the Digg community can submit and share content. Readers vote on the submission by way of "Diggs," which are essentially endorsement votes.

When a company posts a press release, Reddit and Digg should be two of the first places it goes, as they are easy to add a link to. A marketer can use her personal account to share links; a business account is not necessary. In fact, it makes more sense for a personal account to do the sharing, since it then seems less self-serving than a business account sharing its own content. Submit regularly, and do not bunch all the submissions at the same time or it will seem spammy. It is always better to have the submissions appear at different times so they are not competing with each other.

When a business submits to social bookmarking or news-sharing sites, it is best to get multiple people at the business involved. If a site sees the same article being submitted by a dozen or so people, it can jump-start the promotion in the hopes of the article getting listed on the highly trafficked home page.

Review Sites

When it comes to mobile, review sites are so very important to a business. The fact is that people are far more likely to post negative reviews than positive ones. If a person sees a roach at her favorite Chinese restaurant, a picture will be taken, and it will be spewed all over the web in a matter of seconds. That is why having a social media strategy that reviews online reputation management on sites like Yelp, Foursquare, Angie's List, CitySearch, OpenTable, and TripAdvisor are so important. Negative reviews must be responded to promptly. Being confrontational will not work on social media, because everybody is a tough guy when posting online. Instead, answer the concern and explain how safeguards have been put in place to prevent a similar incident from happening again. If the reviewer seems satisfied, ask them to go back and re-review the business or edit the existing negative one.

Feedback on review sites can be the best friend of a business. Therefore, it is critical that a business remind satisfied consumers to write positive reviews as well. Mobile websites, for example, can include prominent links to review sites, and customers should be encouraged with an incentive to post on them. Businesses should have an ongoing system that empowers customers to give positive reviews.

At times, there will be negative comments about a business that are undeserved and even unfair. In some cases, the comments may have even been coerced or placed by a competitor. There is not much a business can do about a poor review other than answer the reviewer. But the very best way to diminish the impact of a bad review is to have a lot of positive ones to go along with it.

REPUTATION MANAGEMENT

A business, however, can be mentioned on more than just traditional review sites. There are countless places on the web where a business can be mentioned, and the comments can be both positive and negative. Keeping abreast of what people are saying online is important either way. This process is known as reputation management and involves monitoring what is being said about a business online and taking action to attempt to make sure that what is being said is in line with the goals of the business. Companies perform various tasks, mostly on social media, that enable them to respond to both negative and positive mentions by burying the negative ones and enhancing the exposure of the positives ones. If the feedback is positive, the business can thank the author and even ask for an important SEO-enhancing link back to the business if such has not already been provided.

Google Alerts is a great way to be informed about what is being said about a business on the web. This service alerts a business to information it should be reviewing. A business should set up multiple Google Alerts about the business itself, the products that it provides, and its competitors. Then, when that particular keyword is mentioned on the web, an e-mail is sent to the person who has set it up, and the business can quickly address the comment.

No matter how ridiculous the criticism might be, it is best that the business always take the high road and respond accordingly. If that does not get the job done, ignore further criticism from the commenter. If it continues and is hostile, personal, or confrontational, the business should not hesitate to block or report the user.

People may be googling your business right now, and the online record of your business is usually permanent. Even if a particular piece of information is removed, it is still maintained in the Wayback Machine. (The Wayback Machine is a digital archive of the World Wide Web from 1996 to the present. It contains over 10 billion web pages.) Therefore, it is critical that your business monitors what is being said about it, addresses any negativity in a professional manner, and makes it an ongoing practice to encourage positive comments and reviews from satisfied customers.

Social CRM

Today, social media and customer relationship management are so intertwined that it is impossible to have one without the other, hence the need for social customer relationship management, or social CRM. Social CRM is the process of engaging with customers on social media with personalized messages that can be created at scale. The key to social CRM is the term "at scale," which indicates that the business hasn't just agreed to respond to a single request that has yelled loudest, but it has built the infrastructure to maintain social media contact with all of the customers who desire it. To perform social CRM at scale, the business must have some necessary tools to avoid the impossible task of looking all over the web for comments. There are numerous providers available online, and many integrate or are extensions of the sales department's CRM solutions.

Social CRM requires that the brand and the consumer have a two-way conversation that shows that the customer is always right and the brand truly cares about the problem. This is costly and timely but is really the only way to be successful with social CRM.

Employees that work on social media need to react in a timely manner, put a human face forward, and answer as an individual on behalf of the company. This means using first names in interactions. Brands need to also realize that there are some cases where answering via social media may not be the best option, and a private e-mail or phone call may be better at facilitating two-way interactive communication.

Representatives also need to know when to throw in the towel. There are many trolls on the Internet who are unreasonable and just out to embarrass the company into giving them something free, so they continue to hurl insults and unrealistic expectations via social media. At some point, continuing to engage unreasonable people does more harm than good. Individuals monitoring conversations such as this will realize that the brand has attempted to solve the consumer's problem, and now the consumer is simply being impossible to deal with.

Not all social media interactions are negative. Brands also need to reward important online brand advocates. Those people that continue to praise a brand are providing an invaluable service at no charge to the company. Sending an occasional gift to these fans is a great way to keep them as brand advocates who will continue to offer the comments that are so very helpful to the business.

TOOLS FOR SOCIAL MEDIA POSTING

Nobody wants to spend an inordinate amount of time posting to social media. After all, for most businesses, social media is simply a component of an overall marketing strategy. If a business does not control the amount of time it spends on social media, an employee's whole day can be consumed by it. Social media is addicting and fun, and many businesspersons gravitate to the job that is the most fun and not necessarily the one that is most important.

Fortunately, there are a large number of tools that can help a business with its social media posts. The beauty of these tools is that a business can dedicate a small amount of time—perhaps one hour per week—and do the posting for the entire week, then just supplement it with timely posts as the week goes on. The two most popular social media posting tools are Hootsuite and Buffer. Both are easy to use and will enable you to set up your posts in advance. They also provide analytics on engagement, so you know what is working and what is not. There are free versions of both, but the freebies do not allow for enough social media sites to be involved, so your business will likely need to use the upgraded versions for a nominal monthly fee. It is difficult to imagine how a business can be successful with a consistent social media strategy without using one of these important social media tools.

TIPS FOR SOCIAL MEDIA POSTING

When it comes to social media, sharing is good and selling is generally not as good. If a business positions itself as the expert in the field, the sales will come because people will want to work with the best. Consider what happens at a trade show. If somebody gives a great presentation, there are audience members lining up to meet with the speaker after the speech because he gave evidence that he was an expert in the field and could offer solutions to the problems encountered by audience members.

It is okay to post a sales-related post every now and then, but if that is all a business does, it will likely alienate many followers and they will choose to opt out, which is a genuine lost sales opportunity. Remember, people do not like being sold to on social media, so most social media selling needs to be subtle. The best long-term strategy for a business is to be perceived as the foremost expert in the field. If that is accomplished, the business will naturally come.

In general, it is always best to be brief on social media. Use bullet points when possible and remember that people like numbered lists. There are tons of posts out there, and if consumers can read yours in less than five seconds, it is surely going to mean greater exposure.

Use #hashtags. They will help your posts get found and increase the number of followers that your business has. Social media posts are only as good as the number of followers that see them, and that amount can increase dramatically with the use of great hashtags. Check which hashtags are trending and gather a list of the most used ones, both overall and within your industry, and use them.

Business social media posts should also encourage consumer participation. After all, it is all about engagement, is it not? One of the best ways to do that is to share photos of happy consumers using the product. Only a select amount of people care about the technology of the product itself; every prospect cares about how it will make his life better or easier.

Regardless of the medium, it is always best to use pictures, graphics, charts, and videos in posts. People are visual and, in regards to social media, generally lazy; they do not particularly want to read. Just be sure you do not randomly grab pictures off the Internet, as many companies are actively enforcing their copyrights on pictures. Copyright infringement of pictures on the web has become big business!

Be consistently active with social media. Working social media every day by the same person can get monotonous, so attempt to get a team to do the work. If social media efforts disappear for a long time, a business will lose followers and appear to not be on top of its game by prospective customers.

One of the biggest questions that social media experts get is about the quantity of messages that should be posted. It varies for each social media site, but the key is to post a lot of messages, assuming they all have some value. This is contrary to what many experts say. Occasional complaints will come in, but it is all about the total number of engagements and shares. So do not sweat it if you lose a follower every now and then. The magic number of how many messages should be sent out is this: send one less than the point where followers get annoyed and stop following the business.

Monitor this and then arrive at the magic number of messages per day for a particular business's needs. Posting often will result in an increase in opt outs, but if the end result is increased engagement and shares, losing a few followers is worth the trade-off.

Don't be afraid to use the same content more than once. If it worked once, use it again. This is truer on some social media sites than others. For Twitter, for instance, reusing content is not a problem, whereas on Facebook it might not be as good of an idea. A great holiday post can be recycled next year. A tweet that was effective can be used many times over until it produces diminishing engagement.

It is common sense, but it is worth mentioning what not to post. Don't post anything political or controversial. Posting on gun control, for example, will likely alienate half of your business's possible customers, so why do it? At the end of the day, it is all (well, almost all) about the money.

Regardless of which social media sites your business plans to actively use, reserve your business name on all of them. It is an easy thing to do, only takes a few minutes, and if your business does not do it, it may regret it later when it does want to expand its offerings.

Social Video

Social media videos need to be short, easy to consume, to the point, and exciting or interesting so that viewers become engaged. Start strong, tell a story, and tug at the viewer's emotions if possible. This will make a video go viral.

Facebook and Twitter have both made major efforts to upgrade their social video platforms. Brands looking to get the greatest amount of shares should post video to the gorilla of social media— Facebook. While Facebook users will watch longer videos, Twitter users have a shorter attention span and prefer videos of 30 seconds or less. Instagram videos can more closely mimic a longer video. Vine and Snapchat videos need to be very short, and this time restriction actually leads to some of the most creative videos available on social media. Businesses looking to add video to their social media marketing strategy need to understand that the video needs to match the medium. A longer-form Facebook video simply is not going to work on Vine. The business can't simply cut out six seconds and expect it to work on Vine.

There is a tremendous amount of competition for a viewer's attention on social media today. And video is, by far, the best way to obtain that attention if it is done right. Brands that can master video production are being greatly rewarded with shares and increased loyalty.

Maximizing Exposure

One of the ways to maximize exposure for a social media account is to join communities. There are different names for these communities depending on which social media site a business is on. On Google Plus, they are known as circles. Other social media sites call them lists or groups. Whatever they are called, they are ways to get a business's message out to an appropriate target market. Some communities are public, meaning that they'll take anybody (even me), while others are private and require an invite or request to join. People always like to get something for free, so contests and giveaways are two more great ways to gain exposure and followers.

Choosing a Handle

The best handle to choose on a social media site is the name of the business. Businesses evolve and so do the products they sell, so unless a business is sure that it will always be in the business of selling the same thing, it should probably stay away from using products in the handle rather than company names. If the company name is already taken, use the name of the company and then a geographic or product reference (if it is a sure thing that the business will always be selling that product). For example,

"@Marios.Morgantown" or "@Marios.Fishbowls" could be used if there's already another Twitter account using the @Marios handle.

The same is true when it comes to personal accounts. For individuals, names are almost always best, even if you have to be "JohnSmith316." It might be cute to use a handle such as "Best900NumberSalesman," but it may not be the best name in the next decade. Instagram is the worst when it comes to cutesy names; it is very difficult to find targeted followers on it. A handle is like a tattoo: it is forever, unless you want to start all over. Today's cutesy name is tomorrow's regret, so stick with the basics.

If possible, use a consistent social media handle on all social media business accounts. A neat tool you can use to check if a particular handle is available across multiple social media sites is Namechk (www.namechk.com).

Creating Your Profile

The goal of a profile is to convince others that this is a profile that they want to be involved with. And just like in life, and dating, a picture is worth a thousand words, and a first impression is very important. Like a personal profile, a business profile should show that it is trustworthy and competent. This starts by putting a properly sized logo in the avatar section of the social media site. Most avatars are square and most logos are horizontal, so there's likely going to need to be some work done by a graphic artist with the all-important avatar. The cover picture is the largest graphic on the site, so use something that depicts the business. Change it often so regular visitors do not get bored. And, whatever you do, do not use the canned pictures that are available from social media sites themselves. Nothing shows a business is more clueless about social media than using the pictures that come with the frames.

Take advantage of all of the copy that is available on a social media profile description. The more copy that it used, the more keywords that can be inserted. Social media optimization is the process of creating a social media profile and posts that will be optimized with keywords to gain higher search and social media site rankings. A business's social media profile may be changed from time to time to take advantage of products that the sales and marketing teams are promoting or to take advantage of hot-selling products based on seasonality or trends. If a business is emphasizing sales of a particular product line, changing a social media profile temporarily makes sense.

Most social media sites enable a business to obtain a vanity URL after it gets a minimal amount of followers. This enables the business to replace a random series of numbers with a URL that properly reflects the business or brand name. Get a vanity URL as soon as possible and before inviting people to join the page.

Posts come and go, but profiles are going to be around for a while. Therefore, it is worth it to spend some extra time in getting the business profile right the first time. Use your best internal writer or consider outsourcing this important task.

Attracting Followers

Attracting new followers to a social media site is an ongoing job. After all, why would a business not want as many qualified and targeted followers as possible? Content creation and posting still requires the same amount of work whether 100 or 10,000 people see the posts. Continue increasing qualified followers or the social media account will become stagnant and benefits will start leveling off.

Of course, the key word here is "qualified." A business owner needs to reach influencers in its marketplace. When social media first started, businesses bragged about how many followers or Likes they had. While gaining a lot of followers is important, it is far more important to have followers that are engaged with your messages and that can influence others.

It is always better to go to a crowded restaurant than one that is empty. The same is true when trying to attract followers to a business social media account. There is no doubt that people are more likely to follow an account that has a significant amount of followers than one that only has a few. Therefore, it may be tempting to buy bogus, fictional followers. In fact, they can be purchased on sites like Fiverr for as little as a "fiver." It might also be tempting for a manager or agency to buy bogus followers to show the boss that they are doing such a great job in growing the audience. But since many social media sites serve posts based on overall engagement, purchasing more followers can actually have a negative effect on overall distribution of organic posts.

There is, however, one social media site where a business might actually want to purchase followers—Twitter. Twitter freezes the ability of an account to follow more people when it reaches 2,000 follows if it does not have at least 2,000 followers. When this happens, a Twitter account is locked out from following more users until the number of followers catches up. Therefore, adding purchased followers to get an account over 2,000 and deleting them later might be a strategy to consider.

Here are some tips on how to attract more followers:

- Follow others—In many cases, you will get a follow back. Follow other businesses in your niche, local businesses, local media, industry media, important bloggers, key influencers, and industry organizations. Important customers and the contacts at those businesses are also a must-follow.

- Comment—If there is something to add to the discussion, go ahead and comment. Praise goes a long way towards gaining future followers.

- Share—It is the biggest compliment one can give to another social media account. Offer incentives, such as contests, to those that share the message.

- Add links to e-mails—Put social media links on an e-mail signature. The people that employees of a business are interacting with are likely to follow back since they are already engaged and interested in the business.

- Place links in newsletters—Add social media links to company newsletters. If a recipient likes what they read in the newsletter, they are apt to click through to follow the business on social media as well.

- Include links in press releases—Integrate social media sites into any and all press releases that the business uses. Not sure which press-release sites to use? Consider the ones that require payment, such as PRWeb and PRLog. There are fewer junk releases, and the results on paid sites are almost always better than on the free sites because they actually reach true journalists.

- Engage influencers—Key influencers are the big dogs in the industry. Influencers are the people that speak at industry trade shows and have huge amounts of followers. Be sure to follow all of them and attempt to engage them as much as possible, in the hopes that they will promote your posts and content.

Influencer Marketing

Imagine how valuable it would be to your clothing company if an Academy Award–winner wore your dress on the red carpet. That dress would be sold out the very next day. It is the same on social media. A business needs to find key influencers in its niche that are willing to be brand advocates that promote the business.

The first trick is finding those key influencers. Some of them are already known, because they are the authors of the books and articles in the industry. They are often bloggers or people associated with trade associations. In the business of mobile marketing, a key influencer would the mobile marketing manager at Starbucks or Domino's, an employee of the Mobile Marketing Association (MMA), the publisher of an industry journal, or the author of a book on the subject. But they are not just famous people. Some of the best advocates for a brand are simply happy customers that a business can find easily by monitoring hashtags or through Google Alerts. Invite them to promote the brand and recognize them with merchandise or shout-outs for doing so.

Potential customers trust third parties, such as influencers, far more than the brands themselves. For instance, imagine you went to a chamber-of-commerce meeting many years ago and Donald Trump spoke about what a great businessman Bob Sacamano was. You'd be a lot more apt to believe him than if Sacamano braggingly told you himself that he was a great businessman.

Influencers are not just people that will drive traffic to a website. They are people that will drive sales. Hence, any business needs to have a definitive social media strategy to attract those key influencers.

SoLoMo

Social media is no longer confined to a standard desktop computer, so brands do not have to wait for consumers to get back to their homes or offices to reach them with their message. There has never before been a medium so adept as mobile at finding a business's best customers on the medium they are already using within striking distance of making a retail purchase.

SoLoMo (pronounced "So-Low-Mow") is short for social–local–mobile and represents a complete paradigm shift for traditional marketers. Instead of the traditional pushing of messages to consumers via old-fashioned, traditional media, such as print, radio, television, and outdoor, the contact message is pulled by the consumer as a result of her social activity in the local area via mobile device.

Social media has become so commonplace that some say people do not really communicate IRL (in real life) anymore. Check out a group of strangers in an elevator. Half are looking at a social media site. Go to a trade show, and half of the audience is only half-paying attention to the speaker because they are multitasking with social media on their mobile phones at the same time. What used to be rude is now socially acceptable.

Local offers remain the most relevant to consumers due to their proximity and immediate availability. Therefore, it should come as no surprise that marketers are anxious to deliver their messages to the most personal—and local—of devices, the mobile phone.

Mobile has created a mind shift over the years. Some social media networks started as primarily desktop and slowly evolved into mobile. Facebook and LinkedIn are examples of this. MySpace began the same year as Facebook and is an example of a social media network that declined in popularity in part because it didn't make a successful migration to mobile. Others, such as Instagram or Foursquare, were almost exclusively mobile from the start.

Let's take a look at an overview of the three elements that make up a traditional SoLoMo strategy:

- Social—How many people randomly choose a restaurant anymore? It is a risky thing to do. Best to first check third-party sources, such as Yelp, Foursquare, Google My Places, or TripAdvisor, to get reviews. After the dinner, the consumer may add another restaurant review so that people can read his opinion.

- Local—Groupon and LivingSocial bring hyper-local e-mail messages to consumer phones almost every day. The local pizza restaurant may send a text message. Keyword searches like "hotel near me" are gaining in quantity. More than 70 percent of searchers are looking for businesses within five miles of their location.[30]

- Mobile—Shoppers today have more information than ever right in their pockets or purses. Routinely, they contact brands multiple times, using different devices for a single transaction. This leads to a glut of information that often puts the consumer in a position of greater knowledge than the store employee.

An example of a SoLoMo strategy would be a mobile app that has access to a consumer's GPS location and that enables the consumer to interact with it. SoLoMo represents the perfect storm of its three elements:

- Social media is the platform to engage the audience.
- Local is the relevant proximity to the business.
- Mobile, not desktop, is the medium of connection with the brand.

Buoyed by the proliferation of smartphones and tablets, a successful SoLoMo strategy benefits acute marketers not only through additional business but also through increased engagement and virality for the brand. It puts the power of information in the hands of the consumers. Connecting consumers to your local brand makes them loyal advocates who will share information about the brand through social media. This turns out to be a win-win in the long run.

The notion of a mobile-first marketing strategy, then, is an obvious choice given the local data that a mobile phone provides. Since the mobile phone is now the predominant way that users access the Internet, one can easily see the importance of it in an increasingly necessary SoLoMo strategy.

Klout

Want to see just how good the social media presence of a business is? Klout is a tool that measures the strength and power of a person's or business's social media presence. Just enter the information, and it will come back with a score that ranks the user versus others on the Internet. Klout does not count for anything that has an effect on the business, but it is generally accurate and totally addictive.

Blogs

A blog is an important but often forgotten part of social media. Every business should have a blog on its business website. It is the daily social communications epicenter of the business.

The blog was invented by Ian Ring in 1997. Shortly thereafter, the term "web log" was used to describe blogs. Later, it was jokingly renamed "we blog" and eventually shortened again to the moniker "blog." Blogs were originally nothing more than online diaries—personal journals that allowed tech-savvy authors to rant about one thing or another. Links were popular within blogs since search engines were decidedly less sophisticated and counted links from a personal blog equal to that of a national news service. Link-building created quite a financial opportunity for bloggers, who had to that point been toiling away for no monetary gain.

Businesses later realized that blogs could be beneficial to them as well. Even if the business wasn't high tech or involved with writing and web design, it could easily maintain a blog as a feature on its site. Writing was a snap, because blog readers do not expect highly technical writing; a conversational tone that could be written by anybody on the staff worked fine. It was this conversational tone that set blogs apart from traditional Internet copywriting.

Thanks to WordPress and Tumblr templates, it has become incredibly easy to have and update a blog, and even to make it mobile ready when installed. It is extremely easy to add a blog to a blogging platform like Blogger on its domain (www.blogger.com). Doing it this way, however, makes little sense, since traffic will be sent to the Blogger domain instead of the URL of the business itself.

It is far better to send the traffic to the business website, so most businesses include a blog as part of a subdirectory on its site. A blog used in a subdirectory is a URL like "www.mywebsites.com/blog." By doing this, the inbound link juice received from articles posted on the blog is generated for the site itself, not the easier-to-use external product found on a blogging site.

Business blogs should maintain categories of posts to make it easier for readers to read other posts related to their area of interest. It is also very important to add an internal search bar so readers can quickly find the content they are looking for. Comments should be encouraged. Readers should have the ability to easily share the content with add-ons, such as ShareThis.

Plugins, bits of software that improve a website's function, are included as a feature on all WordPress templates. At a minimum, the business blog should download a plugin to remove comment spam and should also install the Yoast plugin to provide an easy-to-use template for SEO-related input. There are many other handy plugins available that can improve the quality of the blog and the ease of updating. Scan the list of plugins and choose the ones that would be right for your business blog.

Search engines hate static websites and, for the most part, a business site tends to be rather stagnant. A blog can provide an immediate power boost to a website, since the content is being regularly updated. An easy-to-use blogging platform like WordPress means that non-tech-savvy marketing employees can update the site themselves without any knowledge of HTML. Because blogs are basically the same as traditional websites, the same SEO strategies work for both blogs and the primary website of the company. The blog will need the same strategy for title tags and meta descriptions. Internal linking and garnering links from outside sites also need to be an important part of the strategy. Keywords are also incredibly important, and therein lies an extra opportunity for a site. With a blog, articles can be written to target long-tail keywords that might not be important enough to be included on the primary website copy. These long-tail keywords should be easier to win in the search results than the primary keywords, which are more hotly competitive.

One effective way to get visitors to a business blog is to monitor what is trending online. Take a look at Google Trends and then consider writing a blog post about subject matter in your industry that is currently trending. A blog post also gives a wealth of content that can be shared on social media; sharing new content on social media can be automatically programmed into the blog itself by adding a plugin. Moreover, additional content will subtly drive visitors to the business website, which is, of course, what a business wants in the first place.

To truly judge the effectiveness of a business blog, click-throughs and tap-throughs from the blog itself to the main website need to be tracked. Analytics will also show just how many reads are coming from social media mentions. After a while, they will become significant.

A common question about a blog is: how often should a business publish on it? It is best to start with a comparison of your direct competitors. As a general rule, however, the more often that a business publishes the better, so long as the quality of posts is consistent. If a business is publishing less than five times per month, it is not enough. Up to 10 is more in the range of acceptability. Fifteen per month will clearly have an impact on visits. Whatever your business does, just be sure you're not that business with a blog that hasn't been updated in three years! That says something very poor about the business. If a business is not going to update its blog regularly, it is better to not have one.

Social Live Streaming

You probably know social live streaming as the Periscope and Meerkat apps. It is the evolution of YouTube going live and in real time. These live-streaming apps let users point their smartphones at whatever is happening in front of them, whether they own the rights or not, and broadcast it to a potential audience of hundreds of thousands of viewers. There is no time or phone memory limitation (because it's not saved to your mobile phone), and fellow users can log in and watch the live stream.

Twitter acquired Periscope in January of 2015 and released it in March the same year. Periscope is the early leader of the social-live-streaming category. Meerkat, which started a little earlier in 2015, is independent, although with a significant investment from Comcast. Meerkat started off loosely affiliated with Twitter until the Periscope purchase made it more advantageous for it to be affiliated with Facebook.

Live streaming is not anything new, but what is novel is the ease in which consumers can use the products. It is very simple to download an app, sign in with a Twitter account, click "stream," and post the link. Then anybody in your Twitter community can click on that link and watch whatever you are broadcasting from your phone.

There are numerous applications for businesses and brands to use live streaming:

- group technical support
- interactions with key business personnel, such as the president
- new product demos
- major news announcements
- gauging public opinion on a new product offering
- increasing customer loyalty through VIP offerings
- webinars
- exclusive insider offers

To get started with marketing a live-streaming video, make the announcement in advance to your followers. Use hashtags to try to draw in additional followers and viewers. Find a steady way to hold the mobile phone that is taking the streaming video, like a simple tablet stand; a lot of videos on these sites are painfully unwatchable due to their unsteady nature. Have a staff member nearby to answer any questions from the comments or to record any business leads. Keep a log of those that attend and follow up with them via Twitter, Facebook, SMS, or e-mail.

Social live streaming apps allow viewers to indicate whether they are enjoying the production or not. Viewer comments are seen on the screen. Businesses can respond to those comments as an added selling tool. The amateur producer can see statistics on the production, such as number of viewers and average time spent watching. Productions are saved for 24 hours.

Marketers should take note: Live streaming allows for immediate social interaction with all-important video content. Since most viewers come from the Twitter or Facebook followers of a business, live streaming is a great way to promote content to an audience of those specifically interested in the brand. A promotion is more likely to reach loyal followers than the general public, but live streaming is yet another new tool in the mobile marketing toolbox.

TRACKING THE EFFECTIVENESS OF SOCIAL MEDIA AND CONTENT MARKETING

Results for social media efforts don't happen overnight. It takes time to obtain sufficient followers to have an impact, and it takes consistent effort in posting to get results. Figure on six months of regular effort until real results are coming in that have a positive effect on sales.

Like all tracking efforts, it starts with the establishment of measurable KPIs and the resulting statistical analysis of those KPIs. For measurements to be effective, they have to align directly with the objectives established. Using the age-old SMART method makes the most sense. Be sure that the KPIs for social media analysis are: Specific, Measurable, Actionable, Realistic, and Timed. There should be a process in place in advance to easily measure effectiveness and to make sure that all such efforts can be quantified numerically. "There seems to be more people coming to the store" is neither a valuable nor quantifiable measurement.

Here are some common KPIs that a business may want to track on social media:

- website traffic
- page views
- video views
- downloads
- new followers
- opt outs
- comments
- engagement, such as Likes, shares, retweets, +1s
- conversions

- document requests
- newsletter opt ins
- click-throughs and tap-throughs
- e-commerce sales
- in-store lift
- in-store sales
- coupon redemptions
- predefined key influencer reach

Larger companies will want to track results weekly, and small and medium companies can do so monthly. All of the major social media sites have built-in analytics that will help a marketer track the effectiveness of social media posts. Another way to track social media efforts is to add an Urchin Tracking Module (UTM) to the posts. In 2005, Google acquired Urchin Software; with the acquisition, Google began the process of creating what is today Google Analytics. The UTM is part of the link that is placed on the social media post or guest author post, and it sends signals to the Google Analytics system that a site is likely already using.

Tracking social media to most people means tracking an increase in followers, click-throughs, or other easily measurable stats. While those stats are certainly important stepping stones to increased sales, at the end of the day, it is all about how more additional sales (or savings, in the case of customer service) are being made because of the social media efforts.

TOP SECRET: WHAT DOES FACEBOOK KNOW ABOUT YOU?

Facebook Is Gathering Data Everywhere You Go

You've certainly seen them: those advertisements that run in your Facebook News Feed. They are often in the second position, just below the post from your college BFF. They are targeted! Highly targeted! In fact, scarily targeted to some.

Facebook compiles its interest information from a variety of internal and third-party sources, and it is not as simple as what you have Liked on Facebook or the content you have posted; it is also about what you do outside of Facebook. Ever go to a site and see one of those convenient Facebook posting icons? You do not have to use them for Facebook to know that you've read that article; it already knows. As if that isn't enough information about you, Facebook supplements its own internal small data with external third-party big-data sources that track your household members, income level, and purchasing patterns.

All of this data is compiled by Facebook and is precisely why those paid advertisements that appear in your News

Feed are almost always of interest to you. It is why Facebook advertising is so doggone effective.

What Facebook Knows About You—Check Now!

If you've always wondered how Facebook knows so much about you, here's a way to figure it out:

1. Sign in to your Facebook page.

2. Find a paid advertisement in your News Feed.

3. Click on the "v" button in the upper right-hand corner.

4. Click on "Why am I seeing this?"

5. Click on "Manage Your Ad Preferences."

6. You will now see the page showing what Facebook knows about your interests.

I guess that's how they knew you were an Aaron Carter fan.

Want to learn more about social media marketing? See updated statistics and other important information at RelevanceRaisesResponse.com.

Chapter 6

MOBILE ADVERTISING

There has never been an advertising medium quite like mobile that enables a brand to effectively target the right consumers, in the right place, at the right moment.

WHEN WILL MOBILE GET ITS FAIR SHARE?

*E*ach year, research companies, such as comScore, come out with statistics that analyze time spent with media versus advertising spend. Time spent with mobile continues to dramatically increase each year. Yet while the advertising dollars being spent on mobile are also increasing, brand advertiser investment is nowhere near keeping up with the amount of time consumers are spending with mobile devices.

The most egregious violator is print advertising, which continues to amass large amounts of advertising spend that is, quite frankly, undeserved, at least in comparison to the time spent with print advertising by the public. Look around at lunchtime at the businesspeople eating alone. Are they reading a newspaper or on the restaurant's Wi-Fi? Drive around the neighborhood in the morning and see how many newspapers are in the driveways. It is a wonder that it still makes financial sense to deliver them. Perhaps print advertising still makes sense if the target market is over 60, because the demographic of print readers definitely skews older. For most advertisers, however, older customers are normally less coveted than younger ones, so advertisers' continued fascination with print baffles most in the mobile and digital industry.

Another medium that over-indexes in terms of advertising dollars spent versus time spent with media is terrestrial radio. Although not nearly as dramatic as print's imbalance, many advertisers and agencies still seem to gravitate to what is traditional and what is known. Agencies, many still not adept at mobile, continue overinvesting money in radio because it is a known entity and the relationship with the local radio station is long standing. Plus, the business owner likes to hear his ads between his favorite classic rock tunes. In many cases, traditional advertising agencies are not doing their clients any favors by continuing to place their hard-earned advertising dollars in the same old place. Often, this is done because mobile and digital represents a new world that even agencies have not yet explored. There is often no expertise in-house, so the agency just keeps doing things the way that it always has, with the business owner not encouraging the agency otherwise.

WAYS TO PURCHASE MOBILE ADVERTISING

By far, the most common way to pay for mobile advertising is via a cost-per-thousand (CPM) model. It may seem odd that it is called CPM instead of CPT, but the reason is that the term is truly "cost per mille," with "mille" being the Latin term for thousand. A CPM model offers the lowest cost per impression available to advertisers. It offers maximum brand reach. The negative to a CPM purchase is the possibility of receiving low-quality sites, such as amateur bloggers.

Purchasing advertising by a cost-per-click (CPC) model means that an advertiser pays only when a user clicks or taps on the ad. The positive side is obvious—an advertiser only pays for direct engagement and gets the branding for free! The negative to CPC is that fat-finger clicks, which are common in mobile, result in an extra cost and a worthless visit. CPC is also vulnerable to fraudulent clicks, which result in a similar extra cost and absolutely no meaningful value to the advertiser.

It is tempting for advertisers to lean toward a CPC model over CPM. That way, an advertiser is paying for something closer to the eventual conversion results. That being said, CPC is rarely a better value in the long run. If agencies sell via a CPC model, one can bet that the financial formula is going to be in their favor, because on the back end, nearly all publishers are selling on a CPM model. Therefore, the agency is going to build in enough margin to ensure that it will profit, even in a worst-case tap-through scenario.

Some companies may even offer a more exotic solution, such as a cost-per-inquiry or cost-per-action model. These rare payment offerings are likely to be even more skewed in the favor of the company offering the advertising package. What the seller is logically going to do is estimate the number of inquiries or actions, then mark up the financial model to make sure that they do not get burned in the transaction.

HOW TO ADVERTISE ON MOBILE

There are several ways that a marketer can purchase advertising on mobile listed below, each followed by an example:

- direct mobile websites—buying an advertisement directly from Yelp on its mobile website

- direct in-app advertising—buying an advertisement on the Pandora mobile app directly from Pandora

- mobile social ad networks—buying mobile advertising on sites like Facebook, Twitter, LinkedIn, and Instagram, with the tools that they provide

- mobile ad networks—purchasing advertisements on a mobile ad network, or on a mobile app or mobile website from an agency that has relationships with such networks

Direct Mobile Websites

You can purchase directly from mobile websites themselves. A common place where a small business may purchase directly is Yelp. Yelp has a very aggressive sales team; it seems like every small business has had a visit from a Yelp rep. But, buyer beware: a quick Google search will show many legal cases from small businesses that were not happy with their Yelp purchases.

Many advertisers seek to purchase mobile advertising on sites such as ESPN or CNN. Most of the major sites do not want to deal directly with a lot of customers, so they usually have a minimum investment of at least $10,000 or more per month, which makes such advertising only possible for larger advertisers. Places where a local advertiser may buy direct mobile advertising without a large investment are local newspaper or cable company websites.

Direct In-App Advertising

An advertiser can also purchase advertising directly from app providers, such as Pandora. As more and more brands introduce apps, time spent with apps is increasing dramatically every year. Apps like Pandora have direct sales teams that can help facilitate an advertising purchase directly in-app.

Mobile Social Ad Networks

If a business can only advertise in one place on mobile, the best place is social media, especially Facebook, because social media sites have the distinct advantage of knowing so much about a consumer. Not only does a social media site know about a user's geolocation, but it also has extensive information on the user's demographics, psychographics, lifestyle characteristics, and interests.

Think of everything that a consumer posts on Facebook; Facebook obviously knows that. Then, think of all of the sites that a user visits that have the Facebook share button on them. Because of the code on the site, Facebook knows you were there, whether you clicked the share button or not. Most people are always logged in to their Facebook page because computers remember the passwords. Therefore, a consumer with a Facebook account is always being tracked online. Combine that with the data mining that Facebook provides from third-party sources, and you can see how Facebook advertising is the ultimate when it comes to relevance raising response rates.

Facebook is not the only one. LinkedIn, for example, has a person's entire resume in its database, and it is regularly updated. Talk about business intelligence!

Consider what that means for an advertiser. No other medium in the history of advertising can claim to so effectively target a user's geolocation, demographics, and interests like a social media network. With that competitive advantage, it is no wonder that Facebook has become such a powerful marketing tool and that television is scrambling to try to find a way to compete with social media's big-data capabilities.

Mobile Ad Networks

There are a lot of mobile ad networks out there competing for market share against the giants of Google and Facebook. In fact, one list has over 415 mobile ad networks![31] There are even some companies that are marketing white-label versions of their ad networks so almost anybody can say they are in the mobile ad network business directly. Of course, no customer or agency could ever be familiar with all of the mobile ad networks, so you end up using just a few, mostly based on the availability of inventory, price, service, and personal relationships.

Millennial Media, Jumptap, AdMob, Rocket Fuel, Mojiva, and Tapjoy are mobile ad networks that a lot of advertisers and agencies use. Some mobile ad networks have areas of specialization like InMobi, Flurry, and Chartboost—one that specifically targets gamers. Top video ad networks include Adap.tv (which is owned by AOL), BrightRoll, Videology, and YuMe. For a non-technical newcomer to mobile advertising, there is no easier interface than the Google Display Network, which targets mobile websites, and Google AdMob, which provides in-app advertising.

Quite frankly, the mobile ad networks do not usually get results that are as effective as Facebook because they do not offer the pinpoint targeting or the viewability that is provided on social media. They do, however, offer a much better CPM and provide a lot of branding at an inexpensive rate. If branding is the goal, then mobile ad networks will maximize the amount of gross impressions that a brand receives. Mobile ad networks are also a great way to increase reach and frequency and get the message in front of consumers that are not regular users of social media. Some of the sites where an advertisement may appear may not be of the same quality level as others, but they will still deliver impressions and results, albeit with likely less engagement.

In addition to buying on mobile ad networks directly, there are also aggregators of the many mobile advertising networks. These services, which are almost exclusively provided by agencies, provide a means to aggregate hundreds of mobile ad networks on a single interface. The advantage to such a solution is that an advertiser can buy at the cheapest possible price at any given moment at over 415 mobile ad networks. Using a mobile-ad-network aggregator can really stretch a brand's advertising investment, as the savings are significant and the participating publishers are vast.

PROGRAMMATIC BUYING

Traditionally, media has been sold by ad sales people responsible for negotiating a price for inventory on various mediums. Unfortunately, at least for the job market, with programmatic buying, there is considerably less need for human salespersons.

Increasingly, mobile advertising is being purchased programmatically through ad exchanges using real-time bidding. An ad exchange uses an automated auction format for the buying and selling of mobile advertisements. What this means is that the publisher will accept the highest bid for its advertising space at any given moment. In contrast, a mobile ad network will purchase the ad at the lowest possible price at the same given moment. It is supply and demand at its finest—prices are established according to real-market conditions and in real time. Think of it as a fluid market of mobile advertising, where the price is set based on real-time value at the time of the transaction being made. Programmatic buying has brought speed and efficiency to mobile media purchasing.

Efficient mobile advertising commerce includes several entities: ad exchanges, a mobile ad network, a demand side platform (DSP), an ad server, and a real-time bidding engine. A DSP is a piece of software that enables advertisers to purchase display ad inventory in an automated fashion via real-time bidding exchanges. To take advantage of the power of a DSP, an advertiser will most likely have to use the services of a mobile/digital advertising agency that has access to the DSP. It is not likely that an individual brand will make such an investment.

The DSP enables an agency to maintain efficiency on multiple buys by using a single mobile advertising interface rather than having to deal individually with many different mobile ad networks. By utilizing a host of different mobile ad networks, the agency can benefit its clients by consistently obtaining the best possible rate for the mobile advertising inventory at any given moment.

By utilizing an agency with a DSP, the advertiser gains wide access to maximum inventory and laser-focused targeting. It also gains the ability to serve ads and bid on ads, plus track and optimize the mobile advertisements—all in real time. It is an enormous amount of information to keep track of, and it can only be done through the use of an effective DSP solution. Without DSPs, mobile advertising would be considerably less effective and more expensive, as advertisers would have to work with numerous ad networks, and the advertiser could not be assured that they were obtaining the best price in every instance.

It is difficult to imagine a mobile advertising world without DSPs. DSPs have helped to remove costly salespeople from the equation and have made the system far more efficient by making the process of purchasing mobile advertising like the stock market, where prices are adjusted based on supply and demand and current market conditions.

With a DSP, mobile impressions are auctioned off to the highest bidder at that very moment. The result is a "fill rate," more commonly referred to in a real-time bidding environment as a "win rate" for the advertiser. The win rate is the number of ads purchased divided by the number of attempts to purchase an ad. In other words, the DSP, on behalf of a specific advertiser, contacts 100 publishers and bids on ads from those publishers. Of the 100 ads the DSP attempts to purchase, six are actually purchased. That makes the advertiser's win rate 6 percent. The advertiser can adjust its bid price upward to get an improved win rate or to gain exposure on more premium sites, or it can adjust the bid downward to be more conservative, thus resulting in a lower CPM, fewer gross impressions, and more ads running on less attractive sites.

It may seem like DSP technology is replacing mobile ad networks, but in reality what DSPs have done is blur the lines between the two. DSPs are getting into the ad network business and vice versa. The combination of the two working together is simply the next generation of mobile ad buying.

In addition to DSPs, there is another element to making programmatic buying work for mobile advertising. That side interfaces with the publisher wishing to sell advertising space on their site. This is known as the supply side platform (SSP). The SSP interfaces with ad networks and ad exchanges to make the programmatic inventory available to advertisers. In most cases, publishers are competing against each other by offering the best price, because most advertisers only want their advertisements to be seen by the most coveted person and do not necessarily care on what site it is seen.

PRIVATE MARKETPLACES

Private marketplaces (PMPs), also known as private auction, closed auction, or private access, are a bit of a hybrid between the traditional advertising sales process and the newer programmatic marketplace. In a private marketplace, large buyers and sellers interact in an invitation-only environment that enables both parties to negotiate specific terms for highly sought-after premium inventory. It is the most common alternative to the typical programmatic auction approach that sells inventory via an unreserved auction format in a bidding system where all can participate equally.

Inventory on a private marketplace may be purchased programmatically, but the difference between it and traditional programmatic buying is that it is not an open network that all can participate in. It is "one to a few" in its approach, since it is by invitation only. Ad network companies such as BrightRoll, DoubleClick, AppNexus, and Kantar Media offer private marketplaces to their best customers. Think of a private marketplace as programmatic, but by invitation only. It is a bit of an exclusive mobile advertising party that only the Astors and the Duponts are invited to.

Private marketplaces can be set up several ways. In some cases, the inventory is purchased via fixed price, and in other instances, it is auction style. In most cases, inventory is sold with fixed prices and is reserved in advance. Inventory that is sold in this manner is known as programmatic guaranteed or programmatic reserved.

Publishers like private marketplaces, because those marketplaces give them control over which kinds of advertisers and creative will be displayed on their sites or apps. Publishers want to sell only to the highest-quality brands, as it improves their image as well. *Glamour* magazine, for instance, would enhance its own image by inviting Louis Vuitton, Gucci, and Prada to the private marketplace. In addition, publishers like knowing that a certain amount of revenue is guaranteed and that they will get a higher rate for the premium inventory than they would programmatically. Prices are higher for PMPs because advertisers are competing for the highest-quality ad inventory on some of the most popular and respected mobile and digital properties. These might be advertisements that are above the fold, ads on the *New York Times* website, or special sponsorships. There is definitely prestige involved in PMPs, and that is why advertisers are often willing to pay a premium for the placement. Private marketplaces often result in greater customer satisfaction for the advertiser and the publisher.

Normally, the premium inventory of a top-rated publisher is sold by a direct sales team. One of the added bonuses of PMPs for publishers is that they do not need to have commissionable sales professionals on staff to visit and entertain clients. Instead, that work is done by the PMPs. On the flip side, large advertisers like PMPs because they are guaranteed a certain amount of impressions. If there is additional inventory available, the advertiser often has the option of also purchasing it at an incremental, add-on price. Imagine an advertiser is running a big sale. That advertiser will want to know with some certainty that it will get a certain level of exposure during the sale dates. With PMPs, that audience is guaranteed; with normal programmatic, it is not.

Another advantage of PMPs for an advertiser is that they can actually see their own advertising. With the real-time nature of programmatic, this is not possible, because there is no way to accurately predict where their advertisements will appear.

There is also improved efficiency for advertisers with PMPs because less creative is needed, thus reducing complexity. Advertisers also do not have to worry about ad fatigue (the point where the same advertising creative shows diminishing engagement and returns) with PMPs. The number of advertisements shown to the same users is controlled, and marketers do not need to worry about overexposing the target audience with too much frequency. Reputable brands also do not have to worry about ads showing up on low-quality sites or adjacent to questionable content, since they'll know precisely where the ads will be running.

With private marketplaces, both the publisher and the advertiser know exactly what they are getting and at what price. It is an old-school approach, but in many ways, it can be more effective than programmatic selling and buying.

PREMIUM PROGRAMMATIC

The concept of premium programmatic can also be described as "programmatic plus" and can be called many other names, including programmatic direct, programmatic reserved, and programmatic premium. There appears to be no right answer and no complete consensus as to the naming conventions. This is very strange, but it is one of the many aspects of mobile that is still finding its way, so there is bound to be some confusion in such a nascent industry. Premium programmatic allows the advertiser to pay extra to use its best quality creative in a good placement position with the most desirable audience. Premium programmatic is similar to PMPs in that it is also involved in the selling of premium inventory. In most cases, premium programmatic buys are on an open platform, meaning that inventory is being sold to the highest bidder, regardless of who that advertiser is, instead of being invitation only.

Premium programmatic differentiates itself from the remnant, bargain-basement inventory that is often associated with traditional programmatic inventory. It attempts to preserve legacy value prior to the new digital realities of real-time bidding and capitalize on the scarcity of premium mobile inventory. It works because many marketers believe that having their brand advertised with a quality publisher brings added engagement and positions the brand more positively in the eyes of the consumer. Advertisements are in an environment that the brand would like to be associated with. In advertising circles, this is known as the Vogue effect, in which advertisers benefit more from being in an exceptional medium.

Is It worth It?

One school of thought in the mobile advertising world is that inventory from a well-known or quality publisher is worth more than traditional programmatic inventory. If an ad is seen on a quality site, it exudes added value to the brand. Is the Vogue effect real? This may seem logical for an advertiser like Tesla, but does it make any difference for Sprite?

There are others in the advertising game who do not believe there is any such thing as a premium publisher. If the right person is reached at the right time, who cares whether the ad is seen on *Sports Illustrated* or an American Legion baseball team's website?

Is a mobile ad impression premium just because it was seen on the *Wall Street Journal*?

Premium inventory is defined by the publisher as being so, but publishers always have direct sales teams, too. So one would expect that the best premium inventory is being sold by the humans, not by third parties using partial programmatic tactics. After all, publishers are going to continue to be hesitant to sell their best inventory in an open marketplace where they have less control over the content being placed by the buyer.

PINPOINT TARGETING

When it comes to effective targeting, mobile advertising enjoys the superpower of context. Mobile's uncanny ability to send the best message to the right person in the optimal location at the time when that person is most likely to buy is unsurpassed. Mobile advertising via apps and mobile websites allows for precision targeting that no other medium can match. Marketing pros can target their audience with the following strategies:

- Geofencing—Pinpoint certain zip codes, a specific radius from a business location, or draw a unique polygon around a certain target area so that there's no waste.

- Geoconquesting—Target the competition. If a hospital is hiring nurses, for instance, it could serve recruitment advertisements only to those who are using their mobile devices while at the competitive facility's geographic footprint.

- Demographic targeting—Only want to reach college-educated women, ages 25–34? Mobile can do that.

- Interest targeting—Specific interest groups can be easily targeted with mobile, especially when using social media advertising. Baseball fans attending spring training games in Florida or Arizona that like sunflower seeds? No problem.

- Dayparting—Reach consumers when they are most likely to buy. Mobile offers narrower focusing on dayparting than traditional media. For example, a sports bar could advertise just an hour before the start of the Super Bowl. Mobile does not just allow for dayparting, it allows for timely advertisements, down to the specific minute.

- Retargeting—Once a potential customer visits the landing page, a business can continue to target them by sending advertisements through other websites.

TYPES OF MOBILE DISPLAY ADVERTISING

Banners

Mobile display banners are the standard when it comes to mobile advertising. They are the cheapest form of mobile display advertising. Inventory is plentiful, and so advertisers need to produce multiple sizes to adhere to the many formats that publishers offer.

The mobile banner ad is usually placed at the top or the bottom of the screen, although some opportunities do exist for middle or side screen placement. Banners need to have a small but eye-catching image with concise and powerful text to get the consumer to tap on it. It is best to use unique brand photos rather than stock photography, but either can work. Aspirational imagery works best. Aspirational imagery is a foundational concept across all modern marketing. It suggests that a consumer will relate more strongly to the improvements that your product (product A) will make to their lives than the specific benefits of product B. If you can tap into what your customers want to become, then you can position your product or service as the way to get there. An example of aspirational imagery might be an advertisement for a financial services company that shows a businessperson on his computer on the beach. The image signifies the financial independence that the product will ultimately provide.

With little space to provide much detail, the banner ad is a simple and effective way for a brand to get its product to quickly reach as many people as possible. Standard image ads that run on Google's mobile AdSense platform utilize the following sizes, although this is nowhere near the complete list of sizes that an advertiser may need:

- mobile leaderboard (320x50)
- large mobile banner (320x100)
- small square (200x200)
- square (250x250)
- medium rectangle (300x250)

Since mobile banners have been around the longest, there is not a lot that is sexy about them, but they remain the single most important and used type of mobile advertising. They are cost effective, easy to create, and can be utilized quickly. Since they can be avoided and ignored by users, they are not a problem or annoyance. The negative to banner ads, of course, is that they will not get a huge amount of tap-throughs compared to rich media types of mobile advertising. Since they are small ads on a small screen, it is difficult to make them visually compelling.

One of the tactics that can be used to add a bit of excitement to banner advertising is to use mobile adhesion banners. An adhesion banner is usually at the bottom of the page, and it remains intact regardless of how the user is scrolling. An adhesion banner will always remain above the fold; even when the user scrolls down, it remains in the same position on the mobile screen. Adhesion banners are clearly a premium product that can provide significantly higher engagement. Therefore, they will likely be sold in premium marketplaces.

Interstitials

Interstitial ads are ones that display across the entire screen. They are most commonly used in mobile games. In most instances, interstitials are displayed while the app or mobile website is loading. Often, the user is required to close the interstitial before continuing the intended mobile experience.

Because it is full screen and uses more appealing graphics, an interstitial will have greater tap-throughs and installs than the more passive banner ads that are intermixed with on-screen content. One of the biggest complaints about mobile advertising is banner blindness and that advertisements can't be found on the smaller screen of the mobile device. Not so with interstitials, which take up the entire screen. Interstitials force the user to engage by making a decision to either tap the ad or "x" out of it. On some interstitials, the x out is adeptly hidden, so it takes the user longer to actually tap out of the advertisement.

On the other hand, because of the pop-over nature of interstitials, marketers need to be cautious, because Google now denotes interstitials as not meeting its mobile-friendliness algorithm. Further, interstitial ads can become annoying to users if they are shown the same ad continuously. If ads are in-app, the annoyance factor can create less user satisfaction and lead to app uninstalls. With an interstitial, there is no way that the consumer is going to miss the ad, making it much more likely that they will be annoyed by its presence. Therefore, it is increasingly important that an interstitial offer extremely creative content and a compelling call to action that will encourage the user to tap through before tapping out.

Rich Media

Rich media mobile advertising is mobile advertisements that go beyond just displaying text, images, or video. High-profile advertisers prefer rich media mobile ads because they create an exciting and engaging user experience that conveys the advertiser's message with greater recall. Rich media ads are customizable ads that allow viewers to be drawn to interact with the mobile advertisement. Design of rich media ads, often done in HTML5, is only limited by the imagination of the developer's team. For instance, size often becomes less standard to the designer. Imagine a rich media auto ad with the car scooting along the bottom of the mobile screen.

There are numerous types of creative that can be used for rich media—each can accomplish different things. For example, a user might tap on an ad to make it full screen. These are called expandable banners, and they are the most widely used of all rich media options. Other things that rich media can do include: embed video, add animation and animated GIFs, embed audio, enable radio, add flash games, enable a gyroscope, access the phone's camera, access GPS, add events to a calendar, send an SMS, and enable a tap-to-call.

The high quality of rich media ads helps to boost engagement with the ad. This increased interactivity leads to high tap-through rates and conversions. Also, when consumers have an opportunity to interact with a brand in a fun and easy manner, it is surely going to increase brand recognition and satisfaction. Publishers also love them because they are so entertaining. Rich media is the only kind of advertising that truly improves the user experience on the publisher's mobile site or app.

One of the added bonuses of rich media is that it is nearly impossible for an advertiser to become a victim of fraud. Because a tap-through requires a specific act, it is unlikely that it will be fat-fingered, and it is virtually impossible to create nasty bots that can exploit the more sophisticated interactivity found in rich media ads. While fraud may be more difficult, it is certainly not impossible, so it remains critical for the advertiser to measure all secondary actions after the consumer taps through.

Because of the nature of rich media creative, highly dynamic ad creation is going to require a higher skill set and cost significantly more. They are also going to cost a lot more because publishers charge a significant premium for them. Because the advertiser has so much invested in the creative, it may be more emotionally difficult to remove the ad creative if it is not performing up to expectations. Rich media has to be tested by focus groups and done right the first time. Rich media will not be easy or inexpensive to switch out like it might be with standard banner advertising.

Since rich media ads are nearly impossible to miss, they can quickly become annoying, so precautions should be taken to not continue to serve the same rich media ads to the same users. Advertisers should limit the use of the ads to shorter time periods in order to maximize their effectiveness, as they will quickly suffer from ad fatigue.

Native

Native ads are advertisements that do not really look like ads and are not intrusive, which is why they are found in many popular and well-respected mainstream sites and apps. Native ads do not interfere with the customer's user experience, and, in many cases, users do not even recognize them as advertisements. Rather than present a banner with potentially irrelevant information, native ads attempt to seamlessly integrate with the publisher's app or mobile site and bring added value to the existing content. The basic idea behind a native ad is to make the content relative, thus making the user feel that he is not actually being advertised to. Think Facebook News Feed, Instagram advertising, or Twitter's sponsored tweets. It is usually tremendously targeted to the interests of the user. Moreover, it is packaged into a format that blends in naturally so it looks like just another post similar to the interests of the potential customer.

The origins for native advertising are in traditional media. *Mutual of Omaha's Wild Kingdom* was an early example of native advertising. Today, native advertising allows advertisers to reach their audiences in a relevant and engaging way and possibly avoid ad blockers that may eliminate non-native mobile advertisements.

Native advertising does not always have to be traditional posts with images. In some instances, it is articles as well—articles that are so cohesive with the page content that they appear to be a natural part of the site or app. *Forbes*, for example, accepts native advertising from Fidelity and even promotes Fidelity on its cover. Inside are articles written by Fidelity about retirement. No doubt that Fidelity has found a great platform to get the right message to the right audience—an audience that will be highly engaged by valuable content that discusses retirement.

That being said, it can be expensive for an advertiser to continue to create varied and timely content that fits with all of the mobile sites or apps where it is being presented, but that's just one part of the problem. Remember, native advertising does not come cheaply. In fact, it is sold as a premium to ordinary advertising. This makes native content advertising difficult to scale. That is why it is so important that native advertising target the best audience with content that is ideally suited for it.

Some advertisers, however, can take native advertising too far. Imagine a very creative and entertaining television commercial, but the viewer can't recall the sponsor immediately after it airs. It is the same with native advertising. There's no point in advertising if the consumer is not aware of who the advertiser is. Brands need to be transparent with native advertising and operate with a soft-sell mentality. If readers feel duped by the content, research shows that the native advertising efforts can actually have a net negative effect. When it comes to native advertising, a brand needs to lead with the content and avoid the hard sell.

Video

Video informs and entertains and needs to be integrated into each and every aspect of your digital and mobile marketing efforts. No matter what you do, your job is to tell your story. And more people will listen to your story if it is on video rather than on a page of text.

If a picture is worth a thousand words, then what is a video worth?

Today, more than ever, people demand immediate information and want to be entertained at the same time. So what better medium is there than mobile video for advertisers to resonate with their audience? With the advent of large data packages and prolific Wi-Fi, consumers are watching video regardless of whether they are in their home, at the office, or on the go.

Digital video is, by far, the fastest growing area of mobile advertising. In fact, according to Cisco, by 2019, digital and mobile video will represent 80 percent of all Internet traffic![32] This is largely due to millennials' copious content consumption on mobile and a general trend toward snacking on mobile. Consumers have become insatiable multitaskers and are finding it increasingly difficult to focus on just one thing at a time. That's why they are watching TV and interacting with it on their laptops simultaneously, thus creating a virtual omnichannel tug-of-war.

There are many reasons why an advertiser should consider mobile video. One is the decreased cost of making short-form videos. It probably will not cost as much as you might think. Because of the short form required for mobile video, a long production is simply not necessary to produce results. Most mobile videos are only 30 seconds or less. Many prefer a 15-second format. Remember that Vine's videos are only six seconds long. Because of the short length, brands need to spotlight the top message immediately in the video or it will lose consumer interest quickly.

Video plays automatically on most social mobile platforms, thus reducing friction for the consumer. While the video is usually on autoplay, the sound likely requires a tap by the user so as to not automatically annoy those innocent people around the user.

With video, results are instant, with high engagement, and tap-throughs to make purchases happen immediately. After all, if somebody is tapping on a video, they are already significantly engaged with the video presentation itself, and they are far more likely to be interested in converting.

There are, however, some things that a video advertiser should look out for. Chances are that when a customer sees a video ad once, he will not bother to watch it again, so there is no need to keep serving videos to the same consumers. Booking the best time slot is also important; try reaching people with video in the evening or during lunchtime when they are less conflicted. A working professional or student isn't going to watch a long video when they are busiest, which is normally during the day.

Video works great on mobile for awareness, branding, and calls to action. It helps tell the story of the company in its most entertaining format. The moving image is an effective marketing approach for businesses of all sizes and in all verticals, and it should be a top priority for every heady marketer.

Already, video appears to be a priority, even for small businesses. Over a million small businesses have already posted a video on Facebook.[33] There is no way that there are a million small businesses advertising on television. The opportunity video brings is immense for all size businesses.

Consumers are inherently lazy. They do not want to read; they want to be entertained. Video advertising on mobile is only getting bigger, so start the cameras rolling.

ADVERTISING ON SOCIAL MEDIA

Facebook

Nowhere is the title of this book, *Relevance Raises Response*, more appropriate than with Facebook advertising. Facebook says it best on its site: "Over 1 billion people. We'll help you reach the right ones." What a great and accurate slogan.

As a consumer, it may freak you out a little to know how much Facebook knows about you through its own site and through its third-party data providers. As an advertiser, however, it is Facebook's extensive collection of data that makes its targeting so precise that it is the one "must buy" site for nearly all mobile advertising campaigns.

With Facebook, there are two primary types of advertising available. Open your Facebook page on your desktop and take a look at your News Feed. There will be advertisements there. Although it doesn't seem to be a steadfast rule, Facebook limits the amount of News Feed ads that it serves to consumers to about 10 per day so that they do not get overwhelmed with advertising. Moreover, only 20 percent of the marketing creative can be sales oriented. In other words, Facebook will reject the ad if you have a big "SALE" banner written over it. That's why the News Feed ads do not really jump off the page at you screaming advertising, and it is part of why the native advertising on the News Feed is so very effective. At times, you don't even know it is a paid ad unless you notice the "Sponsored" notation on it.

Take a look at your Facebook page on your mobile phone. Now you see where the sponsored News Feed advertising really shines. It takes up the entire screen of your smartphone! You can't miss that advertising! Now, look to the right on your desktop Facebook page and you will see a narrower column that actually says "Sponsored" on it. These ads are cheaper than News Feed ads, but they are also clearly less noticeable, and they do not show on mobile, from where the majority of Facebook users are visiting. Both the News Feed and right rail advertisements are called dark posts.

What dark posts offer your business is the ability to do A/B testing and to adjust budgets on the fly. The marketer can test various pictures and copy and make sure it is using the best advertisements with the most highly targeted audience. Brands can judge this immediately by engagement—how many Likes and shares the advertising receives. More importantly, the advertiser may also be able to judge by the most important KPI—the cart.

Earlier, we discussed using Facebook Boost Posts. With a boosted post, these tests and adjustments are not possible. Whatever budget is put on the boosted post is what will be invested. No optimization of creative or product selection is possible. The creative and target market that is used at the beginning of the budget is used at the end. That equals potentially wasted dollars for your business, unless you nail it on the first try. Additionally, boosted posts, unlike dark posts, are first posted on your business page timeline and then boosted.

Why does this matter? Think about the Facebook business page itself. Imagine the advertiser is a restaurant that is promoting four different menu items and using three different pieces of copy and three different pictures for each. That's a total of 36 unique advertisements that will need to be created. If the business were to boost them, it would need to post all 36 of the slightly different posts on the restaurant's Facebook business page. Imagine how silly that would look with 36 different, but essentially the same, posts! It would be inundating the business's audience with duplicate content. With a dark post, users will never see all 36 posts on your page, since they are never posted to your timeline.

To begin advertising on Facebook, a business needs to have its own Facebook business page. It is mandatory by Facebook's rules. The business page is tied to the Facebook advertisements. It is possible to set up a generic topic for a business page, but that rarely makes sense, since one of the bonuses of advertising on Facebook is the additional Likes that it will generate for your business. Additional Likes are a bonus that will benefit your company long after the advertising has expired.

More than any other mobile advertising medium, Facebook can offer all of the elements of a successful campaign because it provides such powerful targeting data. Not only does it provide geolocation and demographic information, but, most importantly, it provides a wealth of interest categories. Some of the interest categories are highly targeted, like "currently remodeling home" or "New York Giants superfans." Imagine what it would mean to a wedding business to target women who have just recently changed their relationship status to "engaged." That's some powerful targeting!

Facebook really enables the advertiser to hone in on its audience, gain insight into potential customers, then improve targeting for a more efficient advertising investment. Marketers can target ads based on location, age, gender, language, interests, and behaviors. It can further delineate those ads by creating custom audiences to reach prospects who already know the business, or an advertiser can choose to not target those people already familiar with the business. Custom audiences can be created through current customer e-mail lists or traffic to a business's website or app. This is known as retargeting.

Facebook further enhances its targeting ability by combining third-party data with its Facebook Partner Categories. Instead of having to buy a list of prospects, Facebook has partnered with third-party big-data providers, such as Acxiom, Datalogix, Epsilon, and Polk, to provide a wealth of consumer information gleaned from external data sources like shopping records, credit card data, auto purchases, and government documentation. When Facebook uses third-party data, it is duly noted as "Partner Category" when developing an audience profile.

With Facebook Flex targeting, an advertiser can really drill down to the best possible combination of its geolocation, interests, demographics, and behaviors. An advertiser can choose certain characteristics and exclude others. Imagine a business is selling rifles with safety locks in Chicago. It could juggle a variety of audience profile combinations during its test phase in an effort to find the perfect target audience. That might mean specifying members of the NRA who are married, have children ages 2–15 at home, and are interested in hunting. An exclusion category might be Democrats, since Republicans are far more likely to be gun owners. The more precise an audience profile is, the better you can expect that profile to perform, but the smaller that potential audience will be. The key is to keep extending the size of the audience until the profiles produce results that are no better than break-even.

Purchasing advertisements on Facebook means using its Ads Manager and Power Editor—the tools that Facebook provides to advertisers that wish to market directly through the social media network itself. Creating an advertisement for Facebook involves six elements if the advertisement is going to appear in the preferable News Feed section. From top to bottom, the elements are as follows:

1. Company name—This is used to identify the sponsor of the advertisement and is the same name that is on the Facebook business page. The company name is in bold. Beneath it will be the "Sponsored" notation placed by Facebook.

2. Post text—This is about 155 characters in the Ads Manager, but the Power Editor actually allows for more.

3. Picture—The image takes up the majority of the space, so make it work. If you sell cooling systems, for instance, it is usually better to use happy and attractive people, dogs, and children enjoying the cool air on a hot day than a picture of a boring air conditioner. This is another example of aspirational imagery.

4. Headline—The headline for the advertisement is in bold and cannot go over 25 characters, so use it wisely. One does not have a lot to work with in the headline.

5. Link description—This gives you a chance to tell the consumer what she will get when she taps through to the link listed at the bottom. It is the last chance for a selling message.

6. Link—The actual tap-through link.

Carousel ads allow for the advertiser to place several images on the same advertisement. They do not cost any more than traditional image ads used on Facebook, but their impact has been phenomenal. Carousel ads are really hot now, and initial tests show them engaging with their audience at a rate of up to 10 times greater than ordinary image banner ads. They also work great in a retargeting capacity. According to Facebook, carousel advertisements allow for up to five images and a sixth slide that is the business page icon with "see more at" text below it, but the pictures need to be square instead of horizontal like most Facebook pictures.[34]

Thanks to Mark Zuckerberg's vision, Facebook has recently made strong moves in strengthening its video offerings. Video is an advertiser's dream on Facebook because the audience is already very in tune to watching moving pictures on the social media site. Video will autoplay on desktop and on mobile phones using Wi-Fi. On a mobile phone not connected to Wi-Fi, the user must simply touch the video to play and hear it.

Facebook is now clearly a mobile-first company that realizes the importance mobile video is playing on its social media network. In an effort to go directly after television's domain, it has introduced Target Rating Point (TRP) buying so advertisers can now purchase Facebook video ads on an apples-to-apples comparison basis with television Gross Rating Points (GRP).

A final consideration that is an absolute must with Facebook is using it as a retargeting platform. Retargeting is the process by which visitors to a website that did not buy or perform the action hoped are served with ads on sites like Facebook. Data shows that adding Facebook to a retargeting campaign will greatly increase performance, thanks to the fact that Facebook users check their accounts so often. This makes retargeting on Facebook so effective because the advertiser is likely to reach the prospect almost immediately after the initial contact with the product or service.

Facebook is the gorilla in the room when it comes to mobile and social media advertising. If a business can do only one type of mobile advertising, it should probably be Facebook. This is true for all businesses, but it is especially true for small businesses, thanks to Facebook's excellent geotargeting and interest targeting.

Instagram

The app-centric Instagram platform has been around since 2010, but until recently, advertising on it was really only accessible by invitation only and mainly reserved for the big dogs—kind of like local prime-time television ads. But that all changed in late 2015 when Instagram rolled out its mobile advertising platform to the masses.

According to Instagram, 97 percent of its promotions to date have resulted in "significant lifts in ad recall."[35] Not surprising, given that Instagram enjoys an enormous amount of engagement through Likes of its huge amount of daily photo uploads. Given the success that many brands have had with Facebook advertising, it is not difficult to see why so many advertisers were excited about the opportunities offered by Instagram and its large and loyal base of monthly users. While Instagram costs more than Facebook, the engagement level is considerably greater and the site is less cluttered with posts, making the additional investment well worth it.

Instagram advertising offers similar laser-focused targeting as Facebook, but with the added value of tremendously greater engagement. An Instagram post is up to 10 times more likely to receive engagement than a Facebook post, according to Forrester.[36] The double-tap that initiates an Instagram Like is used much more loosely by social media fans than the good old Facebook Like. Comments are the same story; there are many more on Instagram. Instagram users take a much closer look at the imagery and notice far more details, likely because there are far fewer posts.

It is easy to forget that Instagram is actually owned by Facebook until one sees how similar the platforms are. Facebook has done a great job of aligning Instagram's advertising strategy with its own to offer one-stop shopping for both social networks. In fact, advertisers use the same Facebook tools to create Instagram campaigns as they do for Facebook advertisements. They have access to the same amazing amount of targeting data that Facebook offers, including geotargeting, demographic targeting, and behavioral interest targeting. Unfortunately, there is currently no ability to target ads to keywords or hashtags that are specific to Instagram users.

Like Facebook, the Instagram advertisements take up the entire mobile screen and are nearly impossible to avoid. Advertisements may be image ads, carousel ads, or videos of up to 30 seconds in length. One new feature is that advertisements can be landscape, which shows that Instagram is clearly angling for more video advertising. Videos on Instagram will autoplay, but the user needs to tap the video for sound. A video view is registered in the statistics page only if the user watches for a minimum of three seconds. To record greater engagement, Instagram stats also register those users that watch for at least 10 seconds.

Take a look at an Instagram ad from top to bottom. Instagram has the brand name and its "Sponsored" notation at the very top of the ad. Beneath it is the image. Just below the image and to the right is the call-to-action button, which can be customized. For instance, a restaurant's call-to-action button could say "Book Now" and then lead to an Open Table page. Beneath the image is a description.

Advertisers do not need to have an Instagram account, but it certainly makes sense to have one; the brand will benefit from the additional followers that a paid ad campaign will inevitably produce. Advertisers can see and moderate comments on Instagram ads through the Facebook Power Editor.

Not all is perfect with Instagram advertising, however. There are still some kinks to be worked out. When advertisers create an audience profile to advertise to on Instagram, they appear to get the same market size as if it were a Facebook advertising program. This is impossible, since there are clearly many more accounts on Facebook than on Instagram. In addition, not all Facebook users and Instagram users have their accounts tied together yet. Also, because the Instagram user database is still building, it is sometimes difficult to get enough exposure in a specific geotargeted area if the advertiser gets very granular in its targeting.

For the greatest ROI, it is always best to jump on new advertising mediums early while supply exceeds demand. Instagram's advertising offering is a great new tool for a large or small business's advertising plans, but given its immense popularity, the newlywed effect is not going to last long.

Twitter

People come to Twitter to connect and engage with their interests. In response, Twitter creates opportunities for businesses to engage with their customers through several different paid advertising means.

Promoted Tweets serve specific tweets in the feeds of targeted individuals and businesses that are not currently followers of the account. Advertisers should write new, compelling content for paid advertisements or perhaps use content from a previous tweet that received significant engagement. Include an image that best represents the offering. The tweets will then appear in the home timeline of the users that have been targeted in the Tweet Engagements interface.

When an advertiser chooses to do Promoted Tweets, there is an option to use Twitter Cards. It is worth the extra time to set up a campaign using cards. Cards enable Promoted Tweets to attach photos, videos, and a call-to-action button. Cards take up considerably greater real estate than traditional tweets. Given the clutter on Twitter, more real estate is extremely important—especially when it does not cost a penny more!

Promoted Accounts are similar to Promoted Tweets, except the end goal is logically to gain more relevant followers for an account. By expanding a follower base, a business's community grows, and there are more opportunities to drive desired actions. Twitter also touts the fact that it does not have a system to filter out posts from some followers like Facebook does. On its site, Twitter says, "Plus, there is no formula that keeps your followers from seeing your Tweets in their timelines, so you'll have many moments to engage with them over time."

Engaging copy of 140 characters or less is crucial. A local business, for instance, might create a Promoted Account tweet that asks people to follow it for special deals and coupons. Always include "Follow Us" in the tweet, as that is the intended goal with the Promoted Accounts product. Retweets and favorites can occur from readers on Promoted Accounts as well, so there will be an added viral effect to the paid advertising. There is also an added desktop bonus when using Promoted Accounts. When an advertiser launches a Followers campaign, the Promoted Account message will also appear to the users it has targeted on the side of the home timeline, the Notifications tabs, the People search results page, and the Profile page.

Promoted Trends is another advertising option that is a desktop-only feature. These are the Trends topics that are shown on the left side of a desktop Twitter account. The trends are topical to a user's own specific interests. Promoted Trends are positioned at the top of this list for a 24-hour window and are clearly marked with a promoted icon. Unfortunately, Promoted Trends are not visible on mobile.

One of the shortcomings of Twitter's advertising platform is that some of it was clearly not designed for the mobile user. That's incredibly frustrating, given that the vast majority of tweets are coming from mobile devices!

Here's a tip on advertising with Twitter: Twitter does not seem to have a lot of paid activity yet, and it artificially inflates the suggested bid price. An advertiser can bid a whole lot less and still get the reach it needs. Don't be fooled by the suggested bid price. One can bid half or less and still get significant exposure and traction.

LinkedIn

LinkedIn ads are the perfect place to connect with a professional audience. It is also an important place for finding difficult-to-contact, busy executives. Because members supply their own information, it is safe to say that the information contained within the LinkedIn profiles is largely very accurate, assuming, of course, that it is a verified and legitimate account. Therefore, LinkedIn is all about the right targeting and getting the message to reach the right businesspersons.

Ads on LinkedIn appear on the profile pages of members, on the user's news page, in a user's inbox, on search results pages, and on group pages. The first decision an advertiser needs to make is if they want to advertise in the LinkedIn Feed with Sponsored Updates or in the LinkedIn Pages with Text Ads. The LinkedIn Feed is the area where users' news stories are located. LinkedIn Pages are on the top and the right-hand side. It is cheaper and, not surprisingly, less effective than the LinkedIn Feed.

LinkedIn Feed advertisements are similar to Facebook's boosted posts. It takes an existing post that a business has made and enables the business to pay to expose it to more people in its targeted audience. Advertisers can target by city or region, and then can choose from the following defined groups:

- company name
- company industry
- company size
- job title
- job function
- job seniority
- member schools

- fields of study
- degrees
- member skills
- member groups
- member gender
- member age

After choosing target categories, LinkedIn will give back the potential total audience figures for the campaign. Advertisers can pay by CPC or CPM. A suggested bid and a minimum bid will be provided. Advertisers on LinkedIn can start with as little as $10 per day.

Getting attention on LinkedIn can be more difficult than other social media sites because people are there to do business. It is going to be more difficult to divert them away from sales prospecting with the latest singing dog video. That is why the promoted post option in the Feed will likely get more engagement for the business, because it is more likely to be seen and less likely to be avoided.

YouTube

Advertising on YouTube is fairly simple because direct advertising can be purchased through Google AdWords. The power of YouTube cannot be underestimated. It is the second-largest search engine in the USA, and it offers the advantage of being the only major social media network that is exclusively video.

One of the ways to advertise a video on YouTube is by using TrueView In-Stream Video Ads. TrueView In-Stream Ads run on videos within YouTube or the Google Display Network on both desktop and mobile. On the network, they can run within videos, games, or apps. YouTube videos that are embedded on third-party sites can also show the ads. These are pre-roll videos, or those videos that play prior to the user watching the video that he actually chose to watch. It goes without saying that the videos need to be creative and immediately engaging. Viewers can tap out of the video after watching the mandatory first five seconds, so put the most important content up front. The videos should not be exclusively about self-promotion, or the viewer will be more likely to tap out after watching the minimum five seconds. One of the great features of In-Stream Ads is that YouTube offers a call-to-action feature. There are six different ones to choose from, so you can choose which one is right for your business. The blue buttons that suggest a call to action are very effective. One that is not recommended, however, is annotations (words within the video itself); they do not work on mobile taps.

Another way to advertise on YouTube is to use its TrueView In-Display Ads. These are the ads that will show after a user performs a search. YouTube is very generous when it comes to In-Display Ads. The advertiser only pays when the viewer watches for at least thirty seconds, or half the length of the entire video ad. That being said, the user is far more likely to watch the video since she has just done a search for that specific information. TrueView In-Display Ads have text adjacent to and associated with the video ad. The text has to be exciting, as it and the cover scene of the video will be how the viewer decides whether to click on the video. The headline needs to be impactful, and the two lines of copy beneath it need to provide a powerful description of the benefits of watching the video. Tap-throughs for In-Display Ads can go to the brand's website or the brand's YouTube channel page.

An advertiser on YouTube can target by country and location, age, gender, and specific interests. Specific interests are enabled by the advertiser entering keywords and then YouTube giving statistics on estimated reach based on those keywords. Given that keyword targeting is essentially interest targeting, it seems to work better than any of the demographic factors that are offered. Using keyword match phrases (indicated by putting parentheses around the keyword phrase) further enhances targeted keywords and avoids users searching for content that is related to, but not indicative of, the advertised video.

YouTube offers a great set of analytics. Use them. They will help determine where users are abandoning and what can be done to increase engagement. If a customer likes what they see on a YouTube advertised video, they may become a fan of the business's YouTube channel and even register to receive updates from it. This is one of the added benefits of YouTube advertising. To maximize success on YouTube, consider connecting with new audiences and turning existing viewers into long-term fans. One way to build a YouTube channel audience is to run a paid ad campaign with Google AdWords for video. By doing so, the AdWords videos can promote viewers to follow the business's YouTube channel.

Pinterest

Pinterest began accepting advertising in 2014, and a year later there was still a waiting list of advertisers wanting to give it money and become part of this powerful social media network. There are many reasons to advertise on Pinterest. First and foremost is that it is a huge supplier of social referrals. In fact, while Facebook is the undisputed king of social media referrals, one may be surprised to learn that Pinterest is firmly entrenched as the second-most-popular site for social referrals.[37]

Pinterest buyers are already shopping and ready to reach for their mobile wallets and credit cards. Users are mostly on the site for shopping inspiration, and they want to spend money. An average sale from a Pinterest referral is twice that of a referral sale from Facebook.[38]

On Pinterest, advertisements are subtle, and there are some very specific rules in place as to how Promoted Pins can be purchased. Images in Pinterest advertisements cannot contain any promotional information or calls to action. It clearly wants to keep its advertising looking like the rest of the posts on the site, which is a good thing for advertisers. Pinterest advertising is native and fits in with the overall feel of the site, so most users do not even notice that they are looking at advertisements.

On Pinterest, calls to action in the description of a pin are permitted, but not in the image itself. Users come to Pinterest to look at the pictures and to get ideas. They do not want to be sold to. Pinterest is the ultimate pull strategy social media site. Even the wording that Pinterest uses to describe Promoted Pins is incredibly subtle. It does not use "Promoted" or "Sponsored" in the posts like other social media sites. Instead it uses the copy "Suggested for You." Isn't that nice? It is not an advertisement; it is something that Pinterest thinks the viewer will like, so they are simply suggesting it.

Pinterest is all about the imagery, so a lot of different images are required to produce a great campaign. Advertisers need to vary the images often to find the winning formula. Nowhere is this more important than with fashion (Pinterest's biggest strength), where female appeal to a specific article of clothing can vary widely. Unlike most social media networks, Pinterest is one of the few that thrives on vertical images. Horizontal and landscape pictures do not work as well. Longer vertical images work best because they take up the most ground.

Targeting on Pinterest is not as extensive as on other social media networks. The portal enables advertisers to target pins to users based on geolocation, device, gender, and spoken language. Keywords are extremely important on the site, and Pinterest allows an advertiser to put a massive amount of keywords—up to 150—in an advertised post.

One of the bonuses of Promoted Pins is that they can be saved just like any ordinary post. What that means for advertisers is that users will save the advertised pins, and thus the pins will continue to exist long after the paid advertising campaign has expired. Pinterest claims that saved Promoted Pins give an advertiser a 5 percent bump in bonus exposures that were not paid for.[39]

Buyable Pins are Pinterest's newest product offering. Available on iPhone and iPad in the USA, Buyable Pins let people buy things without ever leaving the Pinterest app. Buyable Pins are denoted with a blue box in the upper right of the pin that says "Buy It." Here, users can see the price, tap it, and make a purchase on their mobile device. Buyable Pins work easily on mobile, and advertisers can take advantage of impulse buyers who are in the mood to make a quick purchase.

Pinterest advertising is hot. Very hot. Its native format and incredibly strong female appeal make it a force to be reckoned with. Its future is much brighter than Twitter's, and it will likely overtake Twitter as the second-most-important social media advertising network on the web. In short, if you are selling something, you should be selling it on Pinterest.

Google Plus

Google Plus advertising is different than the rest because an advertiser cannot purchase paid advertisements on Google Plus itself. Google Plus remains advertising free. What can be done, however, is a business can take a Google Plus post and display it on the Google Display Network. Hence, a post on a business page of Google Plus can be sent out on the Google Display Network to appear on a third-party site that is part of the network. Advertisers handle the advertisements through an AdWords account. Not every brand can use Google Plus advertising, however. In order to set up an advertising account on Google Plus, a business must first obtain 1,000 followers on its business page. Then, and only then, can it begin a Google Plus–based advertising campaign.

Targeting for Google Plus is provided through the Google Display Network, so the targeting is equally extensive. Once the targeted audience is defined, Google will know whom to display the advertisement to on the ad network. The advantage of using Google Plus posts on the network is that viewers can reshare, +1, or comment on the content right in the remote ad; they do not need to click or tap through to the Google Plus business page of the advertiser. This indirectly increases the level of interaction and direct engagement with the ad on the Google Display Network.

Like all of Google's engagement advertising, the advertiser is only billed if a user hovers over the ad for a minimum of three seconds. Charges are not dependent on any action by the user, such as a tap or click.

The Google advertising platform not only tracks engagements, but also gives totals for +1s, shares, comments, and followers created because of the external advertising. Earned Impressions calculate how many additional people saw the ad thanks to the viral shares that are such an important part of every social media network. Earned Social Actions tabulate the total number of +1s, comments, or shares the post received.

Google has kept its Google Plus social media platform free of advertising, at least for now. It is a product that has never lived up to its expectations, so its future is not clear. Therefore, most advertisers would be glad to promote on external sites more than on Google Plus itself anyway.

Vine

Vine does not accept direct paid advertising as such, but it is making money through its social media video site. Here's how it does it. In 2015, Vine's parent company, Twitter, acquired the social media marketing company Niche for an estimated $50 million. Niche has an interesting, well, niche. It matches brands with popular personalities on social media. (If you're over 25, you probably won't know any of the names of these stars.) Then, the popular social media and more traditional stars on sites like Vine create videos that promote those brands. The videos may appear as traditional posts, but they are actually sponsored by the brand, and they have the added bonus of a social media celebrity endorsement. One such celebrity endorser is Robby Ayala, who has several million followers and is also an employee of Niche. If you follow Ayala on Vine, you will likely see several subtle—and not-so-subtle—product endorsements intertwined with his humorous Vines.

Vine's approach to monetization, to date, has been very different than its parent company's. But the normal progression of social media monetization across many sites is to first grow an audience, and then, once that audience exists, make money off of it through advertising. It will be interesting to see if Vine continues with the same non-advertising approach for much longer. If it follows form, it will soon accept paid videos that do not exceed six seconds.

Snapchat

Snapchat certainly has a loyal and engaged following among teens and young adults, so it is a natural place to consider investing advertising dollars. It has done a good job of gaining a significant following and now is monetizing that following with various types of advertising offers. Snapchat only began actively marketing its advertising solutions in July of 2015. It has been cautious to not jump too quickly into the advertising pool, in the chance that it might alienate its core audience of capricious teens and young adults. For that reason, Snapchat is currently only taking the largest of advertisers.

There are several ways a business can advertise on Snapchat. The Stories page, where one would see the snaps from a friend, has a Live Stories feature. Live Stories always coincide with something topical. There is also an entire screen of Discover pages devoted to fifteen different national advertisers. Advertising on Snapchat is very engaging, creative, and, not surprisingly, youth oriented. It has to be. After all, nothing is forced on the user; the user is actually choosing to watch the ad.

The biggest challenge for a marketer advertising on Snapchat, however, is that it is a difficult app to measure results from, since traditional tap-throughs are unable to be measured from the video format. Since it is new to the advertising world, Snapchat does not yet provide any advertising measurements.

The most important thing that a social network needs to be successful is a significant amount of users. After that, it usually starts to find a valuable revenue stream by selling advertising. There's one thing about much-needed advertising, however—users are rarely excited about it. It will be interesting to see how the youth-oriented Snapchat handles walking that fine line with a fickle and trendy audience.

Tumblr

The blog site Tumblr has numerous advertising options available. Engagement is high on Tumblr and it has a very loyal audience, but it is a social media site to consider for large advertisers only.

Sponsored Posts are one way to advertise, and they look the same as ordinary Tumblr posts. They can be targeted based on sex, geolocation, and over twenty interest categories, such as automotive, beauty, education, finance, food, hobbies, pets, shopping, lifestyle, travel, and more. Most categories offer secondary categories so that the advertiser can target an even more specific sub-audience. Video can also be used in Sponsored Posts. Videos play automatically and continue to play while they are on the screen.

Larger advertisers might take advantage of Tumblr's Sponsored Day option. With it, an advertiser can place its brand in the navigation area at the top of the Tumblr portal. When accessed, the advertiser can show any number of articles and advertisements that it so desires. Such sponsorships are sold for 24-hour periods.

Sponsored Blogs are available for in-app advertising and advertising on desktop in the Recommended Blogs section. In mobile apps, the ads are located in the Discovery tab.

Tumblr advertising does not come cheap, so it is reserved primarily for large-budget advertisers. It doesn't even have a do-it-yourself platform, so deals need to be negotiated directly with a company salesperson. Despite these shortcomings, Tumblr's audience is loyal, and it has a bright future for advertisers.

Vimeo

Vimeo has built a business that is very different from YouTube. Against a juggernaut such as Youtube it certainly does not want to go toe-to-toe. For that reason, Vimeo has consistently eschewed advertising and will not run pre-roll ads prior to watching the videos people really want to see.

That being said, Vimeo does have an advertising page on its site, although it does not really say much. It seems to have an approach of: if an advertiser has a creative idea, go ahead and give us a call and we will see what can be worked out. That opportunity should certainly be considered if the advertiser is interested in courting the artsy users that make up the Vimeo audience.

Quora

As a question-and-answer site, Quora offers advertisers a unique opportunity. It is logical to suggest that if an individual is asking a question, he is very possibly in the market for making a purchase in that category. Hence, Quora could offer advertisers some highly focused advertising opportunities.

Quora advertising will be similar to search advertising. Based on the user's question, a paid advertisement in that category will be returned along with the answers to that question. Quora advertising is expected to debut in late 2016.

Ello

Ello's entire strategy is to be the anti-advertising medium. Therefore, if it holds true to form, it will not have advertising on it ever. We'll see.

Messaging Apps

Messaging apps, such as Facebook Messenger, are extremely popular overseas, but they have not been quite as popular in North America. As with most innovations, however, young adults are actively using them, and they should be a consideration for any mobile advertising strategy.

Snapchat is one messaging app that already offers an advertising platform. While it has advertisements in its Discover and Live Stories sections, it has thus far not offered paid advertisements to run in personal snaps. Advertising on Facebook Messenger and Facebook-owned WhatsApp appears to be imminent and logical; Zuckerberg has even said so. After all, Messenger is already actively being used by many businesses to chat with customers, so Messenger-targeted advertising would be quite lucrative.

Those messaging apps with strength internationally are already starting to monetize. WeChat, for example, started selling advertising in 2015. Viber does not currently sell advertising, but it does make money from selling emojis to users.

A lot of messaging apps began as alternatives to personal text messaging and phone calls, but many have now become so popular with users that they are essentially portals. As app portals, immune to ad blockers, they will be seeking new and innovative ways to monetize the users that are flocking to them.

NO MORE FREE ADVERTISING ON FACEBOOK

A short time ago, the news for small businesses was that there was a FREE ADVERTISING source taking hold of North America.

Free advertising could be obtained; all you had to do was build up your Likes on Facebook and post regularly. There were over one billion active users on Facebook. And, best of all, a business could actually run posts when customers were most likely to buy, like a restaurant at 11:30 A.M., just before lunchtime hunger sets in.

Then, Facebook stopped giving away the farm. "Who's going to buy our advertising if we are giving it away for free?" Facebook started decreasing the amount of followers that saw your business page posts. Decreasing, decreasing, and decreasing. Today, only 1–2 percent of your followers ever even have a chance to see your Facebook business page posts.

Moreover, Facebook has reduced page reach and continually upped CPMs for advertisers because it wants to "protect" the News Feed from being overwrought with cheap ads and bad content. Native News Feed ads on Facebook are "premium" inventory compared to most other mobile display ads. Facebook limits advertisements so that users are not overwhelmed with them during a normal browsing experience. In fact, most users will be served only about 10 ads per day in the News Feed.

There are a number of reasons why the ability to post on a business page and reach all of those who have Liked it has ended. First is the sheer volume of posts that are going onto Facebook now that the medium is over 10 years old. About two-thirds of Facebook users access the site on a daily basis, and they average over 300 friends per account. Add those posts to the over 30 million local-business pages that are posting and you can see how your posts are getting lost in the din. There's also the enormous amount of Likes of the Facebook customer. In the USA, the average Facebook user Likes over 70 pages, up from just 4.5 in 2009.[40] Facebook users love to Like. Finally, there is engagement. Facebook's mantra is all about engagement, and its new algorithm is putting more and more links to articles in the News Feed. It is also putting them closer to the top of your page if they are getting lots of Likes and comments. So the most popular posts are the most likely to continue being seen.

Don't think you can try to beat the system, either, by asking more people to Like or share your business page posts. Facebook is on to you and will bury your post if you promote it by using "like-baiting." Like-baiting in an organic Facebook post is adding copy such as: "Like if you like the Chow puppy and Share if you like the Australian Shepherd puppy."

"Dark posts" is the term that Facebook uses to describe the advertising solution that it created in 2013. A dark post will never show up on your business page timeline, and it will not hit fans' News Feeds unless you target them and pay for it, too. A dark post appears in the News Feed, or the advertiser can save some money and put it on the improved, but still less effective, right rail. In many cases, businesses that were not initially successful with Facebook advertising weren't actually using dark posts, but instead used the convenient Boost Post feature. Many small businesses believe that a Facebook Boost is the same as buying Facebook advertising. Facebook boosted posts reach people who Like your page, some of their friends, and also some new audiences. But boosting a post is not the best way to promote on Facebook. Boosting a Facebook post has its inherent drawbacks, such as the inability to utilize A/B testing, change the target market, or change the creative.

It almost seems as though an active Facebook business page isn't worth very much anymore. Will the advertiser eventually hit the point where none of its Facebook business page posts reach its intended audience? Facebook's Director of Small Business Dan Levy would only say that Facebook would always try to do "what's right for the people on Facebook" and that Facebook is always "going to make the changes to keep things engaging for people." A business needs to have a Facebook business page to buy advertising, so it may as well keep it. Just do not bank on it being as valuable in the future as it was a few years ago.

FACEBOOK IS STILL THE BEST FOR SMALL BUSINESSES

Even with the difficulties in making business page posts visible to consumers, Facebook is still the best small-business advertising medium of all time. Running a small business isn't easy. A small businessperson needs to be an expert at sales, marketing, finance, accounting, engineering, and human resources. A small business does not have the deep pockets to compete with the big guys in product development, so it had better be right in what it develops.

At least, this was true until mobile advertising, and specifically Facebook advertising. Mobile is underserved. When it comes to time spent with media, mobile continues to get shortchanged in the overall ad spend! Supply exceeds demand, and that means bargains for advertisers.

Perhaps the best thing about mobile advertising is that with geotargeting, there is absolutely NO WASTE! Imagine a local business that is advertising in the New York City DMA. The business can only draw from five zip codes around the store. Any advertising that it does beyond that area is a waste. Thus radio, which casts its wide net, is out. Why reach listeners in northern New Jersey? WASTE! Then, there is print advertising. Need I say WASTE louder? TV? What business can afford decent production and airtime, only to have to pay for advertising outside of its trading area?

With all advertising, the consumer does not have to just be served the advertisement; they actually need to engage with it as well. That's how a business will acquire new customers. And engagement is precisely what makes Facebook mobile advertising so very powerful.

To recap, with Facebook

- the advertisement takes up 100 percent of the mobile screen so you can't miss it;

- the consumer will definitely see it because it is in her News Feed, right there next to the post from her old high-school boyfriend;

- advertisements are targeted based on location and interests, so it is likely something the user will be interested in, and relevance raises response;

- you aren't allowed to write SALE all over the advertisement—only 20 percent of the ad can be dedicated to sales materials—so the native sponsored posts simply look like messages from businesses the consumer has previously Liked;

- each user is only served about 10 advertisements per day, which means the News Feed will never look like a NASCAR driver's jacket.

Think a small business does not have enough advertising budget to use Facebook? The minimum ad spend is $1 per day. My guess is most businesses can afford that level of investment.

RETARGETING

It is often said in business that it is easier to sell something new to an existing customer than it is to sell something to a completely new customer. But what about those prospects that have knocked on your virtual door but haven't made a purchase yet? That's where retargeting becomes a must-have marketing technique for your business.

Retargeting is a tremendous way to keep in front of customers that are seemingly most likely to buy. It turns window shoppers into real buyers by bringing previous visitors back to a business's advertising message.

Here's how it works. A prospect visits the company's website or landing page. During the visit, the business logs the visitor via IP address or cookies so that it knows that the customer has visited the site. To cookie a desktop visitor, it is only necessary for the business to install a small and simple piece of code that is added to the web page itself. The business is then able to track that same prospect all over the web when they visit social media sites and websites other than the one of the business itself. When the prospect is on another website, such as Facebook or the Weather Channel, an advertisement for the business is served to the prospect.

Imagine a consumer visits Amazon and puts something in the cart, then has second thoughts and abandons the purchase. It is very likely that Amazon has cookied the consumer and will be following them around the web, serving them that specific item, and encouraging them to come back to Amazon to complete the considered transaction. It seems that a consumer can't get that product out of her head—or her browser, for that matter.

But e-commerce sites do not have to retarget just visitors to their own businesses. They can also purchase lists of visitors to other sites that may be interested in the product or service. Such lists are known as remarketing lists for search ads (RLSA). One other way to get a list of prospects to retarget is via e-mail addresses or phone numbers. If a business has a list of e-mails or phone numbers, it can use Facebook's, Instagram's, or Twitter's custom audiences. In this case, it can load the list of e-mails, for instance, into Facebook's platform and match them to their accounts so that the business's advertisement is shown to those specific people. Not all e-mails are going to match, of course. For instance, people usually use a personal e-mail account when they sign up for Facebook, so if the list is mainly business e-mails, it is not likely to match well. Facebook officially requires that a business have at least 1,000 e-mail addresses to use this feature, but—insider tip—there have been instances where it accepted lists smaller than 1,000.

Here's another insider tip for retargeting. Your business probably has a lot of customers that have unsubscribed to your e-mail list, so you can no longer legally send e-mails to them. But you can retarget them by their e-mail address with mobile advertisements. It is up to you whether this is ethical or not, but it is not illegal.

Google offers a similar service called Customer Match in AdWords. With this product, a business can upload an e-mail list and then target a pay-per-click or digital advertisement to those people when they are performing searches or are on a site that is part of Google's Digital Ad Network. Since a business is targeting people that it already has an e-mail relationship with, one would expect this to be a highly profitable group to target. Therefore, a higher bid amount is justified to ensure that your advertisements appear to this target group. It is the same with all retargeting programs. Bidding higher on programmatic makes sense because there is a known prior behavior that lends itself to a greater chance of consumers making a purchase. Remember, retargeting always works best if the advertising is served soon after the initial contact has been made.

When it comes to retargeting, there are several best practices to consider so that a business does not overwhelm its target with advertisements and cost itself unnecessary expense long after the consumer is no longer a legitimate customer:

- Burn pages—After the consumer has made a purchase, they should be taken out of the retargeting database. There is no need to continue marketing to a consumer that has already purchased unless there is an upsell involved.

- Determine burn time—If a consumer visited months ago and still has not made a purchase, it is probably a waste of money to keep pursuing them. Discover the point when consumer tap-throughs start declining and turn off the advertisements after the appropriate amount of days.

- Change the message—If the prospect has seen the retargeting ad several times, there is no need to continue serving the same creative over and over. Vary the advertising; maybe some different creative will work better.

- Track where the visitor came from—If the consumer purchases after seeing a retargeting ad, the point-of-purchase tap-through is certainly important, but the initial point of where that consumer came from is probably even more important. Therefore, it is crucial for a business to track the top of the funnel lead point as well as the ultimate retargeting conversion point. This is simply giving credit where credit is due.

A business should not just think of retargeting for e-commerce sales. It is also a great way to generate leads for the sales team of a service business. Retargeting should be considered even if the website itself does not have an e-commerce focus. It is also a great weapon for a business doing talent-acquisition recruitment. If a job seeker has visited the job page, when a business needs to recruit new employees, it is a great way to serve job advertisements to those same likely highly qualified people that visited in the past. It is always better to attract a person with a job than a person who is looking. There may be a good reason why that person does not have a job already.

While retargeting is a tremendous tool for businesses to continue a relationship with an interested prospect, it is not without its shortcomings. Cookies, for instance, are based on the browser being used. So, if a consumer visits a site on Chrome and gets "cookied," then later switches to Firefox on the same device, he will not be retargetable based on cookies. Similar problems exist for mobile IP retargeting. A man could visit a site on his home Wi-Fi, but then his wife could receive the retargeted ad because she's on the same IP address. Many companies are working to solve this shortcoming today with cross-device retargeting and attribution. When they do, greater relevance will raise response even further.

MOBILE COUPONS

Coca-Cola didn't create the first mobile coupon, but it is widely believed to be the company that created the first coupon. In 1887, the inventor of Coca-Cola, John Pemberton, had a problem. He knew that if he could just get people to try his product, they would love it and continue to purchase it from the pharmacies in Atlanta where it was being served. As the business began to grow, it offered pharmacists two gallons of Coca-Cola syrup in return for the names and addresses of customers that lived near the pharmacy. Then, they would mail a product coupon directly to the consumers. Since it was free, the local residents would come in and try it, love it, and continue to buy it. In turn, the pharmacist would continue to need to buy more Coca-Cola syrup.

Today, Pemberton wouldn't need to get a list of local resident addresses. Instead, he could simply geotarget the area around the pharmacy and serve mobile coupons to those living in the area. Mobile coupons are preferable because they do not require clipping, so the shopper rarely forgets them. They have a higher redemption rate than paper ones—10 times higher than traditional coupons.[41] Perhaps best of all, they are environmentally friendly at a time when protecting the environment should be a major consideration.

Promoting mobile coupons can be done in many ways. An interactive text message promotion or a QR code can be placed at the point of purchase in a store. They can also be included in social media marketing, SMS marketing, or the store's mobile app.

Consumers can save mobile coupons in a variety of ways. A text message or e-mail can include an alphanumeric code that activates the discount. A mobile coupon can be saved directly into the Passbook or Google Wallet of the consumer. It can also be saved in the store app that resides on the phone. Or, perhaps best of all, it can be saved to the loyalty or club card ID of the shopper.

Manufacturer's coupons are the coupons that people remember from their childhoods. They were usually present in the Sunday newspaper inside the comic section (the only part most teenage boys read other than sports). Printed coupons required the consumer to diligently clip them, remember to actually bring them to the store, read through the fine print, and then sort through them for redemption. Manufacturer's coupons of the mobile variety have not yet become commonplace in the location where they are used most, the grocery store, mainly because the scanners used in grocery stores have trouble scanning mobile screens.

Most coupons used in mobile advertising are in-store coupons promoted by the stores themselves. These coupons are known as merchant coupons, and they generally offer a discount via a specific amount or percentage. Merchant coupons work best with mobile because they can be easily validated by the store clerk without worrying about the nuances of differing POS systems in different stores.

Another type of mobile coupon is a promotional coupon. While a merchant coupon is provided as a way to drive awareness for a specific item or a storewide sale, a promotional coupon is not redeemed at the store through any type of scanning. Instead, it provides a coupon code that is used on a tap-to-call, or it simply reminds the shopper to visit the store to participate in a sale or special offer. A promotional coupon can be pretty slick on mobile. It can send a push notification when the customer is near the store, or it can send an SMS reminder prior to the termination of the special event.

Even though mobile marketing has been around for years, the ongoing mythology that a person can simply walk past a store and be served a mobile coupon still exists by those unfamiliar with mobile marketing. To have a mobile coupon "pop up" on a phone, the consumer has to have taken some previous action. In the case of couponing, this action is most likely downloading the store app and then agreeing to accept push notifications from the store.

MOBILE ADVERTISING MEASUREMENT

You can't manage what you do not measure. That being said, measurement is one of the areas that advertisers continue to struggle with when it comes to mobile marketing. The inability for advertisers to directly connect mobile engagement with in-store sales is one of the factors that continues to hold back mobile advertising investment. Advertisers have long accepted the fact that traditional media is largely unmeasurable, but those same people ironically hold mobile advertisers to a much higher standard. Mobile advertising is expected to be precisely measurable, primarily because Internet advertising is so easily measured through the use of cookies.

Unfortunately, when it comes to mobile advertising measurement, the online cookie crumbles. In the desktop world, where users tend to stick to a stationary device and a single browser, cookies are king, but in the multidevice, on-the-go mobile space, cookies are at best inconsistent and at worst completely unavailable on some platforms.

Mobile needs to do a better job of validating itself when it comes to measuring metrics that truly matter. At the end of the day, measuring things like taps, website hits, and app downloads are great, but they do not necessarily translate to in-store sales. What businesses truly want to know is in-store sales lift, not the less meaningful in-store traffic visit figures. After all, despite the proliferation of e-commerce and the fact that mobile is changing everything, over 90 percent of all sales in the USA are still made in brick-and-mortar retail establishments.

Paying for advertising to generate brand awareness is becoming less common. Sure, brand awareness is important, but the executive suite usually wants to use sales figures to evaluate and ultimately justify mobile advertising budgets. If the CEO is going to approve an advertising budget, the CMO better be able to show a sales increase equal to or greater than the advertising investment.

Often, agencies do not help in the evaluation process, either. Agencies tend to evaluate advertising campaigns based on in-store lift, or how many more shoppers walked through the front doors of the store. The long-entrenched feeling of those in the advertising business is that the only thing they can control is the message itself; once the consumer enters the store, it is up to the store personnel to close the deal. The handoff from marketing to sales occurs when the consumer enters the retail establishment.

What is really needed is an evaluation of return on ad spend (ROAS). ROAS is evaluated as the increased sales lift divided by the cost of the advertising campaign. It is usually evaluated in such a way as to indicate that for every dollar spent on advertising, the store returned a sum of x dollars in net sales lift. Note that the only way for ROAS to be evaluated properly is to use profitability on sales items, not increased gross sales dollars. Of course, some consumers are going to buy the advertised products whether they were promoted to them or not. Therefore, to evaluate ROAS, a baseline sales figure, usually traditional sales numbers for that month, is used to establish proper measurement.

Fortunately, there are ways to track sales attribution from mobile, although it admittedly takes a bit of creativity. For instance, the trading area of some stores may be included in the mobile advertising campaign while other store areas are not. Advertisers can then compare the sales lift in the advertised stores versus those that did not benefit from the additional advertising. Another method would be via location-based advertising. Advertising may be given to certain zip codes or within a certain radius of the store. By collecting zip codes of purchasers through credit cards, or simply by asking for it when consumers are paying by cash, an advertiser can compare sales lift in those specific locations versus the non-advertised locations.

If increased net sales are equal to the advertising investment, a business should be extremely pleased. Why? Because there are add-on sales that are imminent. The lifetime value of acquiring a new customer is a factor that even the most advanced data will have a hard time determining, but it is part of the benefit of an ongoing relationship with the brand that clearly exists.

All of the methods mentioned are nice ways to measure mobile advertising effectiveness, but there are so many other factors that enter into the mix that it can hardly be considered to be a foolproof method of ROAS measurement. The only way to truly measure the effectiveness of mobile advertising and the corresponding sales lift is to link a mobile user to sales transaction data. This isn't quite so easy when there isn't a coupon redemption element, but it can be done with a good deal of accuracy by using match keys.

A match key is a common identifier that advertisers use to tie target audiences to mobile advertising campaigns. Match keys are an important consideration for both targeting and measurement, and they provide the scale acceptable to most national brands. The most common match keys used are e-mail addresses and physical home addresses. Since mobile advertising can be tied to e-mail addresses and home addresses, it becomes a metric for later determining if the purchase was made by a consumer that was indeed exposed to the advertising. This is not an easy process, since the average person uses six different e-mail addresses and tends to change often; thus, matching sales to them can be problematic. Home addresses are the more stable match key because most people only have one at a time and they only change, on average, every seven years. In addition, home addresses are more easily integrated into third-party data that can be purchased to give insight into past purchasing patterns and demographics.

At the end of the day, the only thing that matters to a business is increased sales. It is tracking it effectively that seems to be continually elusive to mobile marketers.

AD BLOCKERS

Let's face it. Consumers, in general, do not like dealing with advertising. Sure, they tolerate advertising, but it is not on their list of favorite things. Consumers maintain a ravenous appetite for great online and mobile content, but not much love for the advertising that actually pays for it.

While ad blocking may be new to mobile advertising, it is not new in general. For years, at least since the advent of the VCR, over 50 percent of consumers have been fast-forwarding through the ads,[42] thus making watching *60 Minutes* only a 46-minute-and-25-second commitment. So when mobile ad blockers started gaining traction, many consumers rejoiced. If they can block those annoying pop-ups and other forms of banner advertising that increase load times, why not do it?

The fact is that advertising pays for the ability for nearly everybody to have once unimaginable content available on his or her mobile device for free. Advertising subsidizes the employees that work for the companies that provide the content or the apps. Without advertising, those services would cease to exist. Of course, consumers are not connecting the fact that advertising pays for all of those wonderful, free information services that they enjoy on mobile. That is not their problem, and they are not going to volunteer to see advertisements if they don't have to.

Ad blocking has the potential to threaten the economic viability of the Internet and mobile, and push more content behind paywalls that consumers have long failed to support. It is a veritable war on mobile advertising, and it is led by Apple, of all things.

Some publishers have fought back. The *Washington Post*, for example, will not provide access to its content from any device that is using an ad blocker. Instead, it gives messages to users to turn off their ad blockers, instructs them to supply their e-mail addresses for access to the article, or redirects them to a subscription page. "Many people already receive our journalism for free online, and in the long run, without income via subscriptions or advertising, we will not be able to deliver the journalism that people coming to our site expect from us," said a spokeswoman from the *Washington Post*.

The IAB (Interactive Advertising Bureau) has advocated that the top 100 publishers all stop delivering their content to those using ad blockers. Some publishers are considering suing the ad-blocking companies, citing that cutting out ads is equivalent to somebody clipping the advertisements out of the local newspaper or tearing the ads off of billboards. Actions such as those would cause the publishers to hire a private investigator. Others are taking a more pragmatic approach by using the trend as a wakeup call and attempting to solve consumers' biggest complaints about its products. That includes how to serve ads in a more efficient manner without slowing down page-loading time. Slow load time is the most cited reason as to why consumers are using ad blockers. The problem is that mobile advertisements are overly heavy because they are lugging around so many extra data requests from companies that want to define exactly who is seeing their ads. Another thing that could be done to speed up load times is for ads to only load when they are being seen. There is no need for ads below the fold to load in advance if the viewer is never going to move down that far.

Advertisers could also eliminate the most annoying of mobile ads, such as autoplay videos, pop-ups, pop-unders, and full-screen interstitials. Flashing and blinking ads are also no way for a sophisticated industry to act. Publishers bear some of the responsibility for annoying ads as well. TV networks have long maintained certain standards for the advertising that they accept, yet online and mobile publishers tend to not even review the programmatic ads that are being served to them unless they are part of a premium programmatic buy.

Why would Apple allow ad-blocking technology to exist on the mobile web when browsing on Safari? The fact is that it is a tactical move. Ad blockers do not work on apps, and Apple makes a lot of money off of apps in the App Store, while it doesn't make money at all from mobile web advertising. If advertising on the mobile web becomes less valuable, publishers will more aggressively push users to their apps, which are also able to bypass the ad-blocking software. And, with apps, Apple makes money not only in the App Store, but also with its iAd network, which enables app developers to monetize apps. The end result of this strategy will likely be a good thing for large publishers. App users are generally more valuable than mobile web users, since they are loyal to the brand and plan to access the content more often, but it will be a big problem for small publishers and bloggers who can't afford native app development.

Want to learn more about mobile advertising?
See updated statistics and other important information
at RelevanceRaisesResponse.com.

Chapter 7

MOBILE APPS

A walking billboard that's in the pocket of your customer 24 hours a day.

*T*hat is what an app can be for your business. Imagine how important that is, to be one of the apps that the consumer downloads and keeps on his mobile phone's home screen. What's that real estate alone worth to your business?

HISTORY OF APPS

A mobile app is a software program that can be downloaded and accessed directly from a mobile device. It should come as no surprise that the legendary Steve Jobs was the first person to begin talking about apps. In 1983 at a conference in Aspen, Jobs, just six months removed from debuting MacIntosh, talked about a scheme whereby people could download systems on phone lines, much like purchasing records at a record store. (This was a scene in the October 2015 movie *Steve Jobs*.) It was IBM, however, that gave birth to the modern-day version of mobile apps. Its IBM Simon, first released in 1993, has long been described as the first smartphone. Simon contained some very basic mobile apps, such as a calendar, world clock, address book, calculator, sketchpad, to-do list, and notepad. It also included a touchscreen, predictive text, e-mail capability, and fax capability. Back then, these things were referred to as "features" and were found in the Mobile Office section of the phone. You would think that Simon was a big hit for IBM, but it wasn't. Plagued by a battery that lasted only one hour and a price tag of $1,100, Simon only sold 50,000 units.

The first mobile phone game, Tetris, was introduced in 1994 on a mobile phone called the Hagenuk MT-2000. Three years later, in 1997, Nokia designed a black-and-white version of Snake for the Nokia 6110. Snake has since been embedded on 400 million devices worldwide.[43] The key to attracting such a large audience of gamers and non-gamers to Snake was its simplicity. It was a watershed moment for mobile phones, because for the first time ever, people were actively using their phones for something other than for what they were originally intended for—making phone calls.

Wireless Application Protocol (WAP) was introduced in 1999 and allowed for mobile phones to access information via a wireless network. WAP technology, developed in a cooperative effort between Ericsson, Motorola, Nokia, and UP, allowed devices to connect to the Internet, which was a major leap forward. To enable the ability to present on the smaller wireless screen, a wireless markup language (WML) was developed as a counterpart to the Internet language of HTML.

Always the innovator, Apple launched its music store, iTunes, in 2003, and over one million songs were sold in the first week. Then in June of 2007, a major innovation took place—Apple began allowing outside developers to create Web 2.0 applications, which looked and behaved just like preinstalled apps on smartphones. Simultaneously, the first iPhone was introduced, and 270,000 were sold in the first 30 hours. In July of 2008, the Apple App Store was launched, with 552 apps initially included. Within a week, over 10 million apps were downloaded. By September, that number had reached 100 million.[44] "There's an app for that" was a promotional slogan that began in January of 2009 when Apple began doing extensive advertising for its Apple App Store. It has remained a common catchphrase ever since. By October of 2013, there were one million different apps in the Apple App Store.

Three months after the launching of the Apple App Store, Google Android launched its Android Market, and it immediately became Apple's major rival. The T-Mobile G1, also known as Googlephone, was introduced alongside the Google Android Market. Positioned as an alternative to the dominant smartphone of BlackBerry, the G1 was the first smartphone to run the open-source Android operating system. It quickly became the fifth-best-selling smartphone in the USA. In 2012, Google Android Market was renamed Google Play Store.

BlackBerry debuted as the go-to app solution for business use in April of 2009, when its BlackBerry App World was launched. BlackBerry became the third major player in the app fray, and it dominated the app world initially. Its high-income users were avid downloaders of apps. In fact, of the three major app stores, BlackBerry had the largest revenue per app at $9,166.67, followed by iPhone at $6,480.00 and Google Play at $1,200.00.[45]

Windows became the fourth competitor in October of 2010. Amazon's Appstore for the Android operating system debuted in March of 2011 in over 200 countries with 4,084 apps. Later that year, Amazon launched its Kindle Fire tablet. Kindle Fire relies solely on the Amazon Appstore for its sales.

Games have always been extremely popular apps and are an important part of app history. Angry Birds, from Rovio Entertainment, debuted in December of 2009 and has been the all-time best-selling app ever since.[46] By 2015, Angry Birds had been downloaded over three billion times.[47] Angry Birds combines several key factors that have led to it being such a hugely popular game: simplicity, addictiveness, funness, and low price. Columbia Pictures will debut an animated feature film based on the Angry Birds game on May 20, 2016.

Enter social media. Facebook acquired the Instagram app in April of 2012 for $1 billion, the most ever paid for an app company. That number would have been smashed in November of 2013, but 23-year-old Snapchat cofounder Evan Siegel turned down Facebook's $3 billion offer. Both of these transactions were chump change compared to Facebook's $16 billion acquisition of WhatsApp in February of 2014. When it comes to apps, Facebook is, by far, the dominant player today. It holds down four positions in the top 10 in terms of most downloaded apps with Facebook, Messenger, Instagram, and WhatsApp. Facebook is, by far, the most downloaded app, with Messenger and YouTube fighting it out for the runner-up spot.

In 2015, over half of the time spent with digital was in mobile apps. In 2016, 44 billion app downloads are predicted and more app push messages will be sent than text messages.[48] When you consider the evolution of apps, it is apparent that the World Wide Web is becoming less important because of apps. Apps are becoming the dominant source of media in people's lives.

TIME SPENT WITH APPS

Time spent with mobile continues to grow at a rapid pace and now exceeds time spent watching television, largely due to apps.[49] In fact, according to *Harvard Business Review*, more than four-fifths of time spent with mobile is spent in apps rather than on mobile websites.[50] That time in apps is split between the more than 40 apps that are downloaded on an average smartphone, although only about 15 of those apps are used regularly. More than 95 percent of app usage is spent around five general areas of use. Here are some of the most popular by category:

- social media—Facebook, Instagram, Twitter, Pinterest, Snapchat
- entertainment—YouTube, Pandora, iTunes, Radio, Netflix, Spotify
- communications—Messenger, WhatsApp
- directions—Google Maps, Apple Maps, Waze
- news—Yahoo Stocks, The Weather Channel

Less than 5 percent of time spent in apps is spent with shopping apps, with eBay and Walmart being the leaders. Pinterest is the only one of the top 25 apps that is not owned by a public company. Netflix is the only app in the top 25 that requires a subscription.

It is no surprise that music apps rank highest in terms of session length, since music can be played from a smartphone for extended drives, while working out, or at the office. Music is one of the few categories where mobile users eat a full-course meal rather than "snack" on content.

In general, users tend to snack on apps on their smartphones while they enjoy a full-course dinner on their tablet. Since they are with the consumer all day, smartphones tend to get more launches but with shorter durations. Tablets benefit from longer durations since they are mostly used at home. Phablets, those larger-than-life pocket smartphones, tend to behave more like smartphones than tablets.

APPS BASICS

When a person buys a new smartphone, there are free apps preinstalled on the phone, such as the notes feature, calendar, clock, Passbook, and easy-access links to music and app stores. Some of these apps are valuable and others really are not. Smartphone owners will add additional apps of interest to their mobile devices by downloading from app stores.

The major difference between a mobile app and accessing the web from a mobile phone is that the app is actually a piece of software that lives on the mobile phone. Because it is housed on the phone itself, it can be accessed even when the user is not near Wi-Fi or an Internet signal. To download an app, a user needs a smartphone, tablet, or other mobile device with Internet access. Not all apps work on all phones. If a user has Apple products, she will only be able to download apps that are Apple compatible. It is the same with the other mobile operating systems.

A mobile app will likely need to be able to access some features on the user's mobile phone to be valuable, such as the camera, GPS, and other add-ons to the mobile device. By utilizing the features and functionalities of the mobile phone, the app is able to work in cooperation with the device quite seamlessly. No matter how well a mobile website is designed, it can never take full advantage of the mobile phone features like an app can.

When a user downloads an app, the app will usually ask for permission to send the user push notifications. Push notification messages are similar to text messages, but are sent directly to the mobile phone and will not normally end up in the text message box. A user can accept or reject the ability to receive push notifications.

From time to time, the app will have updates to its software, and this will appear on the mobile phone within the app store button. Sometimes the updates are to make bug fixes or to make the app compatible with new devices. There are often updates to cure potential malware, so it is always a good idea to accept the updates from the app company.

Take a look at a true mobile lover's phone and you will likely see pages and pages of app icons. An app icon is incredibly useful and convenient as a shortcut to the content contained within the app itself. Moreover, it keeps the business's brand and logo in the pocket of its customer until the day it is deleted.

IF IT'S FREE, IT'S ME

Over 90 percent of all apps and 95 of the top 100 downloaded apps are free to the consumer.[51] Some do charge for the initial download, but there is significant price resistance with apps, even when they are sold for less than a dollar. The minimum price for an app is 99 cents in the USA, $1.19 in Canada, 79 pence in the UK, and 0.99 euros in Europe. In the USA, developers can charge up to $999.99 for an app, and there are a few that do charge that much.

Some apps with advanced functionality, such as games, may require a nominal fee to download. Paid apps are known as premium apps. A paid model is the most obvious way to monetize an app, by charging the user when he makes the download. Premium apps provide a straightforward pricing model similar to a Software as a Service offering. (SaaS is software that is hosted remotely and charged to the consumer, usually on a monthly basis.) It is difficult to convince those not familiar with a brand to purchase a paid app, so premium apps are mostly offered to people already familiar with the brand or service. Examples might be a popular game extension or a mobile version of an already-known business product. Premium apps may also be ones that are unique with no competitors, or perhaps the app is being sold to existing customers as an addition to the existing product line.

Paymium is another version of a paid app. It offers companies two methods of making money. With paymium, users pay for the initial download of the app, then pay again for additional upgrades. Paymium is mostly used in the gaming industry. An example of a paymium app is the wildly popular Heads Up! game that Ellen DeGeneres made famous.

The app stores also charge developers for the ability to submit to the app stores. It costs $99 per year in the USA for an individual or business to submit apps to the Apple App Store. Apple also offers an Apple Developer Enterprise Program for $299 per year. An organization only needs the Developer Enterprise Program if it is looking to create proprietary apps designed and distributed exclusively to its own employees. Developers wishing to submit apps to the Google Play Store for Android must pay a $25 registration fee per year and must make the payment using Google Payments. Windows Marketplace charges $99 per year. BlackBerry used to charge $200 per year to submit apps, but it no longer has an annual fee, perhaps because it no longer gets a lot of new apps developed for it, given its declining popularity.

Here's an important fact. On both the Apple App Store and the Google Play Store, the app developer receives 70 percent of the revenue and Apple or Google gets 30 percent. There is no negotiation with either store. Note that the 70 percent also applies to upgrades made on free apps. In other words, if the app is already downloaded and the customer adds a paid feature within the app, 70 percent is remitted to the developer for the add-on sale. The third-tier app stores are also very consistent in offering the same

70 percent back to the developer for paid apps or upgrades within apps.

While Google and Apple both remit the same amount to the developer, they handle rebates quite differently. On the Google Play Store, if the consumer requests a refund within 15 minutes of making the purchase, the entire amount is refunded and the entire transaction is reversed. Not the case with Apple. It sells all apps on an "as-is" basis. If the consumer does not like the app, tough luck. Apple will only rebate the price if the consumer is unable to download it or it does not work properly on the mobile device. If the user pushes for a chargeback, Apple still keeps its 30 percent, and the developer is out the rebate difference. That being said, rebates are not requested often on apps, given that most are a mere 99 cents.

Getting people to pay for apps is not an easy task, since consumers are used to getting apps for no charge. Therefore, there are also freemium apps. A freemium app is free to download, but users may need to pay a la carte for enhancements to the app. Major League Baseball's Home Run Derby app is an example. It gets the user hooked on playing the free version using one of the lesser-known sluggers, then asks the user to upgrade to the better-known players by paying for them. There are also upgrades for sale—such as batting gloves, bats, and shoes—that all help your MLB hitter to swat more home runs.

It is not just games that are using the freemium model. The *New York Times* and *Wall Street Journal* both use freemium by offering limited content for free, but each requires upgrades to access additional content. Local newspapers have attempted the freemium model with limited success, but top-tier publications seem to be capitalizing with what is essentially a paid subscription model.

In other cases, such as with the game Angry Birds, the app is free to download, but comes with advertising included. If the user wants to eliminate the advertisements that come up between levels of the game, he needs to pay for the upgrade. So the Angry Birds app is making money regardless of whether the user has paid for it or not; the revenue is earned through advertising when it is a free app.

The freemium model offers app developers maximum flexibility in monetizing apps. The publisher can use an advertiser-supported model and/or it can sell upgrades to existing users. Upgrade sales do require more effort with in-app marketing to the users in an attempt to get them to make additional purchases.

WHY CREATE AN APP?

A lot of businesses seem to feel that getting an app is a modern-day mobile requirement. It certainly is for some, but not all. The first question that needs to be asked is, "Does my business really need an app?" Will having an app eliminate some pain that the customer feels? It may be surprising to learn in a book about mobile marketing that all businesses do not necessarily need an app. All businesses definitely need a mobile website, but not all need an app.

Many businesses check off the box and develop an app, then learn that it is very expensive to maintain and attract downloads. Putting all of the money into development and having nothing left for marketing is a losing proposition. Moreover, it is expensive to simply keep the app up to date. Apps need to be constantly updated with new software when new phones enter the market. That costs money too. A website can be a one-time development issue, save the annual renewal of the domain and a hosting package, but an app is a commitment of time and money that is ongoing.

A local theatre may need an app because it caters to season ticket holders and a small but very loyal audience of followers. An app could certainly cut down on some of the administration for the theatre by giving information about upcoming shows, sending push notifications, and being a depository for mobile tickets and their sales. A local movie theater, however, is probably a different story. AMC has a very good app at the corporate level, but a local movie theater would likely be better served in advertising on some of the movie-theater apps like Fandango, Flixster, Showtimes, or Moviefone instead of creating its own personal app. Consumers are likely not loyal to a particular theater; they just want to see a certain movie. Plus, these apps have all the movie-related traffic anyway, so why not use the already-popular movie-industry apps?

Businesses that have a loyal following and customers that will check the app regularly probably need an app, assuming that the business will keep the content updated. Businesses that require location-based information probably need an app too. If the experience requires the ability to interact with the features of the phone, an app is absolutely necessary. If a business does not want to do SMS marketing, but does have the need to keep in touch with its best customers, push notifications via an app certainly make a lot of sense.

Benefits of an App

Consumers are spending over two-thirds of their time with digital media on mobile apps, but if that is not enough for a business to consider making an app, consider some of the other benefits of having a business app:

- Brand recognition—Where else can a business logo be attached to a customer's most personal of devices 24 hours a day, 365 days a year?
- Direct marketing—It is a direct link to a customer. By using push notifications, a business can send direct messages to its very best and most loyal customers.
- Loyalty—Forget the old punch card. An app can keep track of loyalty points and encourage the best customers of a company to continue to support the business.

- Communication—Apps improve customer communication. Those that download the app have an inside line to send a message to the business, reserve a table, renew a subscription, request service, or purchase a product without making a phone call and waiting on hold for an annoying amount of time.

- Visibility—If the business is a small- or medium-sized business, an app may be an offering the competition does not have. If it is a large business, then the app just needs to be better than the competition in order to stand out.

TYPES OF APPS

It is important to have a basic understanding of the primary types of app development that are available to you. Consulting with your developer will give you the background you need to decide what type of app you should develop.

Native Apps

Native apps live on the device itself. They are installed through an app store and are developed specifically for just one platform, which provides optimum usability and quality. Native apps can also use the other features that are already on the phone, such as the camera, GPS, and contact list. If you are in an area with no connectivity, a native app will still work, and it will be fast. Think of downloading an app for a national park. The user is in a remote area of the park, but he will still have the ability to find the map...and the way back to camp. That is not just a good idea, it is potentially life saving.

The native platform provides the fastest performance of data and the crispest graphics. It offers fluid animation, which is especially critical in games. Although much of the technology resides within the software, a native app can also access information from the

Internet. Native apps can be found in the app stores and they offer the best performance of any type of development.

A major negative of native apps is the update process. If the business wants to update, it must submit those updates to the app store and then have the update pushed to the users. Another negative for native apps is that the developer has to pay a 30 percent fee to Apple or Google for all purchases made on their app stores. The developer gets to keep only 70 percent of the amount charged to the consumer.

Web Apps

Web apps, also known as HTML5 apps, are really websites that may look like native apps, but they reside on a browser. HTML5 apps are far easier to develop than native or hybrid apps because some of the same skills used in web development are used in them. Most are written in HTML5 and are device agnostic. They are usually accessed from a web page where the user is given the option of "installing" them. The install, however, is not really software for the app itself, but a bookmark to the site.

One of the advantages of a web-based app is that you do not have to go to the app store to find it. It can be downloaded from the web. Because the content is on the web, it is searchable, and that can be a huge benefit for increasing downloads. Also, if the business wants to update it, it is as simple as updating a web page; the user does not have to download a new update. Changes require no submission to the app stores and can be done quickly. Another advantage of web-based apps is that there are no content restrictions. Apple, for example, has been notoriously prudish in its willingness to accept some content. Hence, it was Playboy that was one of the first companies to use web-based apps that avoided the Apple censors.

The negative to web-based HTML5 apps is that there are some vital limitations to them. Specifically, there are limitations to accessing the native device functionality. Also, testing on multiple devices can be a pain. And if the app requires a strict level of security, such as with a banking app, web-based apps are a non-starter.

Hybrid Apps

Hybrids are, as you would expect, a combination of native and web-based technologies, some of which are device agnostic. Hybrid mobile apps are built with a combination of web technologies like HTML, CSS, and JavaScript. In recent years, the line between web-based apps and hybrid apps has drawn closer. In fact, you would be hard pressed to find a newer app today that is not built as a hybrid app. That being said, understanding the difference between native and web-based technologies remains an important distinction, and that is why it is still included in this complicated comparison.

Facebook used to be considered a hybrid app, but it recently moved to become a native app. This distinction may be confusing, because Facebook obviously needs connectivity to load the most recent posts. PhoneGap and Cordova, the building blocks for hybrid apps, exist to access device hardware features, but they still can't emulate them as well as native apps can with their increased speed, reaction time, and animation smoothness. That made Facebook's move to hybrid unsuccessful. Mark Zuckerberg said Facebook's biggest mistake was betting too much on HTML5.[52] According to Zuckerberg, when Facebook shifted back to a native app, people were consuming twice as many News Feed stories.[53]

Instagram, owned by Facebook, is interestingly remaining a hybrid app. That is a good decision in knowing what works best for each app. By using hybrid, Instagram gets the support of HTML5 that better supports an app based around photo and video sharing.

One of the major advantages of hybrid apps is cost savings. With hybrids, developers are able to use existing web development skills to create an app environment. Often, this means the app development can be done in-house as opposed to the more costly outsourcing. What is not known can be built through frameworks provided by companies such as PhoneGap and Titanium. Using these frameworks can significantly cut down on the debugging time that will surely happen when making a hybrid app for all of the many operating systems.

It is nearly impossible for a non-technical person to tell the difference between a well-written hybrid app and a native app. And, in reality, it does not make any difference to the user. Some popular apps that are hybrids are Yelp, Instagram, Basecamp, Twitter, Gmail, and Uber. That is some pretty good company.

DEVELOPING AN APP

App development is a lot more difficult than web development because the coding varies based on operating system, and developers need to know different code to accommodate each of them. This requires experience and also an occasional consultation with the software-development kits provided by the operating system. Work on an app is seemingly never done, and brands will need to continue to invest in them even after the initial development is complete to fix bugs and keep the software up to date.

Development of an app starts with designing app flow. App flow is the sequence of interactions that the user will make from the initial opening of the app to arriving at the actual content provided. In the web development business, app flow is equivalent to wireframing. A business needs to dictate its goals for the app and then work in conjunction with the app developer, who will provide details on the best way to create user-friendly app functionality and flow. Once the entire app flow and wireframe are developed, the development agency should be able to provide a financial proposal.

The cost of an app is as difficult to assess as the cost of building a house. There are app developers that have off-the-shelf products for specific niches, such as restaurants. A restaurant that uses such an app is essentially buying a white-label version of the app with little ability to customize. A typical rate might be a little under $1,000, with an ongoing monthly or annual renewal fee. Most business apps, however, are going to be custom development. A typical business app, developed for both iPhone and Android, can cost in the $30,000 range for the initial development and as much as $250,000 when complex e-commerce and product-line features are added.

The average development time for an app is about three to six months, but that, of course, is highly dependent on complexity and how much competing work the app development team has. Establishing benchmarks for dated delivery of certain tasks during the process is the only way to keep a development team on task.

MONETIZING AN APP

When it comes to monetizing an app, it is very simple if it is a retail store app. With an e-commerce retail app, the goal is to sell more product. With non-commercial types of apps, however, it is not quite as easy. The most obvious way to monetize an app is to sell ads on them. There are many online sites that will help app business owners start to monetize their apps with paid advertising.

Keep in mind, however, that users prefer apps with no advertising on them. Users do not connect the fact that the terrific app was free and therefore the only way a business can get some of their development costs back is to offer advertising. An app marketer will be able to choose what types of ads they are willing to include in-app. Banner ads pay the least and interstitial ads pay the most. Not surprisingly, the user annoyance factor for interstitials is greater than for banners. An app owner must balance the current profit motive with the longer-term goal of gaining additional users by having higher ratings.

Another way to make money from the app is to sell things within the app. An app owner can obtain his own inventory of products or become an affiliate for a related product. Affiliate marketing makes a lot of sense for app providers if they can find products that are similar to the purpose of the app. Advertisements that blend in with the app's content appear to be native and are therefore less obtrusive to users. The negative is that normally affiliates only pay when the product is sold, so there is no guarantee of income like one would receive from straight advertising.

WHAT MAKES A GOOD APP?

A good app responds to some pain that the customer feels. If you have to do business in the downtown area of a city, you know what a hassle it can be to find a parking spot. SpotHero is an app designed to address this specific issue and eliminate the hassle of driving in circles for a half hour to find an available parking spot. If a business is simply developing an app that has the same content as its website, it probably isn't necessary; after all, people can access the mobile website. If the app does not cure some pain, it won't be long until the consumer taps out and deletes it into the junkyard of unwanted and unused apps.

Another reason that a consumer may want to download an app is for increased ease of interacting with the business. If a customer works with the business often, adding an app opens the communication lines with the business for increased ease of purchase or to ask a question. In fact, one of the features of a good app is the messaging feature. Autobytel Inc. provides marketing resources to car dealers, including individual car dealer apps. On each of its apps, it offers a multitude of methods for interacting with customers of an auto dealership, including tap-to-call, tap-to-e-mail, and tap-to-text or chat. According to Yahoo, regarding those apps with messaging features, 62 percent of users were still using them a year after the download. For those that did not have messaging features, only 11 percent of users still opened the apps after a year.[54]

Savings is another attraction for loyal customers. Apps can offer digital versions of loyalty cards to keep top customers involved with the brand. Italian ice store Rita's has a great app that tabulates loyalty points for customer rewards. When a customer purchases a water ice, the clerk allows him to scan a QR code that, via animation, literally punches the virtual loyalty card within the app. Rita's can push savings through special discounts or mobile coupons to its app users. All the while, the business is gathering purchasing pattern information from its best customers. The ability to track, monitor, and measure purchasing information eventually leads to the ability to influence future buying behaviors.

All of us also need to be entertained, and an app can certainly provide that. During down times, people turn to mobile to entertain. Angry Birds and Flappy Bird are two such examples of incredibly popular mobile games. Flappy Bird was a mobile game developed in Vietnam in 2013. The game received a sudden rise in popularity. After just a few months, its developer claimed that Flappy Bird was earning $50,000 a day from in-app advertisements.[55] Flappy Bird was removed by its creator on February 10, 2014, due to guilt over what he considered to be its addictive nature.

There are many businesses that have come up with creative ways to influence app downloads, even from consumers who wouldn't normally do so. Zippo Lighter has an app that allows concertgoers to hold up a virtual lighter. Zippo is an example of a relatively boring product that has given customers a fun reason to download its app.

It is clear that not all apps are satisfying the needs of those who download them. Twenty percent of all apps are only used once.[56] Sports and gaming apps lead the way in the percentage of apps only used once. This shows that mobile marketing efforts need to focus more on development and engagement rather than acquisition.

APP KPIS

Mobile has changed the way that marketers analyze the criteria that measures success on the web, because people use apps much differently than they use the Internet. Mobile users snack on content as opposed to spending long durations online like they once did when surfing on their desktop. With desktop Internet, companies want to know hits and page views. It is quite different with mobile, where a company's focus is on sessions. It is not how many minutes the consumer spends, but how often she visits. More visits means that the app is a remedy to some form of pain, or it is simply wildly entertaining.

By now, it is apparent that all mobile marketing tactics need to have KPIs associated with them. Here are some that relate to apps and should be considered as a guide to the app's potential success:

- Acquisition—the amount of downloads from a particular marketing campaign. Acquisitions should be tracked based on organic search, app store optimization, paid advertising, and any other means of marketing and promotion for the app.

- Advertisement taps—how many users are tapping and opening the ads.

- Attribution—where a user downloaded the app in the first place. It identifies the marketing that caused the download to occur.

- Churn—how many apps are being deleted.

- Churn propensity—how likely a user is to abandon the app in the future.

- Cohorts—a group of subjects that started using the app at the same time. Cohorts may be tracked over extended periods in a cohort analysis.

- Conversion—the ultimate goal of an app. A conversion may be to sell a product, register for a subscription, or take any particular action that is the prized goal of the app owner.

- Conversion propensity—the chance of a user converting at a certain point in the app.

- Cost per acquisition—the cost of the marketing campaign divided by the total number of new acquisitions. It is a measurement of how well each marketing channel is performing.

- Downloads—how many people downloaded the app in the past period.

- Events—particular actions taken by app users.

- Features used—which features consumers are using most often.

- Frequency of use—how many app opens occur over a period of time.

- Funnel drop-off rate—the percentage of users that failed to complete a step in the conversion process at a particular point in the funnel.

- Retention—the number of users that return to the app within a given period of time after the initial download. Keeping a customer is always more important than attracting a new one.

- Screen flow—analyzes how users navigate from screen to screen and what their exit points are in order to find problem areas. It gives data as to the typical visitor interactions in the app.

- Screens—how many times users reached a particular screen in an app and how they navigated to the next screen.

- Session interval—the amount of time between sessions. It is a very important KPI to track immediately after the release of the app because it signals the immediate value gained from the app. If a consumer does not visit a second time soon after downloading, there probably was not value received on the initial visit.

- Session length—the average time the app is used in total or per open session. It is the time from app open to app close. Session length makes a lot more sense with mobile apps than it does with the Internet, where a customer could have a web page open as one of many tabs but is not paying any attention to it. It enables the marketer to understand which audiences are spending the most time in the app and why. It would be impossible to compare time of use figures across application verticals. One would not expect a mortgage company's app to be accessed nearly as often as a radio app.

- Time in app/time on screen—the amount of time that a user is in the app over a period of time. For example, users average 27 minutes per month in the app. If users are opening an app often but for short periods of time, thought can be given as to how to offer new content that might keep the users involved longer per session.

- User lifetime value—the average value of a user from the date of download until the date of uninstall.

- User segments—different groups of users that are served different content based on shared attributes. For example, different content may be served to Europeans than Americans, or different methods of conversion might be available after regular business hours than during business hours.

- Users—how many current users there are and their demographics. Users are typically defined as monthly, weekly, or daily average users. Users are the who, where, and when of the app. User metrics are often broken down by age, gender, location, country, and hour of day of use.

App developers often contract with third-party analytic tools to track in-app activity. Basic statistics related to total downloads are available in the app stores.

ACQUISITIONS

It is hard to get noticed on the app stores when there are over two million apps residing there. The best way to get noticed, stand out from the horde, and gain ground in app store rankings is to generate a lot of downloads.

App installs that come from the app stores are known as organic installs. Users find the app after doing a keyword search in the app store or by entering the app name in the search box based on a word-of-mouth recommendation. For most apps, more than two-thirds of installs come from an app store search.[57] Organic installs can be most affected by outstanding app store optimization. The factors that make up ASO are similar to those in SEO, but with one major difference—the number of app downloads is a major factor in ASO. That is why it is so important to also do some marketing for the app outside of the app store itself, especially shortly after release.

"Paid installs," or non-organic installs, are driven by paid and unpaid promotions that take place outside of the app store itself. A common method of driving paid installs is Facebook advertising, and an unpaid promotion might be various public relations efforts. Since there are many options available for paid promotion, close attention is paid to maximize ROI for advertisements. In the app world, ROI translates to CPA.

THE APP STORES

It seems like everybody is making apps today, even the USA government, thanks to an ongoing initiative that suggests all federal agencies have apps. You can even get the IRS2Go app. Given how much time Americans are spending with their apps, it should not be surprising how many apps there are. The Google Play Store has the greatest amount of apps—well over a million of them. The Apple App Store has slightly less, but also has well over a million apps available. On top of these, there are the other app stores listed earlier.

In most cases today, app developers are creating apps only for iPhone and Android. With the cost of app development being so high, it does not make financial sense, at least in most instances, to create apps for BlackBerry and Windows anymore. Remember that, unlike web development, each app development is unique software development and will cost incremental money. With the small amount of users on Windows and BlackBerry, it is difficult to justify additional development for these operating systems.

Usually, the developer of the app will submit the completed software to the app stores. It should be submitted under the name of the business sponsoring the app, not the app developer. With iOS, after submission, the app will go through a certification and App Store review process to ensure that it does not violate any rules, functions well, and is not malicious. If all works out, one can expect an iPhone app to be available in the Apple App Store in about 10 days.

Apple iTunes Connect is a dashboard that allows a business to manage its apps, view reports of the performance of the app, and manage renewals. When a business enrolls in the Apple Developer Program, it receives access to iTunes Connect as well.

Google Android is easier on new apps. Google's review process is not quite automatic, but it is predominantly automated, meaning that there likely will be no human review of the application process. Instead, Google uses sophisticated software that reviews the app code to attempt to weed out those apps with malicious intent. Because of the more automated process, the quality of its apps versus their intrinsic costs is not something that is enforced nearly as well as it is in Apple's approval process. Because of this, more apps make it through the approval process at Google, and thus there is a greater proliferation of low-quality apps. App submissions fly through the Google Play Store and should be available for public download within two days.

Android also allows for its apps to be promoted in other countries and in other stores. Of the third-party options, the Kindle platform is the best option for selling Android apps. Kindle works well for selling premium apps, since its users are already used to purchasing books on the Kindle. The Nook Store is another possibility for marketing Android apps. Although the Nook product is in decline, this app store remains a viable secondary option for download of Android apps.

App Store Optimization

When you are competing against a million other apps vying for the consumer's attention, it is important to have a well-thought-out strategy for marketing your app at the Apple and Google stores. This is known as app store optimization and is similar to SEO, but it only targets the app stores. Since two-thirds of all apps are discovered through an app store search, ASO is the single most important thing an app owner will do to market the app. While every marketing strategy is going to be different when it comes to ASO, there are some basics that you need to get right to have any kind of chance.

It all starts with keyword research. This is the same kind of keyword research that a marketer did in the past for website SEO, but there are differences between app searches and web searches. A website can have many different pages on it, with each page targeting specific keywords. An app has only one page, so it needs to align all of those keywords within a single app. The good news is that app stores allow an app owner to put up to 1,000 keywords in the app description, so there is plenty of space for long-tail keywords. That being said, app searchers tend to input single word or shorter keyword phrases like one would expect on a traditional desktop web search. An app business owner can use the traditional SEO keyword search tools—like the Google Keyword tool or the tools from Moz or Ahrefs—or it can invest in a keyword search tool that has specific results for the app stores, like KeywordTool.io and Sensor Tower.

Like with traditional SEO, it is good to have a primary keyword for the app in the title of the app. Although there are many apps with names that are generic and have nothing to do with the functionality of the app, it is a surer bet to include keywords in the app title. And, as stated above, the app stores allow for 1,000 keywords to be inserted into the description of the app. Here is not the place to be cautious. Use as many keywords as you can think of, and not just the obvious ones. Ask yourself what problem or pain your app solves and how people might search for it in the stores. Think of the description section as the one that requires the most creative writing in order to persuade the potential downloader to choose your app instead of the others competing for his attention. Use bullet points for ease of reading, and think great copywriting over keyword stuffing. Finally, there are the app visuals, which are possibly the most important aspect of the description. The best app screenshot images will immediately tell the reader what the app is all about and present the value proposition of what the app will do for the customer.

After the description for the app stores is completed, it is time to start working on getting positive reviews. When the app initially launches, have colleagues, friends, and family download the app and review it to kickstart the review process. Reach out to satisfied, regular users of the app and directly request reviews. There are also places where app marketers can purchase reviews, but that is something that is not recommended. In addition to being unethical, it also reeks of something that may one day be punished. Remember, a business is dealing with Google here, and it has already severely punished Internet sites that have built scammy links.

It is extremely difficult for an app to get a following, even if it represents a well-known brand. External paid installs prop up the total downloads, which ultimately translates to higher ASO. It is a snowball effect. Be sure to save some money for advertising and not spend all your budget on development, or you will end up with a great app that nobody knows about.

MARKETING AN APP

While ASO is certainly important, marketers must not rely solely on promotion within the stores to maximize downloads. There are over two million apps in the stores, and finding a particular app is similar to finding the proverbial needle in the haystack, despite the best ASO efforts.

It is not easy to get consumers interested in downloading another app on their mobile phone when they are already using an average of 26.7 apps per month, according to a Nielsen study.[58] A company needs to have developed a structured marketing plan in advance of the release of the app. It needs a plan to tell existing customers and prospects good reasons why they need the app and where the app can be downloaded. It needs to evaluate all of its current marketing channels to determine which ones would be best for promoting an app.

There is no doubt about the power of creating buzz on social media for an app launch. It is an important part of the initial publicity required. And nobody does app marketing better than Facebook, which earns a significant part of its ad revenue from brands pushing app downloads. Social media will probably be better for facilitating app downloads than outdoor advertising, since a social media user is likely on her mobile phone already, as opposed to a driver, who is hopefully not on his phone. Google AdMob might be the best place, since it enables an app marketer to advertise within other apps that consumers have already downloaded.

Of course, Internet advertising is not always the best source for app downloads. If the app has a huge budget, it may very well be television that results in the most downloads. Game of War did a great job of promoting its app with eye-catching Kate Upton and Mariah Carey as the stars of the commercials.

Acquisition costs will not always be high-priced efforts, like the television advertising for Game of War. Publicity is a major driver of new app downloads, so use press releases and other public relations efforts to get the word out. The ROI provided by public relations efforts will likely be the best of any of the promotional efforts.

When marketing an app, it is absolutely critical to get off to a quick start to break through the supply of apps in the app store. If an app is buried below thousands of others in the rankings, it is going to be difficult to find. Therefore, app marketers must get the word out quickly. Start-ups in the app and web business have been known to use growth hacking, which encourages downloads and use through non-traditional marketing that is either free or very inexpensive. Two well-known brands that used growth hacking in their early days are Facebook and AirBNB. Facebook gave away embeddable badges that users could put on their websites or blogs to link back to their Facebook page. AirBNB started by searching for real estate rentals on Craigslist and then sending messages to the owners to promote their units on its site.

Downloads beget more downloads, thanks to the viral effect of the purchase and the improved ASO. The viral effect of apps is an important phenomenon to take advantage of. An app should encourage existing users to share the app with friends or on social media (think Candy Crush). This is a great way to take advantage of the viral publicity that a mobile app can provide.

Research from Localytics found an added bonus to advertising apps. App users that were acquired as a result of being discovered via a mobile ad network were more likely to come back for multiple uses on the app than those that found it from an organic search on the app store.[59] This is likely due to the fact that the ad creative did a good job in preselling users on the benefits of the app and that the advertising was highly targeted.

Another great way to drive traffic to an app is to find the URL of the app download in the iTunes or Google Play listing for the app. Keep in mind this is not the URL for the business, but the URL that is used by the app stores. Then, when the business does content marketing on its own blog or on external sites, it can link to the app stores' URL listings. The goal is to get multiple rankings on the search engines for the app. Those rankings might be the page on the business website that promotes the app download and the app stores' direct URLs for the download.

For Apple and Android apps, there are over a hundred countries where the app can be listed. If an app makes its money on advertising, there is no reason not to list the app in all countries, especially populous countries like China and India. Of course, if the app has an e-commerce element to it, this may not be practical. There are also many secondary Android app stores, and therefore many places where an Android app can be marketed. Amazon, Kindle, Nook, AppBrain, and GetJar are a few alternate places where an Android app can be marketed in addition to its logical home base in the Google Play Store.

There is a defined cost to acquire app downloads, and it is measured by a cost per install (CPI) index. The CPI per vertical market varies, but according to Fiksu, it averaged $2.98 per user in 2015, and it is rising every year as businesses expand their use of mobile advertising.[60]

LAUNCHING A NEW APP

Not all businesses are able to launch a new product with a theater full of early adopters and reporters like Steve Jobs did with his Apple products. It is unlikely that an ordinary business will enjoy an onstage presence with an audience of thousands eagerly waiting to see the new product demonstration.

A big app launch party is probably not the best way to go for most new app products. It is probably better to do a soft launch and rely on friends and family and ASO tactics to gain newbie users. Then, once all bugs are fixed, selling points are confirmed, and target audiences are analyzed, do the larger app launch with the marketing budget attached. It is no different than when a new restaurant opens. Train the staff with friends, family, and media VIP invitations, then open the restaurant to the public with an advertised grand opening.

It is critical to create buzz prior to your formal launch release date. Think e-mail marketing, press releases, and all the same strategies you would do if you were having a store grand opening. This is the time for the staff to celebrate its achievement. This is the time to gain positive publicity.

USER RETENTION BY PUSH MESSAGING

Look at any statistics showing time spent with mobile and one will see that much of that time increase is attributed to increased use of apps. But, while people may have a lot of apps on their phones, many are never used. That means consumers are using only a few apps but using them often. The apps being used often are considered to be "sticky." Instagram, The Weather Channel, and ESPN are sticky apps.

Given the high cost to develop and then get a consumer to download the app, it is easy to see why a business does not want to see its app eventually deleted due to lack of use. That is why engagement with users is so very important. Mobile engagement with apps typically starts the moment a user downloads an app. It is essential that the user see the value of the app immediately. To prove the value of your business's app, it is important to give tutorials during an app's first use about the cool things it can do.

A great promotional tutorial should conclude with the benefits of opting in to push messaging. Then, an iPhone user should be asked if they want to actually receive push notifications. If they say "no," wait awhile, and then ask again after they get more familiar with the features of the app.

One way to keep users coming back for more is to send them push notifications. A push notification is a text that appears on the lock screen of the mobile device. There are also banners that appear at the top of the device if it is in use and alerts that pop over the screen until dismissed. It is a real-time notification from the brand to the customer that it has an important message for her. Push notifications are in part how marketers can avoid getting their apps lost among the ocean of icons that appear on a typical smartphone. By using push messages, a brand gives the customer a good reason to come back to the app by directing the user to a desired action.

According to the Good Push Index, 70 percent of app users will either delete or not use the app if no push contact has been made within 30 days.[61] Without push notifications, consumers are three times more likely to abandon an app after one use. Just like with

SMS marketing, it is important to send push messages often, but not so often that they bombard the user. Users will not permit an unlimited amount of push notifications, so every message should count, or users may react negatively and delete the app. If a brand sends too many messages at the wrong times and attempts to always sell a product, it is far more likely that the user will delete the app.

The app does not have to be open to receive a push message. A push notification appears on the screen of the user's mobile home page. Users have the ability to swipe right to go directly to the content related to the push notification. So if the user swipes right, it will open the app and lead him to the right page for the pushed content. From top to bottom, the message on the smartphone home screen includes a logo and what brand is sending the message, then the text display. On iPhone, it shows the first 60 characters of the push notification; on Android, it is limited to the first 45 characters. App users on iPhone must first agree to receive push notifications before an app can send them. Android users, on the other hand, are already opted in to receive push notifications and must opt out to have them stop. It is kind of like the legal comparison between text message marketing and e-mail marketing—iPhone is opt in messaging and Android is opt out messaging.

There have been several studies reporting on the number of app users that agree to receive push notifications. Results vary, but as a general rule, one can assume that about half will agree to receive pushes from the brand. That varies by industry, of course. A ride-sharing app, for instance, is highly functional and nearly all users will opt in to push notifications, because the app itself relies on them to tell customers their car has arrived. Food and beverage is the category that is second most likely to allow push messaging. After all, what could be more important than eating? Social media has the lowest rate of opt ins for push notifications.

Most push messages are "batch" messages. In other words, a message will be sent to all of the app users or cohorts at the same time. The other type of messages is "triggered" messages, which are sent after customer actions, such as accesses to a certain screen.

Push messages can also be categorized as "transactional" or "engagement." A transactional message is expected by the user and may be something like a notification that the ordered product has shipped. Or it may be a message from an airline to notify the user that her flight is delayed. An engagement push message is a marketing message. It can be a mobile coupon or an ad to download the Kim Kardashian: Hollywood app. An engagement push message is a surprise.

Push messages offer brands a rare opportunity to establish relationships with users. They are not a one-size-fits-all strategy. Different messages should be sent to different users, and users should be segmented according to various interests. It is always best if push messages are personalized and tailored to the recipients. This eliminates the "spray and pray" method and creates a more targeted "right time, right place" strategy. It is not surprising that personalized messages are more than twice as likely to be opened than mass batch messages. That is where audience segmentation comes in. When a push message is not relevant, it can be viewed as spam. If that happens too often, users may turn off notifications for the app. That is why all push messages should be targeted and relevant to the users receiving them.

Personalization does not always mean saying the user's name and offering something unique to just that user. In some cases, personalized engagement messages can be made based on the usage level of the user. Introductory messages need to be sent to new users of the app. Upsells or loyalty promotions may be provided to regular and highly engaged users. Those who signed up for the app and have not been active should receive messages that tell them the features of the app, because maybe they will use the app if they know more. Those who used to be regular users but are not anymore should receive promotional messages encouraging them to come back.

There are certain types of push messages that will almost always work well. Timely reminders are one of them. They can remind users of an upcoming event or even get back in touch with them for incentives on completing the purchase of a product that was left in the cart. Every app user likes to feel special, and exclusive offers are a great way to clear remaining merchandise. Critical information is always, of course, good information to be sent via push. For instance, an airline can notify passengers of a gate change via push notification. Finally, an app push is a great way to get dormant app owners to come back. Tell the customer that they will get something special or find something unique by opening the app again.

An app owner can also use push notifications to gain more positive reviews. By targeting the segments that use the app most often and are likely the most satisfied with the app, apps can obtain all-important positive reviews, which will result in greater downloads.

Open rates for push messages are an important consideration, and the results may seem counterintuitive. Most apps currently send push messages in the evening, likely with the thinking that people are more relaxed and willing to engage with the content. Seems logical, but actually the afternoon has the greatest tap-through rate. The same study shows that weekend tap-throughs are fewer than weekday. Friday is the best day of the week, followed by Tuesday. Messages of less than 10 words have a higher tap-through rate than those with 11 or more words.[62]

Push notifications are not a replacement for SMS marketing. While they are likely cheaper than SMS messaging, there is still a hard cost for them, since most apps use push notification tools that are purchased from a company, such as Urban Airship. That being said, they cater to a different audience, and to maximize reach, businesses should use both push notifications and SMS.

There are times when a message needs to be sent, but a push notification may not be the best way to engage the consumer. For instance, attempting to describe a new feature that the customer may or may not use probably would not make sense via a push notification. In such an instance, it would be better to serve the user the information via an in-app notification, also known as native app content. While push notifications can sometimes seem too, well, pushy, native app content just seems like it is part of the regular show. It is not interruptive and not at all invasive from the user's perspective.

One of the great ways to get positive reviews is to use in-app notifications to gauge just how satisfied the user is with the product or the app itself. If the response is positive, then this is a person that should be targeted to provide an app review or a positive review on sites like Yelp. Often, in-app notifications are used to encourage users to download the newest versions of the app. Loyalty programs and mobile coupons are also ways to engage app users with in-app messaging.

Linking an app to a user's favorite social media site is another way to keep them engaged. This is known as social proof. Social proof is the theory that people will engage in an activity more if they see that their peers are also involved. For example, an app might show the user a list of his Facebook friends or Twitter followers that are also using the app. The navigation app Waze does this by showing where a user's Facebook friends are on the map and what time they may be arriving at the same destination. This can be a valuable feature in addition to offering social proof.

Personal content is also important and keeps users engaged. On Netflix, for instance, it recommends movies that the user may like based on movies that she has already watched. It may be movies with the same stars or with similar themes. Offering local content is another way of providing personal content to the user, and it leads to increased user satisfaction.

Businesses that offer apps need to have a long-term commitment to them. Nobody wants to continue to use an app that has the same stale content, appearance, and user experience. If the app is boring, it will soon be deleted. See what content users are accessing the most and continue to enhance it. Solicit feedback from users so that the business can find out what users desire and about any bug fixes that are required. App updates will ideally occur at least quarterly to continue to engage users.

Downloads may be nice, but engagement with those downloaders is far more critical. If engagement does not occur, a business app will ultimately be deleted when the smartphone owner does his next purge of unused apps.

APP ANALYTICS

More companies and brands are investing in mobile apps today, so tracking the effectiveness of those efforts is critical. Brands need to not only realize their app's initial success figures, but also find a way to estimate the lifetime value (LTV) of a consumer that is engaged with the app.

Fortunately, there are numerous tools available for mobile app analytics. These analytics tools enable the data-driven marketer to gather insights and act on them. Some basic analytics are available from the Google Play Developer Console and iTunes Connect, such as overall and category rankings, downloads, revenue, device access, and geolocation of users. Another thing that app store analytics providers can determine is fill rates. Fill rates are the number of ads delivered properly to the app divided by the number of ad requests to the app from multiple ad platforms. An app would like to have a fill rate of as close to 100 percent as possible, since that means more advertising revenue. Of the two app store analytics providers, Google's statistics are far superior to iTunes's, which is more of a management platform than a measurement platform.

Suffice it to say that the data offered by the app stores themselves is hardly enough for a serious marketer. Third-party app store analytics providers like App Annie can provide more detailed data, such as ranking history, search keywords, competitors' daily app downloads and revenue, app sales and revenue in hundreds of countries, engagement, reach, retention figures, user demographics, cross-app adoption, and users' opinions of the app's quality. Third-party analytics providers can also track the health of a user base by calculating app usage metrics. They can also offer insight, such as whether version updates have an impact on the average session duration. These are great tools for A/B testing of app software enhancements. Just like with mobile advertising, an app should improve with each new content upload.

Further analytics can be built into the software itself. These in-app analytics report on how users are engaging with the app by tabulating statistics on screens viewed, exit locations, clicks, time spent, and purchases. Proper analysis and enhancements based on these analytics can help optimize the user experience and thereby improve retention rate.

The sister to in-app analytics is performance analytics. These measure the technical side of the app. Load time and uptime are examples of performance analytics. Apps with technical deficiencies do not survive for very long. Performance analytics help ascertain if customers are leaving or dissatisfied by pinpointing problem areas for the app that are in need of bug fixes.

The newest and most promising form of analytic data is known as predictive analytics. These analytics, almost always provided by outside companies, couple big data with machine learning algorithms in an attempt to statistically predict the outcome of an offering. A machine learning algorithm provides computers with the ability to learn when exposed to new data and statistics. In a competitive advertising situation, for example, a brand would know how much to bid for an advertisement to target a specific user based on his resemblance to the profiles of an app's top customers.

Having insight into the inner workings of the app allows the brand to adapt to changing scenarios and keep the users coming back again and again. No matter how much research and how many test markets were done prior to the launch of the app, there is no guarantee of success if no follow-up analytics and testing are done. Only by analyzing key KPIs and coupling them with user feedback can an app grow to be as good as it possibly can be.

Want to learn more about mobile apps? See updated statistics and other important information at RelevanceRaisesResponse.com.

Chapter 8

MOBILE COMMERCE

Retail businesses have multiple touch points with their customers on the path to purchase. The businesses that provide a true omnichannel approach to those touch points will be most likely to succeed in the age of mobile.

M-COMMERCE

Everybody has heard of e-commerce, but considerably fewer people identify with m-commerce. M-commerce is the selling and purchasing of goods and services through mobile devices, as opposed to traditional e-commerce, which occurs on desktop devices.

To be clear, m-commerce is not a separate entity from e-commerce. It is actually a subset of e-commerce sales and is calculated as part of e-commerce sales. M-commerce is the evolution of e-commerce. Historically, if businesses could make a little extra selling goods on the small screen of the smartphone, then that was great. Today, however, entire businesses, such as Uber, are m-commerce-only platforms.

While m-commerce sales have a few years to go to catch e-commerce sales, which make up two-thirds of all online sales in North America, the gap is clearly narrowing each year. There are several reasons for this:

1. Responsive and adaptive web design is now the norm for most m-commerce sites, and this evolution has helped eliminate sites not being optimized for mobile—previously the biggest factor in making it difficult to shop on a smartphone.

2. Larger mobile screen sizes are becoming more commonplace. This includes not only tablets but also phablets—the half-tablet, half-phone hybrid.

3. There is greater use of smartphones for everyday purposes, and making purchases via mobile is one such purpose.

4. Over time, the public has shown increased confidence in making online transactions on a mobile phone.

Despite the increase in m-commerce sales, however, shoppers are still considerably more likely to make a purchase from a desktop than a mobile phone. This is not only true in overall purchases, but also in the percent of conversions from desktop compared to mobile. While the gap narrows every year, consumers are still more likely to want to make the actual purchase from a desktop.

There remain several reasons for m-commerce's inability to match e-commerce sales figures. Consider the following:

- The smaller screen and lack of a keyboard make it more difficult to fill out a form and make a purchase. Just entering a 16-digit credit card number correctly without fat-fingering any of the numbers is difficult to do on the first try.

- A mobile phone is often not near Wi-Fi, as opposed to a desktop, which always has Internet access.

- Many mobile phones do not accept cookies, so it is difficult to prefill some of the forms. There is one promising exception, however, as Safari now offers prefill forms on its mobile browser—an enhancement that should improve this factor.

- E-commerce sales offer credit card and PayPal payments. M-commerce payments rely on mobile wallets, which are still emerging in the USA.

- Consumers have not been purchasing on mobile devices for as long as they have on desktops, so there is still some reluctance to do so, especially by older customers.

Not surprisingly, when it comes to making purchases on mobile, tablets act more like laptops and desktops, given their larger size. iPads convert best of all, followed by Android tablets. Of smartphones, Androids convert to sales better than iPhones. This is surprising, given the higher income levels of iPhone users, but Android also skews younger, so that does give an edge to it when it comes to mobile sales conversions. In general, desktops tend to convert more often during working hours, but mobile takes over during leisure time.[63]

When it comes to m-commerce, North America trails other countries in the percentage of online purchases made via mobile. In Japan and South Korea, more than half of all online transactions are made by mobile. Percent of purchases made by mobile in the United Kingdom are not far behind those of the Far Eastern countries. According to Forrester, it will take the USA until 2018 for half of its online sales to be made via m-commerce.[64] Japanese mobile consumers are over three times more likely to convert to a sale than USA consumers. If USA mobile conversion rates rose to those of Japan, then mobile would account for over half of all e-commerce sales in the United States.[65]

Opposite to what is going on in retail stores, mobile users visit online retailers more often and they buy more often, yet the average ticket sale is decreasing slightly on mobile. That is because mobile users are in a hurry when it comes to m-commerce, and they don't take the time to shop for add-on items.

Mobile Web or App?

Retailers, and businesses in general, continue to struggle with which mobile channel is more important to them—the mobile web or the app? There is really no right answer to this. In most instances, both are needed to maximize sales. Assuming that the ultimate goal for a business is to have both, it almost always makes sense to have a mobile-optimized website before an app. Having a mobile website today is more like keeping up with the rest of the world rather than adding something to give the business an edge, whereas an app may be more useful for developing something for a very specific purpose that cannot be effectively accomplished via the mobile web.

A business may want to move the app up on the to-do list if it has a requirement to offer personalization to its customer base. An app also better facilitates complex calculations, processing, and reporting. And an app may not require a network or wireless connection.

Certainly, a larger share of retailers have deployed mobile websites than apps, but many retailers remain convinced that the desktop website is the most important part of its online e-commerce marketing strategy. After all, desktop websites still convert to sales the best, followed by mobile websites and then apps. But ultimate conversion is not indicative of the entire picture. Mobile is highly instrumental at the top of the path to purchase sales funnel. For instance, there are not a lot of auto sales made online, car unseen, but much of the initial research on automobiles is made online at the top of the funnel, at the information-gathering stage. That research often occurs on mobile. If the initial mobile contact with the auto brand is not a positive one, the vehicle buyer may never make it into the end-game purchasing funnel that will most likely take place at the local dealership.

THE TRADITIONAL SALES FUNNEL

AIDA, coined in the late 1800s, is the precursor to the traditional sales funnel. AIDA stands for the four stages that a consumer goes through after seeing an advertisement. You probably learned this in your freshman marketing class (and have since forgotten it):

1. Attention   **3.** Desire

2. Interest   **4.** Action

The concept of AIDA still makes sense today, but at some point, the marketing funnel changed and became a bit more sophisticated. It moved more to a funnel shape, where potential customers are squeezed out of the purchasing process as the funnel becomes narrower on the pathway to the actual sale.

1. Awareness	4. Action
2. Consideration	5. Loyalty
3. Preference	6. Advocacy

Both of the staged paths to purchase listed above are linear, meaning the consumer passes through each stage on the way to making the ultimate purchase.

Things are much more complex today because the consumer is using multiple forms of traditional and digital media to gain information prior to the purchase. When a customer enters the store today, he is already armed with an incredible amount of information learned before making the selection of the product. Rarely does a consumer just show up anymore and make the decision entirely at the store with the help of the salesperson. Customers are using multiple devices and going through numerous interactions, both online and offline, prior to making the purchase online or at a brick-and-mortar store. In today's world, a linear path to purchase is highly unlikely to occur. Online and brick-and-mortar retailers that are able to work cohesively to connect the dots between various interactions with the consumer will be the winners in today's sophisticated path to purchase model.

DRIVING SALES TO RETAIL STORES

Overall, in-store traffic is down and online research is up, thanks to the phenomenon known as the mobile mind shift. Yet, while in-store traffic is down, consumers are spending more when they visit brick-and-mortar stores. That is because before the consumer ever arrives at the store, she has done research and made decisions. In most cases, she already knows what she wants.

Consumers increasingly crave more information before making a product choice. Most importantly, they want information immediately, wherever they are. Google coined these information-gathering times as "micro-moments" and refers to them as the footsteps that lead people to your store or e-commerce site. Non-Googlers may call them influence points. Micro-moments, or influence points, provide marketers with an open invitation to engage with customers and prospects.

One of the best examples of taking advantage of a micro-moment is a mobile advertising campaign from Red Roof Inn. Red Roof Inn learned that 90,000 people were stranded at airports each night due to flight delays that caused the passengers to miss connections. So the hotel chain developed a system to track late-night flight arrivals, and then it would trigger geotargeted mobile search advertisements for Red Roof Inns that were near airports where travelers were stranded until the next morning's flight. "Stranded?" in the banner ad was surely going to attract the attention of the disgruntled traveler looking for an inexpensive place to stay and disappointed that he would not be making it home that night.

The path to purchase in a retail store has changed drastically because of mobile and the numerous micro-moments that make up the ultimate goal of the business making a sale. Mobile has caused retailers to find new and innovative ways to reach what is essentially a moving target of consumers who are researching and shopping 24/7, regardless of where they are. This fusion of digital marketing and a physical retail store is referred to by a new buzzword: phygital marketing.

For an old-school retailer, it can be a daunting task to think of ways to compete when mobile shoppers can purchase products at home, in the office, or on the road. After all, a small business retail store is only one store and it is only in one place. For a small business, competing against mobile can feel like a hockey team playing with two players down in the penalty box. Thankfully, there are always two ways to look at things—challenge or opportunity.

With mobile, a customer is always on a potential path to purchasing a product. Every time they interact with their mobile device, they can be getting closer to purchasing from a retail store. What a retailer has to do is bring the store to them.

Mobile's unique ability to geolocate consumers is one of its most prized traits. It used to be assumed that all consumers reached via mobile were on the move, but that has certainly changed. For several years now, more smartphone use has occurred in home rather than out on the go.[66] Customers consuming business information at home are more likely to be in the earliest stages of making a purchase. Those being reached on the go are far more likely to be looking to make an immediate purchase at a retail store. Understanding the intent and immediacy needs of the customer engaging with a business's information becomes an important part of delivering the right message in the right location at the right time.

One example of a retail store being in the right location at the right time is with a local consumer searching on Google at work for a new dress to wear to a special event that night. Time is certainly at a premium since the event is only hours away, so the woman has to act quickly, thus making a strictly e-commerce purchase a non-option, due to delivery time. If the shopper finds what she wants on mobile, and knows it is available in her size at her local store, she is highly likely to purchase it at that moment. Not knowing if the product is available, however, is a huge deterrent to traveling to the retail store. After all, the event is that night and there's really no time to do traditional shopping. Therefore, it is imperative that inventory at the brick-and-mortar store be linked to the searches going on online and on mobile. If she likes it, and it is available in her size, she'll be ordering it on her mobile phone and picking it up on the way home.

Those consumers finding information via mobile while at a brick-and-mortar store are the most perplexing to mobile marketers. Half are there to make an immediate purchase and others are still in the "just looking" stage. About a third are still investigating their options.

When not showrooming (checking for the best price online), shoppers in the retail store are usually using their smartphones to garner more information. They are far more likely to be looking at the app or mobile website of the store they are in rather than a competing store's app or website. This presents a powerful opportunity for retailers to connect with consumers on their mobile phones when they are actually present in the store and most likely to buy from that store.

When it comes to considering a small- or medium-cost purchase, no matter where they are, people are using mobile, often because they are very close to making a decision on the purchase. About two-thirds looking at restaurant or retail information, for example, expect to make a purchase within an hour. This makes mobile a huge opportunity to drive immediate engagement and sales right away.

Smartphones have become an integral part of the decision-making process. In some cases, especially with millennials, they are the only touch point in the information-gathering and sales process. Take the restaurant vertical, for instance. Across all age groups, about two-thirds of those choosing a restaurant do so only with input from a smartphone. Even for a big-ticket purchase like a used car, one in six purchasers is deciding based solely on input from a mobile phone.[67]

Mobile is playing an increasingly important and varied role in the path to purchase. E-commerce and m-commerce sales alone do not tell the entire story or show the entire picture, because mobile is just one element on the path to purchase. Retailers that fail to measure the influence of mobile risk missing its true ability to drive in-store sales.

OMNICHANNEL MARKETING

There used to be a time when purchases occurred only in brick-and-mortar retail stores. Then, with the emergence of e-commerce, purchases were also supplemented online. This type of buying still occurs today, of course, but now people use multiple devices in a single path to purchase cycle. Sixty-five percent of those journeys begin with mobile, according to Pew.[68]

Consumers today are inundated with information, and they are making more informed buying decisions than ever before. Shoppers are taking advantage of an array of screens and touch points, and purchases are no longer being made in the consistent, linear fashion that they used to. In response, companies are attempting to adopt an "omnichannel" approach to their marketing. Omnichannel marketing refers to a business providing a consistent message to consumers across any online device or offline interaction with the brand. It seeks to provide the customer with a seamless shopping experience, regardless of the point of contact with the brand.

Most businesses today are using multichannel marketing as a stepping-stone to their goal of becoming omnichannel. They have a mobile-optimized website, social media accounts, a mobile advertising campaign, video marketing, an e-commerce site, customer service reps, in-store sales associates, and more ways to interact with consumers. But they are handled by different people and different departments, each with their own KPIs and often inconsistent strategies. The business may have fantastic mobile and other marketing elements, but if they do not work together with the same message and with the same goals, it is not legitimately an omnichannel approach.

That's why more and more marketers are seeking to partner with publishers that can provide cross-channel marketing buys for their advertising. While technically also multichannel marketing, cross-channel marketing goes one step further by providing cohesive and seamless marketing strategies across different channels. Same person, same message, different mediums. An example of a cross-channel advertising buy is TMZ, which can provide television commercials in the show itself and in-app advertising for the same brand, both providing the same message.

Almost two-thirds of businesses are using at least nine channels to interact with customers, so it is easy to see just how complex a cross-channel approach can be to implement.[69] Effective analysis and action requires some way to integrate internally generated small data, also called first-party data, and externally purchased third-party big data into the mix. Small data is typically cookie or login data that has been generated from direct interactions with the customers. Big data is a modern marketing buzzword for large and complex sets of data that are impossible to manage without some highly responsive management and analysis tools. Big data is absolutely vital, however, to execute a frictionless cross-device strategy, where the brand is able to say, "I know you are the same person regardless of which device you are using."

Some combinations of cross-channel marketing work better than others. The five most popular pairings, in order, are: desktop–mobile; TV–mobile; desktop–TV; radio–mobile; desktop–radio. Video makes a lot of sense for cross-channel marketing, because a 30-second commercial can be shown on television and a 15-second, short-format commercial with similar content can be played on mobile. Seamless and integrated.

Omnichannel marketing is the next level of multichannel and cross-channel marketing strategies. Omnichannel marketing is about marketing across different channels, where the greatest success comes from creating cohesive cross-channel marketing strategies. This seamless approach to marketing across various channels guides potential customers towards engagement and moves them down the sales funnel.

When it comes to an omnichannel approach, Starbucks is a company that clearly gets it. Starbucks has physical rewards cards for those people who like carrying plastic when getting their coffee fix. The plastic rewards cards are integrated with the Starbucks app, which also keeps track of an individual customer's loyalty points. Cards can be reloaded in the app, on the website, via phone call, or in the store. Promotional messages seen in the app are the same as the point-of-purchase messages that can be seen in the store. Starbucks is omnichannel across its entire marketing strategy.

In an ideal world, a business would be able to track a user across all channels like this. Let's say Lloyd Braun wanted to buy a great book about mobile marketing. After doing a Google search on a desktop, Lloyd finds the book on the author's company website. This is known as a touch point, because it is a time that the brand has engaged directly with the customer. Lloyd reads about the book on the website, but decides to go to Amazon to see if there are better books on the subject. Lloyd then goes to his Facebook page on his tablet and sees an ad from the company selling the book. This time, he taps through and decides to buy it, only to have his battery run out. So he switches to his smartphone and goes to Facebook and there it is again. He's been retargeted. He finally gets to make the purchase.

The reason that the book was able to be sold is because the company knew where to find Lloyd across all of his devices. In the past, a consumer's multiple touch points were not effectively linked. Therefore, marketers did not have the ability to receive a message on one channel and take that intelligence over to another channel where Lloyd was also engaged. Today, however, by combining company data, big data, and marketing automation tools, a business can provide a holistic view of all of Lloyd's activity on multiple devices and through varied touch points.

In reality, although strategies are improving, mobile consumer data remains notably difficult to mine. Cross-channel metrics are difficult to discern because consumers have multiple devices at home and at work. They have social media accounts with different handles and different usernames. They have multiple e-mail accounts, and some even carry two smartphones. In some cases, multiple family members or coworkers further confound the picture because they share devices. This leaves most marketers flush with data but lacking of any real insight. While big data to track consumers like Lloyd across multiple touch points is improving, omnichannel marketing still suffers from a lack of consistent data across multiple devices and engagements that can occur both in and out of stores. Even if the company uses a data management platform, it has difficulty connecting the dots for a single consumer as he makes his way through the path to purchase because of the enormous amount of devices to track. Often, those devices are using mediums like apps, where tracking is difficult due to a lack of cookies. Add to that the offline connections that are made and it is a mass ball of confusion for marketing executives.

To truly implement an omnichannel approach, data needs to be unified to a single customer across the many silos that marketers are tracking. It becomes difficult to find a cohesive approach, because online advertising uses cookies, mobile uses a combination of cookies and other identifiers, and offline activities use customer names, phone numbers, home addresses, and e-mail addresses. Businesses need to have a data strategy in place to attempt to get started in providing a seamless and consistent consumer experience from beginning to end. Because information is being gathered from multiple sources, integrating that data is the difficult part as the purchase journey continues to become more complicated. Although not easy to make it fully functional, an omnichannel marketing approach should be the goal of all sophisticated marketers.

MEASURING LIFETIME VALUE

If marketing is being measured, it should always be improving. In today's environment, however, measuring the effectiveness of various mediums is not so easy, because each contributes to some degree to the consumer making a final purchase. With a true omnichannel approach, a brand is leading the customer down the path to purchase through multiple touch points until that customer makes a purchase. That makes tracking the value of each individual element in a cross-channel marketing approach difficult to quantify. A marketer needs to know what is working—and what is not working, as well—in regards to the end-game sale.

Let's assume that Sue Ellen Mischke has downloaded a brand's app on her Android smartphone. She checks out a product on the app and then goes to the nearest retail store to buy it because she does not want to wait or pay for shipping. To the unsavvy marketer, the retail store deserves all the credit, but Sue Ellen first found out about the product in the app. Doesn't the app deserve some credit for creating that sale? If Sue Ellen had not downloaded the app, she may never have even known about the product in the first place.

Here's another example. Sid Farkus is on his laptop, sees a digital ad on the *New York Times* website for a new massage chair, and he puts the item in his cart. Then, he has second thoughts about making such a silly purchase and abandons the item in the cart. Luckily for the brand, it is using an omnichannel approach and begins its retargeting campaign. A week later, on a particularly stressful day, Sid is on his smartphone browsing his Facebook account. He is served a retargeting ad showing the massage chair, and he buys it. Where is credit for that sale given, to the initial interaction on the laptop from an advertisement purchased on the *New York Times* or to the retargeting ad on social media? Is there some kind of shared credit given? These are perplexing problems for marketers even if they are able to tie the initial touch point to the final action.

The most important thing to learn is that multiple touch points contribute to the ultimate sale, and credit needs to be assigned to each in determining the LTV of the customer. Marketers need to connect the dots between the app download and the purchase made in the store when making this designation. In the case of Sid, the value of the app install to the business could end up being much greater than originally anticipated, since the sale was not recorded in-app, but it was a primary reason the sale was made.

The end game in determining the value of the app, or any other element in a cross-channel approach, needs to compare the cost of the development, maintenance, and promotion versus the LTV of acquiring that customer. You cannot simply compare the initial sale against the cost of acquisition, since theoretically that same customer will be back in the future to make additional purchases. Projecting future business is difficult, so start with some historic assumptions and then evaluate each marketing element to determine the true LTV of the customer acquisition. Put simply, in the case of the app: if the LTV of the customer exceeds the cost per install, then the marketer is doing something right.

DRIVING SALES IN RETAIL STORES

With all of the opportunities available to consumers to purchase online, it is a wonder that there are still retail brick-and-mortar stores out there. But the fact is that over 90 percent of all purchases still occur in a retail store.[70]

Retail stores are not going away anytime soon, but the way that they interact with consumers is clearly changing. While the vast majority of sales still occur in brick-and-mortar stores, the decision to purchase increasingly flows through smartphones—about a quarter of all sales are influenced by what happens on a smartphone prior to visiting the store.[71]

Marketers must leverage the constant connectivity of consumers, and the geolocation capabilities of their mobile phones, to send relevant messages to targeted users. If brands eschew using mobile to contact customers, they run the risk of losing those customers to competing online stores and turning their retail stores into nothing more than showrooming locations.

One advantage that retail locations have is that employees can directly interact with customers that are walking into the store for the first time. Retail associates can tell a lot more about those customers than an online store can. Certainly, the personal touch from a qualified sales associate is a key aspect (touch point) of keeping that purchase in the brick-and-mortar store and not allowing it to go online. People want to purchase from local stores, help the local economy, and create jobs, so if they get extraordinary service, they will likely buy there.

Beacons

Beacons are an element that really capitalizes on the convergence that makes up SoLoMo. A beacon is a pretty simple thing. It is a small sticker-like item that broadcasts a Bluetooth signal and recognizes when a mobile device is nearby. Consumers that have Bluetooth turned on, have downloaded a mobile app, and have granted permission to be reached will get messages when within a particular radius of the beacon. They work in concert with specific campaigns to enable the app to identify points of interest and point the consumer to specific content. When used properly, beacons can become very valuable tools, especially for retail stores, because they do such a powerful job of providing in-store engagement. Beacons, when coupled with a store app, provide an avenue for retail stores to effectively communicate the right thing to the right person at the right time.

But beacon technology is just technology without a strong marketing plan that includes a clearly defined set of goals. In fact, the device itself isn't anything more than Bluetooth technology; it is the marketing message and strategy behind it that matters. Moreover, shoppers need to embrace several layers of permission-based marketing (Bluetooth, app download, push message permission) to receive messages. And when done, it is important that brands and retailers avoid the creepy factor that comes with in-store promotions that border on stalking in the consumer's mind.

Beacons are not just about a location strategy in a retail store or offering a mobile coupon when a shopper is near a particular product. In fact, offering a discount might just cost the store money if the consumer was going to make a purchase anyway. Instead, offering shopping assistance may be more highly valued than promotions. For example, if a customer is near the Rapid Peeler kitchen gadget display, an engaging video could be sent from the beacon that explains how the item works.

Macy's, Lord & Taylor, and Hudson Bay Company are examples of retail department stores that are using beacon technology. Macy's partnered with location-based coupon company ShopKick for its beacon program. At these stores, when a customer enters the store, she might receive a valuable coupon. Or when the customer is in a particular section, she might receive a demo video of uses for a product. Most importantly, for the store at least, it can track a customer's movement within the store itself, which can provide excellent data for the retailer.

Showrooming

It's frustrating for retailers. A consumer comes to the retail store for a hands-on approach to finding the product that works best for him. He interacts with the store personnel. Then, when the choice is made, he scans the product barcode with an app such as Red Laser or Amazon Price Check to find the best price online and makes his purchase online. This is known as showrooming. With showrooming, a brick-and-mortar store becomes an unpaid showroom for consumers to sample and evaluate products firsthand, only to make a virtual purchase from a competitor. Without a strategy to combat showrooming, a retailer will see inevitable declines in sales.

Some brick-and-mortars are more prone to showrooming than others. Those with unique brands and private labels are less likely to be severely affected because online price comparisons are nearly impossible. At the same time, discount brick-and-mortars, such as dollar stores, are also less likely to be adversely affected because their products are already inexpensive and their customer base not common users of modern smartphone technology.

The biggest threat to brick-and-mortar stores is the king of online selling, Amazon. Much to the frustration of retailers, Amazon has boldly and actively encouraged shoppers to showroom. Its mobile

288 | Bob Bentz

app, Amazon Price Check, has supported barcode scanning since 2010. In an effort to combat brick-and-mortars' common practice of matching online prices, Amazon has offered up to an additional 5 percent reduction for consumers that use the Price Check feature while in-store showrooming. So even if a brick-and-mortar matches the Amazon price, the online retailer is going to one-up it.

Amazon recently took showrooming to a new level when it began offering image recognition with its Flow feature. With image recognition, a customer can simply take a picture of a product and Amazon Flow can recognize it by a logo, artwork, or another unique visual feature. This makes showrooming even easier and eliminates the minor inconvenience of finding a barcode and scanning it. With image recognition, the savvy showrooming customer can take a picture without ever removing the item from the shelf and find a competing price at Amazon. Consumers that are active showroomers want to save money, and about half of them are already members of Amazon Prime. With Amazon Prime, members often get a cheaper price online, no sales tax, and free shipping to boot. What's a retailer to do?

Retailers are unlikely to be able to go toe-to-toe with Amazon, so they need to change the buying experience in stores. They must get with the program and embrace mobile use by customers while in-store, because showrooming is not going away. Mobile does not have to be a threat to brick-and-mortar stores, but a complement.

It makes sense to offer in-store Wi-Fi if the brick-and-mortar has a solid anti-showrooming strategy. When the customer logs in while in the store, it is obvious why they are doing so, and the store can then provide additional incentives for making a purchase in the store itself. The consumer also will not think that the retailer is hiding anything by giving them easy access to all of their potential purchasing options.

With mobile, retail clerks do not need to even have a sales counter. Apple stores do not have them. Rather, sales associates are fitted with tablets with mobile POS data anywhere in the store. This enables them to be freed from the sales counter and out interacting with the customer, providing a value-added service as knowledgeable shopping assistants. When the customer finds the perfect item, the associate is able to check inventory and place orders without leaving the customer's side. Take a clothing retail associate in a department store, for example. The retail associate can help the customer create an outfit by mixing and matching from different brands sold by the store. Such personal service, and the corresponding difficulty in shopping online for the different brands, makes showrooming significantly less likely to occur. A consulted sales associate is the number one thing that will compel a showrooming customer to make a purchase in-store instead of online. A brand can take advantage of that in-store knowledge by offering an appointment to be set online for an in-store consultation.

A solid social media strategy is another way that a brick-and-mortar store can combat showrooming. Consumers usually begin the journey to purchase online, and if that is where the influencers are, then that is where the brick-and-mortar store needs to be too. Retail store brands need to access the review sites, blogs, and industry sites where consumers are researching and formulating their plans. If they do not reach the consumers early in the path to purchase, it is going to be far more difficult to change their opinions on where to buy later. This goes back to social CRM discussed earlier.

Another way to combat showrooming is with a strong loyalty program. Reaching a certain threshold of points is a great incentive to keep consumers buying from a brick-and-mortar. Retailers need to be consistently reminding customers of their loyalty program and giving updates on point totals by prominently displaying them whenever possible. It certainly helps to update the customer on his loyalty points with a push notification when he first enters the store. Everybody wants to get something for free, and reminding the customer of his loyalty point totals is one way to engage them and encourage them to purchase more today.

Most people like to keep money in their immediate area to help spur the local economy. Showroomers are no different, but they need to be reminded about the benefits of buying from a physical store as opposed to Amazon or another online store. The recently conceived Small Business Saturdays do just that—build the local economy.

Consumers using their mobile phones in a store are actually more likely to buy there than online. Sixty percent of showroomers end up buying at the retail store in which they are doing the price checking.[72] But they do insist on getting the best price. Unfortunately for the brick-and-mortar store, that means a price match guarantee policy is its last resort against competing with online conglomerates and niche stores. A brick-and-mortar store that price matches to online will surely get the sale, since the consumer is already in the store and does not want to pay for shipping or wait for the item to arrive.

Webrooming

Webrooming, remote showrooming, or reverse showrooming is the opposite of showrooming. With webrooming, the customer uses online research to find the best price in advance of going to the brick-and-mortar. They then ask the retailer for the same best price that they found online. Webrooming is actually more common than showrooming, according to a Harris poll.[73] While most brick-and-mortars see showrooming as a threat, they have embraced webrooming.

There is good reason for brick-and-mortars to embrace webrooming. In many cases, the convenience of e-commerce really is not worth it to all shoppers. Many consumers still want the hands-on intimacy that only a brick-and-mortar can provide. There is also the added advantage of not having to pay for shipping, not waiting for delivery, and having the ability to return the item to the store and avoid the potential hassle of boxing and shipping it back.

First and foremost, a retailer with an in-store and online presence needs to have the same inventory available in both places. Nothing is going to disappoint the online customer more than when she comes into the store only to find that the product of interest is only available online. If the brick-and-mortar store is out of a product, it needs to arrange to have the product shipped to the consumer in the same convenient fashion that the consumer would enjoy if she had ordered the product online in the first place.

Another way a brick-and-mortar store can capitalize on webrooming is to offer in-store pickup for an online purchase. Consumers are impatient; they want things now. By offering in-store pickup, the retailer offers immediacy and eliminates shipping costs. An added benefit can be offering ancillary products in-store when they come to pick up. If she bought a sweater online and goes to pick it up, the salesperson could suggest a matching scarf or jewelry as an upsell.

Offering online coupons for in-store purchases is another method of bringing customers to the store. It also may enable the retailer to bridge the gap between the higher costs it naturally incurs in a brick-and-mortar store.

Mobile Payments

Mobile payments in North America continue to lag in comparison to other countries, especially Europe. Mobile payments are often referred to as proximity mobile payments, where customers can pay for a product or service via tapping or waving their mobile phone over a proximity payment mechanism.

The major players in the proximity payment industry are mobile wallets such as Apple Pay, Android Pay, and Samsung Pay. Each uses near field communications (NFC) technology, which allows two devices placed closely together to exchange data. In order for this to work, both devices must be equipped with an NFC chip. With each of the mobile wallet systems mentioned, merchants need to adopt POS systems that can accept mobile wallet payments. Adoption by major merchants remains a barrier to use.

As with most new innovations, younger consumers have less apprehension when it comes to making mobile payments, whereas security concerns remain a pronounced concern among older customers. One of the things that mobile payment providers are going to need to continue to enhance is the security system that monitors such transactions. A proven track record will cause more people of all ages to get involved with mobile payments.

Currently, the vast majority of payments using mobile wallets are for goods priced below $20.[74] Perhaps that is because restaurants, such as McDonald's and Panera, are well-known users of proximity mobile payments, or that users are reluctant to pay for more expensive goods with mobile wallets.

People carry their smartphones everywhere they go. In addition to being their primary device for listening to music, taking pictures, and accessing the Internet, the smartphone can now also be their wallet. Is there really a need for having all those plastic cards in a wallet when the mobile phone can pay for things? Digital wallets and mobile payments just make sense, and their added convenience and increased security will ultimately lead to greater use. Mobile payment mechanisms will ultimately be seen as being more secure as well. A consumer's credit card information is likely stored at over a hundred businesses, from the local supermarket to the dentist to e-commerce sites. That makes credit card data extremely vulnerable. Think of all the businesses that have been hacked recently. Think of all the times your credit card information has already been stolen.

Digital wallets do not provide this same reusable credit card information to businesses because they use tokenization. Tokenization is the process of substituting a sensitive data element, such as a credit card number, with a non-sensitive equivalent, referred to as a token, which has no exploitable value if it falls into the wrong hands.

The smartphone itself also provides added protection that makes mobile payments more secure than credit card payments, at least if all of its tools are used. One of those tools is biometric authentication, which is a fancy name for accessing a smartphone with a fingerprint scan. This protects a user's phone and its ability to make fraudulent transactions, even if it is lost or stolen.

Retailers, who have long loathed paying transaction fees for accepting credit cards, have recently gotten involved with mobile payments. Walmart Pay was introduced in 2016 in its stores. It enables its more than 22 million Walmart App users to pay for products in-store while using the app. For Walmart, its mobile payment app allows it to take on Apple Pay, Android Pay, and banking payment systems, and it saves on transaction fees to boot.

There is one business that, until recently, hated mobile wallets—banks. Banks are being cut out of the mobile payment process now that payments are transacted through mobile apps administered by digital merchants. Naturally, banks are interested in protecting what was once their exclusive credit card revenue. One recent entry into the mobile payment fray is Capital One Wallet, which lets Android users tap their phones on terminals to make payments.[75] Since consumers are already comfortable with mobile banking apps, some may be more apt to use the mobile payment mechanism provided by their bank than by their carrier.

That's also the thought behind Chase Pay, which will debut in 2016. It will use its substantial credit card customer base to introduce its new mobile payment solution. Chase has nearly 100 million customers in the USA, and all of those with smartphones will be eligible to use Chase Pay. Chase's greatest advantage is that it is not tied to any smartphone manufacturer and therefore will function on all operating systems. In addition, Chase will not use any registration process for the service; all of its customers will be automatically signed up if they own a smartphone.

Chase also believes that making mobile payments convenient for retailers is an important part of the equation, and it has specifically targeted gasoline and convenience stores as participating retail locations. It will use older QR code technology to facilitate transactions at checkout rather than the NFC approach used by Apple Pay and Capital One Wallet. This means that the retailer does not require the latest generation of payment terminals that are needed for NFC-based payment solutions. Moreover, as opposed to Capital One Wallet, Chase Pay won't be tied to any particular operating system and will therefore work on both Apple and Android. An added bonus is that mobile users will be able to earn reward points on their credit cards. Chase has high hopes for its mobile payment solution and has set a goal to have 47 million of its 94 million credit card owners using it. If accomplished, it will bring mobile payments into the mainstream with its convenient payment mechanism.[76]

KEY FACTORS TO DRIVING E-COMMERCE ONLINE AND OFFLINE

We live in a world that went digital a long time ago and has gone mobile more recently. Remember the days when a person was actually afraid to enter his credit card online or on his smartphone? This is certainly no longer a concern, and people today routinely do it for paying bills or stocking up on razor blades. What consumers are asking for, however, is a seamless experience that begins with a search and ends with a purchase, either online or in-store. Marketers that can provide the best omnichannel approach on the path to purchase are going to be the ones that win in mobile.

Cross-device, omnichannel marketing always begins with some form of content, whether that is a mobile e-mail, SMS, mobile advertisement, or online review. All can be effective, since consumers continue to crave shopping information on their smartphones. In fact, 91 percent of shoppers have used their smartphone to read information from a retailer in the last four weeks. A surprising 89 percent of shoppers are willing to provide retailers with personal information if the retailer will maintain the highest standards of privacy and if it will help their shopping experience, according to Kelton Global.[77] Shoppers today will not hesitate to provide their personal information in exchange for being provided with better-targeted promotional content. Relevance raises response.

Want to learn more about mobile commerce?
See updated statistics and other important information
at RelevanceRaisesResponse.com.

Chapter 9

THE FUTURE OF MOBILE

Relevance raises response.

SO WHERE IS IT ALL GOING?

*I*t wasn't long ago that users were loving the fact that they could play Snake on their mobile phone, and sending a text message with LOL in it was the ultimate coolest thing ever. Today, the lightning speed of mobile adoption in every aspect of our lives has changed marketing, and our lives, forever. So let's look into the Magic Mobile Ball and see what the future holds.

SEARCH

Search, as we know it today, means entering a keyword and obtaining results back on your desktop or mobile device. Siri and OK Google voice search have moved that process into voice recognition to initiate a search. Expect Google's next move to include improved voice recognition in smart cars where drivers can't type.

The proliferation of apps poses a serious challenge to Google and all other search engines because they have not been able to easily index the content that is inside of apps. This is a major problem for Google, because the future of mobile search is in apps. In December of 2015, Google announced it would begin providing in-app search results on its SERPs. Expect the ability to search within apps to be an increasingly important factor in search.

THE INTERNET OF THINGS

The Internet of Things (IoT) is the integration of physical things that we use in our everyday lives to the Internet network. It is already commonly integrated in the smart house, where homeowners can turn the lights on and off and adjust the temperature from the convenience of their mobile devices. The Internet of Things will continue to expand in all industries, from farming to power generation.

The Connected Car

An extension of the Internet of Things is the connected car, and it is already at a dealership near you. The connected car allows you to connect to the outside world and enhance the in-car experience while driving your car using Internet connectivity. This includes on-board diagnostics, infotainment, and embedded tablets. With the connected car, a user can locate her automobile in the parking lot of a crowded mall, activate the climate controls prior to entering the car, and automatically report an accident involving the car.

VIRTUAL REALITY AND AUGMENTED REALITY

Virtual reality and augmented reality have been around for a while now, but they are really here now with the introduction of Google Cardboard. Google Cardboard offers the ability to superimpose a computer-generated view of a user's real world to create a new and unique vision using just a smartphone and the lenses provided by Google Cardboard. Compared to Google Glass, which retailed for $1,500, Google Cardboard, unveiled in June of 2014, is a much more affordable ($25) cardboard version. The user inserts a smartphone behind the lens and then uses an app to experience the video images. The low price point and easy distribution of Google Cardboard makes it a potential game changer for advertisers and brands.

MONITORED HEALTH

Mobile devices have a chance to save lives. Imagine the next generation of the Fitbit and wearables that will be able to monitor your heart rate and predict an impending heart attack or stroke.

SMARTER ADVERTISING

Mobile brings a powerful array of laser-targeting features that were not available at any time in the past. But, to date, advertisers have not been able to take full advantage of them. That is all going to change as marketers continue to become more sophisticated in their ability to manipulate big data and target specific users with even more advanced location-based services.

One recent change that will help with omnichannel marketing is AT&T's announcement of NumberSync. It will allow a customer's smartphone, tablet, and other devices to share a single phone number. That is certainly going to make it easier to provide an omnichannel marketing approach.

VIDEO

People are inherently lazy, and they aren't going to read if they can be entertained with a video. More and more brands, both large and small, will expand their video capabilities to offer more engaging advertising that goes far beyond the traditional banner ad. This will be driven in part by faster 5G services that will enable videos to load faster and easier.

MULTISCREENING

People don't just watch TV anymore; they watch TV while multitasking with other media. This makes multiscreening either a distraction for maintaining viewer attention or a pathway for creating greater engagement.

TV programs are going to find better ways to integrate multiscreening than just voting on *American Idol*. Viewers are going to be able to choose the outcomes of episodes or vote on who should hook up on *The Bachelor*. But it will be TV advertisers that lead the way with the most innovative multiscreening opportunities. Viewership of TV ads is way down, and the industry is too innovative to continue to let that wane.

Mobile and television are going to become closer bedfellows through joint ventures and possibly even mergers or acquisitions.

Along with big-data providers, the mergers will enable an advertising powerhouse by sending advertisements to smartphones and tablets simultaneous with the viewing of television commercials.

THINK MOBILE, ACT LOCAL

There has never been a better medium for small businesses than mobile advertising. It enables the small business to advertise only in its immediate trading area, thus making it the most efficient advertising tool ever. Expect more small businesses to jump on board the mobile train. Print and radio are increasingly fragmented and lack geotargeting abilities.

Think mobile first. Your customer already does.

MOBILE WALLETS

The idea of using a mobile phone to pay just makes sense. It is far safer than credit cards, and the user doesn't have to worry about losing them or her account getting hacked.

More businesses will enter the mobile wallet battle. Expect retailers to offer their own direct mobile payment solutions to engage their most loyal users. Those payment mechanisms won't only be in the mobile phone; they'll also be embedded on key fobs and loyalty cards.

The ultimate winner in the mobile wallet game is not going to be Apple Pay or Android Pay. It's going to be the bank's mobile wallet offering, because it will be seamlessly integrated into a customer's existing mobile banking efforts.

RELEVANCE RAISES RESPONSE

Marketing is an ongoing contest for people's attention, and mobile provides the mechanism that, in the history of promotion, is the closest a brand has ever been able to get to its customer. With mobile, customers can act on any message at any time, no matter where they are. They can take immediate action to research, find, or buy something. When a consumer can act in the moment, his expectations are high and his patience is low. That makes the credibility and relevance of the mobile message of the utmost importance. Ultimately, brands that do the best job of engaging consumers with a relevant mobile message will win.

As a modern marketer, every digital strategy made today should be thinking tap first and click second. It's the only way for a brand to live "in the moment." Perhaps 2010 was indeed the year of mobile. Who really knows? Whatever year it was, today we are clearly no longer living in the year of mobile.

We are living in the age of mobile.

Remember, you can keep up with the latest trends on mobile marketing at this book's website, RelevanceRaisesResponse.com.

ENDNOTES

1. Statista, "Statistics and Facts about Social Networks," 2015, http://www.statista.com/topics/1164/social-networks/.

2. Everett Rosenfield, "Facebook Quarterly Results Beat on Most Metrics," CNBC, July 29, 2015, http://www.cnbc.com/2015/07/29/facebook-earnings-50-cents-per-share-vs-expected-eps-of-47-cents.html.

3. Jerry Dischler, "Building for the Next Moment," Google: Inside AdWords, May 5, 2015, http://adwords.blogspot.com/2015/05/building-for-next-moment.html.

4. Mary Meeker and Liang Wu, "2013 Internet Trends," Internet Trends D11 Conference, May 29, 2013, Slideshow, http://www.kpcb.com/blog/2013-internet-trends.

5. International Telecommunication Union, Statistics, https://www.itu.int/en/ITU-D/Statistics/Pages/stat/default.aspx.

6. Stephen J. Blumberg and Julian V. Luke, "Wireless Substitution: Early Release of Estimates from the National Health Interview Survey, July–December 2013," National Center for Health Statistics, July 2014, http://www.cdc.gov/nchs/data/nhis/earlyrelease/wireless201407.pdf.

7. Rick Pantaleo, "The Cell Phone Turns 40," *Voice of America*, April 3, 2013, http://www.voanews.com/content/cell-phone-turns-40/1634074.html.

8. eMarketer, "Consumers Get Engaged with Rich Media," October 23, 2014, http://www.emarketer.com/Article/Consumers-Engaged-with-Rich-Media/1011282.

9. Bob Bentz, results of ATS Mobile mobile campaign designed for Subway.

10. Google employee, speech given at the Search Engine Strategies Convention, New York City, April 2, 2014.

11. Aaron Smith, "U.S. Smartphone Use in 2015," Pew Research Center, April 1, 2015, http://www.pewinternet.org/2015/04/01/us-smartphone-use-in-2015/.

12. xAd, "Mobile Path to Purchase," 2015, http://www.mobilepathtopurchase.com/wp-content/uploads/2015/11/Mobile_Path_to_Purchase_2015.pdf.

13. Internet Society, "Global Internet Report 2015," 2015, http://www.internetsociety.org/globalinternetreport/assets/download/IS_web.pdf.

14. Miranda Miller, "72% of Consumers Want Mobile-Friendly Sites: Google Research," Search Engine Watch, September 26, 2012. http://searchenginewatch.com/sew/study/2208496/72-of-consumers-want-mobilefriendly-sites-google-research#.

15. Jerry Dischler, "Building for the Next Moment," Google: Inside AdWords, May 5, 2015, http://adwords.blogspot.com/2015/05/building-for-next-moment.html.

16. Greg Jarboe. "Google Searches with 'Near Me' Surged 34 Times since 2011," Search Engine Watch, April 15, 2015. http://searchenginewatch.com/sew/news/2404050/google-searches-with-near-me-surged-34-times-since-2011.

17. Zachary Davies Boren, "There Are Officially More Mobile Devices than People in the World," *Independent*, October 7, 2014, http://www.independent.co.uk/life-style/gadgets-and-

tech/news/there-are-officially-more-mobile-devices-than-people-in-the-world-9780518.html.

18. "International Smartphone Mobility Report, Jan. '15," Informate, March 2015, http://informatemi.com/blog/?p=133.

19. Becky Bushnell and David McKnight, "Mobile Interactive Messaging: The next Big Thing in Association Marketing?" VantagePoint, Winter 2013, http://www.ercsms.com/wp-content /uploads/2013/01/VP-Mag-SMS-Article-only.pdf.

20. Silverpop, "2013 Email Marketing Metrics Benchmark Study: An Analysis of Messages Sent Q1-Q4, 2012," IBM, 2013, http://www.silverpop.com/Documents/Whitepapers/2013/WP_ EmailMarketingMetricsBenchmarkStudy2013.pdf.

21. Cinzia Cecchetto, "Five Metrics to Assess the Effectiveness of SMS Marketing," Oxygen8, http://www.oxygen8.com/uk/five-metrics-to-assess-the-effectiveness-of-sms-marketing/.

22. Electronic Code of Federal Regulations, Title 47, Chapter I, Subchapter B, Part 64, Subpart L, §64.1200, http://www.ecfr. gov/cgi-bin/text-idx?SID=1a87132685d9f86900858503d1d3a b9e&mc=true&node=se47.3.64_11200&rgn=div8.

23. "Dunkin' Donuts SMS Text Message Campaign," Successful Startup 101, January 7, 2016, http://www.successfulstartup101. com/dunkin-donuts-sms-text-message-campaign/.

24. Bob Bentz, results of ATS Mobile mobile campaign.

25. Pew Research Center, "Social Networking Fact Sheet," accessed January 20, 2016, http://www.pewinternet.org/fact-sheets/social-networking-fact-sheet/.

26. Thorin McGee, "Daymond John: The Shark on Marketing," *Target Marketing*, September 1, 2015, http://www. targetmarketingmag.com/article/daymond-john-the-shark-on-marketing/.

27. Olivia Parkes, "Facebook Trend Forecast: 2015-2016," Mini Me

Marketing, September 9, 2015, http://www.minimemarketing. co.uk/tag/facebook-marketing/.

28. Giselle Tsirulnik, "Adding Facebook Like to Mobile Site Can Boost Sales: Steve Madden," *Mobile Marketer*, September 28, 2010, http://www.mobilemarketer.com/cms/news/social-networks/7519.html.

29. Pinterest for Business, "Rich Pins," accessed January 20, 2016, https://business.pinterest.com/en/rich-pins.

30. Google and Nielsen, "Mobile Path to Purchase: Five Key Findings," Google Think Insights, November 2013, https://ssl.gstatic.com/think/docs/mobile-path-to-purchase-5-key-findings_research-studies.pdf.

31. Abhinav Gulyani, "Extensive List of Mobile Ad Network Companies," *No B.S.: Kick Ass Online Marketing for Smart People*, September 27, 2014, http://gulyani.com/complete-list-of-mobile-ad-networks-companies/.

32. Cisco, "Visual Networking Index: Forecast and Methodology, 2014-2019 White Paper," May 27, 2015, http://www.cisco.com/c/en/us/solutions/collateral/service-provider/ip-ngn-ip-next-generation-network/white_paper_c11-481360.html.

33. Sheryl Sandberg, Facebook Q1 2015 earnings call, transcript at http://files.shareholder.com/downloads/AMDA-NJ5DZ/0x0x823326/a88e8ecf-8532-4f35-b251-4f95c2a4c6b3/FB_Q12015_Transcript.pdf.

34. Garett Sloane, "Facebook's Carousel Ads Are 10 Times Better than Its Regular Ads," *Digiday*, October 19, 2015, http://digiday.com/platforms/facebooks-carousel-ads-10-times-better-regular-ads/.

35. Instagram for Business, "Instagram: Open to Business of All Sizes, Everywhere," Instagram, September 2015, http://blog.business.instagram.com/post/128686033016/150909-advertisinglaunch.

36. Nate Elliott, "Instagram is the King of Social Media Engagement," *Forrester*, Nate Elliot's blog, April 29, 2014, http://blogs.forrester.com/nate_elliott/14-04-29-instagram_is_the_king_of_social_engagement.

37. Danny Wong, "In Q4, Social Media Drove 31.24% of Traffic to Sites," *Shareaholic*, January 26, 2015, https://blog.shareaholic.com/social-media-traffic-trends-01-2015/.

38. Mark Hayes, "How Pinterest Drives Online Sales," Shopify, https://www.shopify.com/blog/6058268-how-pinterest-drives-ecommerce-sales.

39. Pinterest for Business, "Promoted Pins: Reach Your Audience and All Your Marketing Goals," Pinterest, https://business.pinterest.com/en/promoted-pins.

40. Justin Lafferty, "How Many Pages Does the Average Facebook User Like?" *Ad Week*, April 11, 2013. http://www.adweek.com/socialtimes/how-many-pages-does-the-average-facebook-user-like/418322.

41. *Business Insider*, "How Mobile Coupons Are Driving an Explosion in Mobile Commerce," June 3, 2013, http://www.businessinsider.com/mobile-coupons-driving-mobile-commerce-2013-5.

42. Consumer Electronics Association, *Video Content Discovery and Purchasing Trends*, Consumer Technology Association, 2014, http://www.cta.tech/News/News-Releases/Press-Releases/2014/Digital-Video-Content-Is-a-Supplement,-Not-Replace.aspx.

43. Microsoft Devices Team, "10 Things You Didn't Know About Mobile Gaming," Windows, January 16, 2013, https://blogs.windows.com/devices/2013/01/16/10-things-you-didnt-know-about-mobile-gaming-2/.

44. Lax Friedman, "The App Store Turns Five: A Look Back and Forward," *Macworld*, July 8, 2013, http://www.macworld.com/

article/2043841/the-app-store-turns-five-a-look-back-and-forward.html.

45. Hakunamatata, "A Quick Look: Mobile Application Distribution," December 20, 2013. http://www.hakunamatata.in/blog/general/A_Quick_Look_Mobile_Application_distribution.

46. Brian Patrick Eha, "The Dominance of 'Angry Birds': From Startup to Animated Series," March 14, 2013, http://www.entrepreneur.com/article/226107.

47. Nick T., "Angry Birds 2 Review: A Fresh Take on a Winning Formula," Phone Arena, July 30, 2015, http://www.phonearena.com/news/Angry-Birds-2-Review-a-fresh-new-take-on-a-winning-formula_id72129.

48. Leena Rao, "Users Will Download 44 Billion Mobile Apps by 2016," TechCrunch, April 28, 2011, http://techcrunch.com/2011/04/28/users-will-download-44-billion-mobile-apps-by-2016/.

49. Greg Sterling, "Time with Mobile Apps Now Beats TV as Apps Become the New Networks," *Marketing Land*, September 16, 2015, http://marketingland.com/time-with-mobile-apps-now-beats-tv-as-apps-become-the-new-networks-142780.

50. Sunil Gupta, "For Mobile Devices, Think Apps, Not Ads," *Harvard Business Review*, March 2013, https://hbr.org/2013/03/for-mobile-devices-think-apps-not-ads.

51. Flurry Insights, "The History of App Pricing, And Why Most Apps Are Free," July 18, 2013, http://flurrymobile.tumblr.com/post/115189750715/the-history-of-app-pricing-and-why-most-apps-are.

52. Christina Warren, "Zuckerberg's Biggest Mistake: Betting on HTML5," *Mashable*, September 11, 2012, http://mashable.com/2012/09/11/html5-biggest-mistake/#y8OJrXKhSGqU.

53. Drew Olanoff, "Mark Zuckerberg: Our Biggest Mistake Was Betting Too Much on HTML5," TechCrunch, September 11, 2012, http://techcrunch.com/2012/09/11/mark-zuckerberg-our-biggest-mistake-with-mobile-was-betting-too-much-on-html5/.

54. Matt Kapko, "Messaging App Usage, Retention Rates Dwarf All Other Apps," CIO, March 26, 2015, http://www.cio.com/article/2902399/mobile-apps/messaging-app-usage-retention-rates-dwarf-all-other-apps.html.

55. Ellis Hamburger, "Indie Smash Hit 'Flappy Bird' Racks Up $50K Per Day In Ad Revenue," The Verge, February 5, 2014, http://www.theverge.com/2014/2/5/5383708/flappy-bird-revenue-50-k-per-day-dong-nguyen-interview.

56. Localytics, "The 2015 App Marketing Guide: The Data Trends and Takeaways You Need to Consider in 2015," 2015, http://info.localytics.com/4l-2015-app-marketing-guide-mobile-data-trends-takeaways.

57. John Koetsier, "App Store Optimization: Money for Nothing, and Installs for Free," VentureBeat, November 20, 2015, http://insight.venturebeat.com/report/app-store-optimization-money-nothing-and-installs-free?utm_source=vb&utm_medium=boilerplate&utm_content=editorial-post&utm_campaign=app-store-optimization-report.

58. Nielsen, "So Many Apps, So Much Time for Entertainment," June 11, 2015, http://www.nielsen.com/us/en/insights/news/2015/so-many-apps-so-much-more-time-for-entertainment.html.

59. Localytics, "9 Things To Consider before, during and after Launching Your App," June 26, 2014, http://info.localytics.com/blog/9-things-to-consider-before-during-and-after-launching-your-app.

60. Kendall Briar, "Fiksu Indexes: Marketers Growing More Willing to Invest Upfront to Reach the Right People at the Right Time on Mobile," *Mobile Advertising Watch*, August 28, 2015, http://mobileadvertisingwatch.com/fiksu-indexes-marketers-growing-more-willing-to-invest-upfront-to-reach-the-right-people-at-right-time-on-mobile-19626.

61. Urban Airship, "The Good Push Index," 2015, https://marketing.adobe.com/resources/etc/commerce/products/exchange/urban_airship_engagementplatform/doc11425336491470/Good%20Push%20Index-%20How%20targeting%20boosts%20push%20messaging%20response%20rates_Final.pdf.

62. Dave Hoch, "6 Data-Driven Best Practices for Push Messaging Content," Localytics, November 6, 2014, http://info.localytics.com/blog/6-data-driven-best-practices-for-push-messaging-content.

63. Criteo, "State of Mobile Commerce, Q1 2015," March 2015, http://www.criteo.com/media/1896/criteo-state-of-mobile-commerce-q1-2015.pdf.

64. Forrester Media Center, "US Mobile and Tablet Commerce to Top $293B by 2018; Total Ecommerce to Hit $414B," May 12, 2014, https://www.forrester.com/US+Mobile+And+Tablet+Commerce+To+Top+293B+by+2018+Total+eCommerce+To+Hit+414B/-/E-PRE7004.

65. Criteo, "State of Mobile Commerce, Q1, 2015,"

66. Harvard Business Review Staff, "How People Really Use Mobile," *Harvard Business Review*, January–February 2013, https://hbr.org/2013/01/how-people-really-use-mobile.

67. xAd, "Mobile Path to Purchase."

68. Chris Newbery, "The Path to Purchase: Tracking the Consumer Journey," *Marketing Tech*, January 9, 2015, http://www.

marketingtechnews.net/news/2015/jan/09/path-purchase-tracking-consumer-journey/.

69. Aberdeen Group, "State of the CEM Market 2014: It's All About Better Use of Customer Data," March 2014, http://aberdeen.com/research/8867/ra-customer-experience-management/content.aspx.

70. A.T. Kearney, "On Solid Ground: Brick-and-Mortar Is the Foundation of Omnichannel Retailing," 2014, https://www.atkearney.com/documents/10192/4683364/On+Solid+Ground.pdf/f96d82ce-e40c-450d-97bb-884b017f4cd7.

71. Wurmser, Yory, et al., "Omnichannel Trends 2015: Mobile Is the New Retail Hub," eMarketer, December 2014, http://www.social4retail.com/uploads/1/0/9/8/10981970/emarketer_omnichannel_trends_2015-mobile_is_the_new_retail_hub.pdf.

72. Courtney Flaherty, "Deloitte Annual Holiday Survey: Smartphone Shoppers Help Make Retailers' Registers Jingle This Season," Deloitte, http://www2.deloitte.com/us/en/pages/about-deloitte/articles/press-releases/smartphone-shoppers-help-retailers-register-jingle.html#.

73. The Harris Poll, "Showrooming and Webrooming: A Tale of Two Trends," December 3, 2013, http://www.theharrispoll.com/business/Showrooming_and_Webrooming__A_Tale_of_Two_Trends.html.

74. Retail & E-commerce, "Mobile Payments Will Triple in the US in 2016," eMarketer, October 26, 2015, http://www.emarketer.com/Article/Mobile-Payments-Will-Triple-US-2016/1013147.

75. Olga Kharif, "Capital One Pushes into Mobile Payments with Android App," *Bloomberg Business*, October 14, 2015, http://www.bloomberg.com/news/articles/2015-10-14/capital-one-pushes-into-mobile-payments-with-android-app.

76. Brielle Jaekel, "Will Chase Dethrone Apple with Bank-Branded Mobile Payment Adoption?" *Mobile Commerce Daily*, October 28, 2015, http://www.mobilecommercedaily.com/will-chase-dethrone-apple-with-bank-branded-mobile-payment-adoption.

77. RetailMeNot, "The Impact of Mobile Marketing on Retailer Sales," October 2015, http://www.retailmenot.com/corp/static/filer_public/0e/e8/0ee82d9a-9706-4e9c-b0cb-8591ad07639b/rmn-wp-valueofmobilemarketing-web-120415.pdf.

ABOUT THE AUTHOR

ob Bentz is the president of Advanced Telecom Services, Inc., established in 1989, with offices in suburban Philadelphia, Toronto, London, and Prague. Bentz helped lead the team from a startup with no outside investment to a multinational company with $62.2 million in annual sales. Today, in addition to operating as the parent company Advanced Telecom Services, the company operates under the name ATS Mobile (its technology provider) and Purplegator (its agency and consulting solutions entity).

Consumer interactivity has been the common element in the four decades of the company's existence. Over the years, Bentz has seen the business continue to thrive while serving the same markets—advertisers, agencies, brands, and media. What has changed, however, is the medium in which the interactivity has been delivered. He has seen it evolve from the landline phone to the Internet and, most recently, to the mobile phone.

The author got his start in mobile in 2002. After visiting the company office in London, he learned about a cool new phenomenon going on in the United Kingdom called ringtones. Keep in mind that in 2002, Europe was three or four years ahead of North America in terms of mobile.

While the company had missed its opportunity in the UK market for ringtones, it vowed that it would not miss the opportunity in the

United States. So the company established two of the first ringtone sites in the United States—RingingPhone and MonsterTones. The ringtone business was ultimately sold to the publicly traded Zim Corporation.

After the sale, ATS was left with the knowledge, expertise, and technology to deliver information and entertainment to the mobile phone, so it decided to branch into offering mobile marketing solutions, specifically SMS text message marketing, through its 84444.com and 84444.ca (Canada) sites, which are still operational today. Today, the company provides all things mobile, from the most complex (app development) to the simplest (SMS) and everything in between, such as geotargeted mobile advertising.

This is the second book written by Bob Bentz. The first book, *Opportunity is Calling: How to Start Your Own 900 Number* was written in 1993 and can be found at Amazon.com.

Bentz resides in suburban Philadelphia. He is a loyal season ticket holder to the Phillies, Eagles, and West Virginia Mountaineers. He is also a baseball coach who has coached six players who went on to play professionally. He loves backpacking and fostering rescue dogs until they find their fur-ever homes.

Please follow Bob Bentz at his personal website and on social media:

- BobBentz.com
- LinkedIn: http://www.LinkedIn.com/in/BobBentz
- Twitter: @BobBentz

Remember, this book will also be continually updated with more information at:

http://RelevanceRaisesResponse.com

ACKNOWLEDGMENTS

To all those who reviewed and helped me edit the book, I give you my deepest gratitude. This book is more than just one person's efforts; it is the efforts of the many great friends and family that helped to review it for me: Barbara Bentz, Brittany Bentz, Brooks Bentz, Bryan Bentz, Brad Bierman, Barbara Breeser, Scott Bronenberg, Frank Butler, Michael Candelori, Dr. Michael Cowpland, Bret Dunlap, Chester Elton, Jeff Horton, Frank Mazza, Velina Rusjakova, and Jenna Silliboy.

The book was published by Judy Weintraub and the staff at SkillBites. It was edited by Elizabeth Thorlton.

The front and back covers were created by Michael Candelori.

Thanks to three gentlemen who wrote the forewords for the book: my long-time business partner, Bret Dunlap, Senior Vice President, Mobile Division, Autobytel; Chester Elton, author of *The Carrot Principle* series about motivation that has sold more than a million copies; Dr. Michael Cowpland, CEO of Zim Corporation and founder of the highly successful Corel and Mitel Networks.

The book website RelevanceRaisesResponse.com was created by Cuan-Chai Megghross and Chris Wall. This site will be updated with the latest statistics and information about mobile marketing so that your book never goes out of date.

Business manager for the book was Margie Varallo.

There are probably not a lot of people who acknowledge canines in their books, but my dogs have always given me so much more than I could ever give back to them. A big juicy bone of thanks to my housedogs over the years: King (German Shepherd mix), Beauregard (Golden Retriever), Braxton (Rough Collie), and Barkley (Golden Retriever). Also, to my current best friends Pilgrim (Chow mix) and Hope (Australian Shepherd mix). Further, to the dozens of dogs that we have fostered from shelters until they've found their fur-ever homes, and also to those less fortunate. Please consider adopting a shelter dog today.

In a perfect world, every home would have a dog and every dog would have a home.

Finally, to my wife, Barbara Komisar Bentz, who has constantly encouraged me to write more. She continues to say that I could write the next *Marley and Me* about all of the funny stories we've experienced through our passion of rescuing dogs. I don't know if I could do that, but I promise that someday I will try.

Bob Bentz

ADDITIONAL RESOURCES

AppsFlyer. "The Beginner's Guide to Mobile Advertising Analytics." August 2015. https://facebookmarketingpartners.com/wp-content/uploads/2015/07/The-Beginners-Guide-to-Mobile-Advertising-Analytics_Updated.pdf.

Barbeau, Pierre. "6 Key Reasons Why a New App Fails." *Mobile Commerce Daily.* September 18, 2015. http://www.mobilemarketer.com/cms/opinion/columns/21314.html.

Borrell Associates. "The 2010 U.S. Local Mobile Advertising & Promotions Forecast." 2010. https://www.borrellassociates.com/aboutus/pressreleases/167-borrell-associates-releases-2010-local-mobile-advertising-a-promotions-forecast-ad-spend-to-double-in-2010.

Boyle, Cathy. "Mobile Website, App or Both? How Channel Choices Are Made." eMarketer. June 2015. http://west.gannettuscp.com/images/uploads/attachments/eMarketer_Mobile_Website_App_or_Both-How_Channel_Choices_Are_Made.pdf.

Bustos, Linda. "The Showrooming Threat: 5 Ways to Fight Back." *Get Elastic.* November 19, 2014. http://www.getelastic.com/showrooming/.

Cass, Andrew J. *The mCommerce Blueprint: The Definitive Guide to Mobile Marketing for Small Business.* One Lifestyle Marketing, 2015.

Chan, Nicole. "Reasons Digital Wallets Are Destined to be 'the' Payment Process." Retail Customer Experience. September 4, 2015. http://www.retailcustomerexperience.com/blogs/why-digital-wallets-are-destined-to-be-the-payment-process/.

Criteo. "State of Mobile Commerce Report." Q3, October 2015. http://www.criteo.com/resources/mobile-commerce-report/.

CTIA, the Wireless Association. "CTIA Short Code Monitoring Program, Short Code Monitoring Handbook." Version Number 1.5.2. Effective October 1, 2015.

Deloitte Digital. "Navigating the New Digital Divide: Capitalizing on Digital Influence in Retail." May 2015. http://www2.deloitte.com/content/dam/Deloitte/us/Documents/consumer-business/us-cb-navigating-the-new-digital-divide-v2-051315.pdf.

DiSilvestro, Amanda. "The Pros and Cons of Adopting Apple Pay for Your Ecommerce Business." Search Engine Watch. October 27, 2015. http://searchenginewatch.com/sew/opinion/2432048/the-pros-and-cons-of-adopting-apple-pay-for-your-ecommerce-business.

Duggan, Maeve et al. "Social Media Update 2014." Pew Research Center. December 28, 2009. http://www.pewinternet.org/2015/01/09/social-media-update-2014/.

Dunlap, Bret, and Jay Friedman. *30 Days to Mobile Marketing Expertise*. Goodway Group, 2013.

Dushinski, Kim. *The Mobile Marketing Handbook: A Step-by-Step Guide to Creating Dynamic Mobile Marketing Campaigns,* 2nd ed. New Jersey: CyberAge Books, 2012.

eMarketer. "Cross-Device Marketing Roundup." Presented by Atlas and Liverail. October 2015. https://www.emarketer.com/public_media/docs/eMarketer_Cross_Device_Marketing_Roundup.pdf.

eMarketer. "Push Marketing Roundup." Presented by Silverpop. September 2015. https://www.emarketer.com/public_media/docs/eMarketer_Push_Marketing_Roundup_2015.pdf.

Eslinger, Tom. *Mobile Magic: The Saatchi & Saatchi Guide to Mobile Marketing.* Hoboken: Wiley, 2014.

Fitzgerald, Toni. "What's Driving Digital Ad Gains: Retail." *Media Life Magazine.* May 20, 2015. http://www.medialifemagazine.com/whats-driving-digital-ad-gains-retail/.

FunMobility. "Mobile Advertising Trends Report." 2015. https://www.funmobility.com/resources/whitepapers-webinars-quick-guides/mobile-advertising-trends-report-2015/.

Garris, Molly, and Karen Mishra. *A Beginner's Guide to Mobile Marketing.* New York: Business Expert Press, 2014.

Genadinik, Alex. *Mobile App Marketing and Monetization.* Semantic Valley LLC, August 24, 2014.

Gibson, Ben. "Tackling Showrooming, Shopper Abandonment: New Mobility Tools for Retail CMOs." *Innovation Insights.* January 22, 2015. http://insights.wired.com/profiles/blogs/overcoming-showrooming-and-shopper-abandonment-new-mobility-too-1.

Hasen, Jeff. *The Art of Mobile Persuasion: How the World's Most Influential Brands Are Transforming the Customer Relationship through Courageous Mobile Marketing.* Frontier Press, 2015.

Hazzard, Michael. "The Definitive TCPA Guide for Text Message Marketing." Tatango. June 26, 2014. http://www.tatango.com/blog/the-definitive-tcpa-guide-for-text-message-marketing/.

Heneghan, Bill. *Marketing on the Move: Your Customers Are Mobile. Are You?.* Bill Heneghan, 2014.

Kawasaki, Guy, and Peg Fitzpatrick. *The Art of Social Media: Power Tips for Power Users.* New York: Portfolio/Penguin, 2014.

Kahuna. "Top 8 Push Notification Campaigns Your App Should Be Running." 2015. https://www.kahuna.com/resources/top-8-push-notification-campaigns-your-app-should-be-running-right-now/.

Klein, Jeff. *Mobile Marketing: Successful Strategies for Today's Mobile Economy.* Power Play Marketing, 2013.

Landau, Jeanne. "Support Services: Today's Shorter Attention Spans Scream for Memorable Response Tools." *Response Magazine.* July 1, 2015. http://www.responsemagazine.com/direct-response-marketing/support-services-today-s-shorter-attention-spans-scream-8741.

Lavine, Adam. "The Road to Redemption." FunMobility, 2013. http://pages.funmobility.com/rs/funmobilityinc/images/FunMobility-Mobile-Coupon-The-Road-to-Redemption-Whitepaper.pdf.

Levis, Shannon, and Alli Brian. "New Data Shows up to 60% of Users Opt out of Push Notifications." *@andrewchen* (online newsletter). http://andrewchen.co/why-people-are-turning-off-push/.

Lobaugh, Kasey. "Retailers: It's Time to Capitalize on Digital Influence." Deloitte Digital. May 13, 2015. http://www.deloittedigital.com/us/blog/retailers-its-time-to-capitalize-on-digital-influence.

Localytics. *8 Critical Metrics for Measuring App User Engagement.* 2015. http://info.localytics.com/4d-8-critical-app-engagement-metrics.

MacGougan, Patrick. "Average Cost per Loyal App User Drops in July." Go-Mash Mobile. August 27, 2015. http://go-mashmobile.com/mobileapps/news-mobileapps/average-cost-per-loyal-app-user-drops-in-july-4844/.

MailChimp Research. "Email Marketing Benchmarks." January 13, 2015. http://mailchimp.com/resources/research/email-marketing-benchmarks/.

Marin Software. "The Essential Guide to Native Advertising: The Rise of a Digital Ad Format and Best Practices for Commanding

Audience Attention." 2015. http://www.marinsoftware.com/resources/whitepapers/the-essential-guide-to-native-advertising-the-rise-of-a-digital-ad-format-and-best-practices-for-commanding-audience-attention.

Martin, Chuck. *Mobile Influence: The New Power of the Consumer.* New York: St. Martin's Press, 2013.

Martin, Chuck. *The Third Screen: The Ultimate Guide to Mobile Marketing*, rev. ed. Nicholas Brealey Publishing, 2011.

Martin, Erik J. "The ABCs of A/B Testing." *EContent Magazine.* September 2, 2015. http://www.econtentmag.com/Articles/Editorial/Feature/The-ABCs-of-A/B-Testing-105882.htm.

Morrison, Maureen. "The CMO's Guide to Messaging Apps." *Advertising Age.* September 14, 2015. http://adage.com/article/cmo-strategy/cmo-s-guide-messaging-apps/300331/.

"New Research Shows How Digital Connects Shoppers to Local Stores." Think With Google. October 2014. https://www.thinkwithgoogle.com/articles/how-digital-connects-shoppers-to-local-stores.html.

Neustar. "Whitepaper: The Omnichannel Data Management Platform." 2015. https://www.neustar.biz/resources/whitepapers/omnichannel-dmp-whitepaper.

Richards, Michael. *Social Media: Dominating Strategies for Social Media Marketing with Twitter, Facebook, YouTube, LinkedIn and Instagram.* Michael Richards, 2014.

Rothenberg, Randall. "Ad Blocking: The Unnecessary Internet Apocalypse." *Advertising Age.* September 22, 2015. http://adage.com/article/digitalnext/ad-blocking-unnecessary-internet-apocalypse/300470/.

Rothman, Dayna, and Ellen Gomes. *The Definitive Guide to Mobile Marketing.* Marketo. 2015. http://www.marketo.com/assets/uploads/The-Definitive-Guide-To-Mobile-Marketing-Marketo.pdf.

Salz, Peggy Anne. "Winning Big with Long-Tail Apps." *EContent.* September 01, 2015. http://www.econtentmag.com/Articles/ Column/Agile-Minds/Winning-Big-With-Long-Tail-Apps-105890. htm.

Samuely, Alex. "How to Marry Mobile with Location for Bricks- and-Mortar Advantage: Swrve Exec." *Mobile Commerce Daily.* September 18, 2015. http://www.mobilecommercedaily.com/how- to-marry-mobile-with-location-for-bricks-and-mortar-advantages- swrve.

Schadler, Ted, Josh Bernoff, and Julie Ask. *The Mobile Mind Shift: Engineer Your Business to Win in the Mobile Moment.* Cambridge, MA: Groundswell Press, 2014.

Schaeffer, Chuck. "How to Solve the Retail Problem of Showrooming." CRMsearch. October 30, 2015. http://www.crmsearch.com/showrooming.php.

Sidney-Smith, Ray. *SoLoMo Success: Social, Local and Mobile Small Business Marketing Strategy Explained.* W3 Publishing, 2014.

SlickText. "The Advanced SMS Marketing Guide." Slick Innovations, LLC. June 25, 2015. http://www.slicktext.com/advanced-sms- marketing-guide/sms-marketing-keyword-selection.php.

"The Definitive Guide to Mobile Ad Measurement." 4INFO. March 2015. http://www.4info.com/4INFO/media/4Info/Resources/Whitepapers/ 4INFO_DefinitiveGuideToMobileMeasurement_20150521.pdf.

"The New Digital Divide: Retailers, Shoppers, and the Digital Influence Factor." Deloitte Digital. 2013. http://www2.deloitte.com/ content/dam/Deloitte/us/Documents/consumer-business/us-rd- thenewdigitaldivide-041814.pdf.

Verto Analytics. "US Digital Content Market, May 2015." http://www. vertoanalytics.com/2015/06/us-digital-content-market-report/.

Wolf, J. *Social Media: Master, Manipulate, and Dominate Social Media Marketing with Facebook, Twitter, YouTube, Instagram and LinkedIn.* J. Wolf, 2015.

Zimmerman, Jan, and Ng Deborah. *Social Media Marketing All-in-One for Dummies.* Hoboken: Wiley, 2015.

INDEX